P9-AZU-364

ALBERT SHAW LECTURES ON
DIPLOMATIC HISTORY

Under the Auspices of the

WALTER HINES PAGE SCHOOL OF
INTERNATIONAL RELATIONS

The liberality of Albert Shaw, Ph. D. 1884, has made it possible for The Johns Hopkins University to provide an annual course of lectures on diplomatic history. The lectures, while still included in the regular work of the Department of History, have since the establishment of the Page School of International Relations, in 1930, been placed under its auspices.

ALBERT SHAW LECTURES ON DIPLOMATIC HISTORY

1899. JOHN H. LATANÉ. The Diplomatic Relations of the United States and Spanish America. 1900. (Out of print.)
1900. JAMES MORTON CALLAHAN. The Diplomatic History of the Southern Confederacy. 1901. (Out of print.)
1906. JESSE SIDDALL REEVES. American Diplomacy under Tyler and Polk. 1907. (Out of print.)
1907. ELBERT JAY BENTON. International Law and Diplomacy of the Spanish-American War. 1908. $1.75.
1909. EPHRAIM DOUGLASS ADAMS. British Interests and Activities in Texas, 1838-1846. 1910. (Out of print.)
1911. CHARLES OSCAR PAULLIN. Diplomatic Negotiations of American Naval Officers, 1778-1883. 1912. $2.25.
1912. ISAAC J. COX. The West Florida Controversy, 1798-1813, 1918. (Out of print.)
1913. WILLIAM R. MANNING. Early Diplomatic Relations between the United States and Mexico. 1916. $2.50.
1914. FRANK A. UPDYKE. The Diplomacy of the War of 1812. 1915. (Out of print.)
1917. PAYSON JACKSON TREAT. The Early Diplomatic Relations between the United States and Japan, 1853-1865. 1917. $2.75.
1921. PERCY ALVIN MARTIN. Latin America and the War. 1925. $3.50.
1923. HENRY MERRITT WRISTON. Executive Agents in American Foreign Relations. 1929. $5.00.
1926. SAMUEL FLAGG BEMIS. Pinckney's Treaty: A Study of America's Advantage from Europe's Distress, 1783-1800. 1926. Second printing 1941. $3.00.
1927. BRUCE WILLIAMS. State Security and the League of Nations. 1927. $2.75.
1928. J. FRED RIPPY. Rivalry of the United States and Great Britain over Latin America, 1808-1830. 1929. $2.75.
1930. VICTOR ANDRÉS BELAUNDE. Bolivar and the Political Thought of the Spanish American Revolution. 1938. $3.50.
1931. CHARLES CALLAN TANSILL. The Purchase of the Danish West Indies. 1932. $3.50.
1932. DEXTER PERKINS. The Monroe Doctrine, 1826-1867. 1933. (Out of print.)
1933. CHARLES SEYMOUR. American Diplomacy during the World War. 1934. Second printing 1942. $3.00.
1935. FRANK H. SIMONDS. American Foreign Policy in the Post-war Years. 1935. $2.00.
1936. JULIUS W. PRATT. Expansionists of 1898 The Acquisition of Hawaii and the Spanish Islands. 1936. $3.00.
1937. DEXTER PERKINS. The Monroe Doctrine, 1867-1907. 1937. $3.50.
1938. ARTHUR PRESTON WHITAKER. The United States and the Independence of Latin America, 1800-1830. 1941. $3.75.
1939. WILLIAM SPENCE ROBERTSON. France and Latin-American Independence. 1939. $3.75.
1941. THOMAS A. BAILEY. The Policy of the United States toward the Neutrals, 1917-1918. 1942. $3.50.
1942. WILFRID HARDY CALLCOTT. The Carribbean Policy of the United States, 1890-1920. 1942. $3.50.
1946. MALBONE W. GRAHAM. American Diplomacy in the International Community. 1948. $3.25.

AMERICAN DIPLOMACY IN THE INTERNATIONAL COMMUNITY

LONDON: GEOFFREY CUMBERLEGE
OXFORD UNIVERSITY PRESS

THE ALBERT SHAW LECTURES ON DIPLOMATIC HISTORY, 1946
THE WALTER HINES PAGE SCHOOL OF INTERNATIONAL RELATIONS

AMERICAN DIPLOMACY IN THE INTERNATIONAL COMMUNITY

BY

MALBONE W. GRAHAM

Professor of Political Science
University of California, Los Angeles

BALTIMORE
THE JOHNS HOPKINS PRESS
1948

PRINTED IN THE UNITED STATES OF AMERICA
BY J. H. FURST COMPANY, BALTIMORE, MARYLAND

To

G. M. G.

ACKNOWLEDGMENTS

I am indebted to a number of others in connection with the preparation of these lectures. Chief among them are professional librarians, who were invaluable aides in getting directly at the sources for minute and sometimes almost inaccessible details. I wish, first and foremost, to put on record my sincere appreciation of the good offices and friendly interest of Dr. Luther H. Evans, Librarian of Congress; and of Mr. David L. Mearns, Director of the Reference Department, for his direct aid in running down obscure sources. My thanks go also to Mr. George L. Sioussat, Head of the Manuscripts Division, and to Mrs. Dorothy Eaton, expert on the handwriting in the original folios of the *Journals of the Continental Congress.* I wish to record my appreciation of the continuous cooperation of Mr. William B. Stern, Foreign Law Librarian of the Los Angeles County Law Library, both in general and for almost magically producing highly inaccessible materials, and for his aid in a long intellectual man-hunt which we both found exhilarating. I wish to acknowledge also the meticulous and valued assistance of Mr. John C. Hogan, formerly of the Los Angeles County Law Library staff.

Innumerable courtesies were extended to me by Dr. Lawrence Clark Powell, Librarian of the University of California at Los Angeles. My appreciation goes also to Dr. Richard Archer, Supervising Bibliographer of the William Andrews Clark Memorial Library,

Mr. Everett Moore, Head of the Reference Department, and Mrs. Jean Anderson, Miss Gladys Coryell, Miss Hilda Gray, and Miss Ardis Lodge, all Librarians in the Reference Department of the University Library.

My heartfelt thanks and appreciation go to my colleague Professor Louis Knott Koontz of the Department of History, for his continuous encouragement and tireless interest, and for numerous constructive suggestions made during the reading of the manuscript in preparation for publication.

Finally, to Professor Malcolm C. Moos of the Johns Hopkins University goes my everlasting gratitude for lifting from my shoulders many of the minutiae of publication and for seeing the manuscript through the press.

M. W. G.

For permission to quote from works listed below, grateful acknowledgment is hereby recorded to the following publishers:

Doubleday and Company

Ray Stannard Baker, *Woodrow Wilson: Life and Letters*

Harper Brothers

Henry L. Stimson, *The Far Eastern Crisis*

Houghton-Mifflin Company

Stephen Gwynn, *The Letters and Friendships of Sir Cecil Spring Rice*

Charles Seymour, *The Intimate Papers of Colonel House*

INTRODUCTION

The purpose of these lectures is to trace the influence which the United States, as an independent political entity, has exerted on the institutions of the international community, from the beginning of American independence down to the period closing World War II. At the same time they endeavor not only to register the degree of acceptance by the United States of the preexisting political, diplomatic, and legal usages of nations, but also to record the impress of contemporary outside forces, at each stage of our national development, on the malleable and ductile practices of the infant American Republic. The golden thread of continuity is to be found in the relationship, the two-way influence, of the United States on the Community of Nations and of the International Community on the United States.

If the period traversed were one of stagnancy in human annals, the narrative might be simpler, the analysis more lucid. But the United States has been no idle factor in the collective life of the states of the modern world. It has gone through two convulsive episodes in human history, during which the locus of authority both within and between states has appreciably shifted from one social class to another, and its diplomacy has mirrored in the international *Salle des Glaces* the conflicting ideologies actuating it at any given period of its national history.

The first broad phase marks the entry of the United States on the international stage. In a world which, for well over a century, had known the emergence of no new national entities and was in fact busily engaged in reducing to vassalage, if not extinction, various long-established state entities, the sudden appearance, out of a congeries of discrete colonies, of a dynamic young confederacy is an event of the first magnitude. But the process by which the United Colonies becomes the United States and the United States in turn becomes an integrally accepted member of the Family of States runs so zig-zaggedly across the boundaries of previously accepted constitutional and international normalcy that it is at times difficult to see the process as a whole and discover the distant points reached, or measure objectively the degrees of tacit acceptance of the United States, or account for the time-lags in certain quarters of the globe where there was lengthy symbiosis without official contact. In the main, this initial great phase covers the period from the first moves of overt resistance against Great Britain to the close of the Napoleonic wars. The role of the revolting colonies is initially one of "militia diplomacy," as Francis Wharton once reprovingly dubbed it; [1] it ends with the United States fully accepted by the entire European Family and playing the role, as much by right of mere seniority as by primogeniture, of introducer and sponsor of new members from the Latin American world. In the process, the United States adopts its own distinctive national policies, but also hardily puts forth its own conception of the international

[1] Francis Wharton, *Revolutionary Diplomatic Correspondence of the United States*, I, 290-294 (Washington, GPO, 1889).

legal and political order. Even at the end of this first phase, to use the words of a great President,

"The stage is set, the destiny disclosed." [2]

The United States has come through revolution to its own framework of policy, frankly hostile to a decadent and tyrannical Europe, while no less ardently friendly to the "new created world" then taking shape at its right hand.

The emergence of the different members of the American Family of Nations ushers in an important, and rather crucial, phase, covering the exfoliation of the American community and the first period of contacts with it, centering chiefly around the great Congress at Panama. It is a period of tense internal conflicts over human freedom which are fiercely reflected in foreign policy. While the United States is perfectly willing to affirm, as the *Leitmotif* of its policy, the opposition to the extension of the European System to the New World, the stalemate of domestic political forces as yet precludes a national consensus regarding the extension of the democratic freedoms of the New World to the Old. Thus it is only as minority factions are peculiarly articulate regarding some European issue, or the protagonists of human freedom reach into the international sphere to curb the slave trade, that there is a stirring consciousness of vague inter-dependency among nations in dealing with problems of more than local or national extent.

[2] Address to the Senate, July 10, 1919, *Public Papers of Woodrow Wilson*, III, Pt. I, 551.

With the outbreak of the republican, and national, revolutions in Europe, in 1848, there is vouchsafed an initial opportunity to affirm, in a public way, our national faith in the power of the democratic movement and process to renovate Europe. The enunciation of the democratic *Credo* by a great Whig and his supporters, after the high tide of democratic hopes, and even in the hour of their recession, marks the transition of the United States from the defensive position of a weakling state to the vigorous, polemic pronouncements of a commonwealth of transcontinental proportions. Even inchoately, the first decade after the Mexican War finds the United States increasingly assertive of its ideas in the international sphere.

Across this long period of two thirds of a century (1848-1914), the shadow of the Civil War falls obliquely. There are obvious and inescapable recessions, in an hour of national weakness, from the bold, forward positions taken in Webster's day. Nor is it merely a reversal of form from the principles of peacetime diplomacy. There are basic decisions, taken with the life of the nation at stake, which shape the course of diplomacy and, in a measure, the Law of Nations, for decades to come. The impact of the domestic struggle reaches very far—witness the changes of emphasis on recognition, on neutrality, on virtually every aspect of maritime war. It is evident also in the strategic preconceptions of the years immediately following Appomattox. For three decades the very weakness of the nation is the primordial cause of our diplomatic retardation, of the *lenteur* and drift in international policy, while the nerve, bone, and sinew of our national being are slowly healing. But there is latent strength and occasional strong conviction, efficiently if not always effectively asserted in affairs concerning us, oftentimes at very long range—witness the matters of minority guarantees after the Congress of Berlin, our interest in the handling of Morocco in 1880, our deep preoccupation with the partition of Africa in 1884-6, and our very active share in the settlement of the Samoan question at the end of the 'eighties. Nor is our solicitude for "oppressed nationalities" in the succeeding decade, whether in Armenia, Cuba, Finland or South Africa, less articulate. Only the opportunity for international institutional solutions is lacking.

Following the Spanish-American War come two relatively swift opportunities, both at The Hague, in 1899 and 1907, to work for a more durable medium in which international relations may operate. Here the United States, though a newcomer to the field of organizational diplomacy, treads firmly. Given, for reasons peculiar to its own internal development, to an adulation of judicial settlement, the United States seeks to write large, upon the international blackboard, the principles of international adjudication. Hence its passion for a Permanent Court of Arbitration, a Court of Arbitral Justice, an International Prize Court, and, obliquely, a Permanent Court of International Justice. In the relatively calm atmosphere of the *ante bellum* days before 1914, the putting forward of proposals for the development of international judicial institutions seems enough.

World War I abruptly ends this alluring interlude. With the breakdown of the Old Order in Europe, there is relatively swift perception that it cannot be restored by a mere reversion to the *status quo ante.* Accordingly the quest is for more substantial foundations for the future. Initial recourse to an ancestral policy of neutrality soon shows its moral emptiness, its juridical vacuity, as a foundation for a new order compatible with the principles long since espoused by earlier, almost forgotten forebears. Not even armed neutrality suffices. When the proving time comes, it is by nationally laying hold of fundamental principles, " shot through " with our consistent tradition and ethic, but expressed in terms of wider than national application, that a rational conception of a viable international legal order emerges. There has to be a clean break with imperialistic dynasticism; we are impelled to espouse, on a world-wide scale, the principle of nationality that gave us birth. Thus, in an hour more significant for us than any since the Declaration of Independence, the United States enters the lists, prepared to destroy two empires and decentralize two more.

The application, particularly as regards Europe, of the twin principles of self-determination and democratic national self-government on the one hand and of formalistic juridical internationalism on the other, is the *Leitmotif* of the fifth, brief but important, phase covering the period from April 6, 1917, to the close of the Wilson Administration. It is a phase indisseverable from the principles and personality of Woodrow Wilson. It consists of the long endeavor (1913-1918) to articulate the principles of the democratic doctrine, and the even more difficult moves during the closing months of the war and the sessions of the Paris Peace Conference, to translate them from abstractions into concrete terms of the settlement. This involves the dual effort of American diplomacy to disengage from the wrecks of the imperial edifices the recognizable state fragments making up the mosaic of the new Community of Nations, and then to establish the institutional framework for holding the whole together. This grandiose enterprise is largely effected on both scores despite the political, though not economic, defection of the United States from the amorphous coalition of the Allied and Associated Powers, and despite the exclusion of Soviet Russia from the settlement.

The last phase of the evolution of the relations of the United States to the Community of Nations begins with the endeavor of President Harding to have no dealings with the League of Nations, "world governing with its super-powers" and ends with the adoption and implementation of the United Nations Charter. In this period, much, much water flows down the streambed of history. To begin with, the United States is recurrently forced to give economic support and underpinning, between 1922 and 1933 to the diplomatic settlement it politically disavowed in 1920. When these fail, the United States is compelled to resort to a series of expedients in the hope of averting the major issue of its fundamental political relationship to the rest of the international community. With the outbreak of hostilities in

Europe in 1939, all hope disappears and the undertaking of a new endeavor on a global scale is seen as imperative.

The ensuing developments embrace the endeavors of American diplomacy, primarily under the leadership of President Roosevelt, to broaden the terrain of action to include a global settlement, and to establish the necessary institutions to give dynamism, momentum, and vitality to the peace to which he looked forward. And yet even this short span of time, covering, as the calendar goes, the liberation of a half dozen nations and the destruction of two more empires, subdivides sharply. It breaks up, under close scrutiny, into the phases of an enforced neutrality, undertaken in concert with the other American Republics and maintained, however reluctantly, as the juridical postulate of common action until the beginning of the *Blitzkrieg* in the West. Once again a day of the politics of strategy outweighs sixteen decades of the strategy of politics. With the swift changes in the relationships of power in the Atlantic Basin, it becomes necessary to formulate action, no longer for isolation or insulation, but for defense on a hemispheric basis. And it is not merely the defense of territory, with which the entire system of neutrality is bound up, but the defense of ideas and ideals, of values which transcend alike comfort and security, of principles whose survival becomes essential to the maintenance of the American tradition.

A second time-span covers the transition from the Collective Neutrality that is weighed in the balances of history and found wanting, through the working hypothesis of Hemisphere Defense, supplemented by specific aid to those whose defense is deemed essential to the defense of the United States, to the common war effort, denominated a policy of Continental Solidarity.

The coming of the war to America transforms the largely unilateral quest of the United States for new approaches to a global settlement into a large-scale endeavor to achieve a general reorganization in cooperation with our allies. Although the consultations are by no means confined to our principal allies, it is clear that the United States is compelled, in order to catch up with the procession, to move at an accelerated pace, if only to make up for lost time—the sterile, pitiful decades when we refused to acknowledge in policy, and when we even opposed in law, the logical consequences and implications of our changed world position. The working bi-partisanship initiated by Cordell Hull activates the change to a new conception of global cooperation, and under the impetus of war, the process appreciably accelerates. It is out of this new " critical period " that the cooperative foreign policy, working under the United Nations Charter for every broadening objectives, has emerged.

CONTENTS

LECTURE 1

The Entry of the United States into the Family of States, 1776-1810

The appearance of the United States of America on the stage of international politics at the beginning of the last quarter of the Eighteenth Century was an event of the first magnitude. It was a novelty, politically speaking; it posed a completely new problem in diplomacy; it abruptly altered the preconceptions of the European Continent as to the orbits of international commerce, and it suddenly overthrew many of the postulates of the geo-political thinking of the day. But the catalogue of innovations does not end there, for ideological forces arising from the American Revolution were destined to have far-reaching effects on the internal constitutional structure and the international practices of already existing states. All these aspects of the emergence of a new political community deserve consideration in any attempt to evaluate changes effected in the legal system, the practices of diplomacy, the closed economies and the deep-rooted dynasticism of the Old World, by the arrival of the first-born in the New.

It is perhaps fitting to recall initially the salient traits of the world scene in the period immediately preceding the colonies' bid for independence. First and foremost, it was a world of imperial states. The colonists, certainly down to 1763, were inured to the conception of multi-national statehood, for they had known no other situation under the British flag. They had grown up accustomed to the extension, on the North, of the French Empire over new areas—over those of the Algonquins, the Hurons, and even as far as the land of the Assiniboines. They were familiar, to the South, only with colonial administrations which steadily superimposed a European and African culture on the native Caribs, or, as in the Dutch West Indies, mixed East Indian stocks of much older history with the African and aboriginal inhabitants. Still further South, they knew only of the rule of the Spaniard or of the Portuguese over enslaved populations. Of trends toward colonial autonomy or other forms of self-governance in these other areas they knew absolutely nothing, for there was nothing to learn. Whether they gazed at the map of Europe, or Africa, or Asia, the situation was the same. In Northern Europe they saw the declining empire of the Vasa kings; in Central Europe, the almost incomprehensible structure of the ramshackle Holy Roman Empire, with Hapsburg Crownlands lying outside its formal boundaries on the one hand, and Hohenzollern appanages on the other. Beyond these confines stretched the domains of the Russian Tsar across the vast Continent of Asia, across the Straits into the frigid northlands of the North American Continent, down to the lands

"where rolls the Oregon"

and even further. Over the shorelands of much of the Mediterranean the power of the Ottoman Empire held sway, including the subjugated Christian populations of the Balkans, and the long arm of the Islamic theocracy stretched into the deep hinterlands of Africa and Anatolia and the Middle East. Even in the half-legendary Cathay, it was imperial rule over far-flung peoples that was exercised by the Manchu rulers. In only two areas of the earth, both European, were other forms of governance known and fully recognized: First, the ancient republican cantons of the old Swiss Confederation, immured for centuries in their impregnable position in the Alps, and, second, the United Provinces of the Netherlands, with a venerable, aristocratic tradition of municipal self-government which, however, did not extend to the colonial domain in Indonesia, Africa, or America. Small wonder that to many of the colonists, particularly those of conservative persuasion, the concept of a world of nation states seemed very far distant!

In the second place, the world of the 1770's was overwhelmingly monarchical and dynastic. Royal power, aggressively organized, was the principal medium by which the existing agglomerations of land and power had historically been built up; all previously known confederacies and republics were relatively small, compact, and contiguous, their cohesion more a matter of community of material interests than the result of adhesion to common political ideals. The outlook for large, sprawling, underpopulated republics had no viable historical precedent, and the durability of ideologically grounded unions was open to serious question. Thus the prospect of uniting the British colonies in America over any extended period of historical time on the basis of a republican ideal must have seemed to all but an eccentric minority as very fatuous indeed.

In the third place, the world at the time of the American Revolution was largely one of closed economies. The very issues over which the quarrel with Britain began are eloquent witness. Nothing could have been more consciously designed to aggrandize the trade of the metropolis than the mercantilist philosophy which insisted on rigidly closed trade orbits between the mother country and its colonies, particularly in time of war, as the Rule of the War of 1756 palpably demonstrated. And yet only the most draconian legislation, stringently enforced, could confine to such rigid trammels the outreaching thrusts of steadily expanding economic interests, such as the molasses trade; and only autocratic regimes could enact such legislation and enforce it. Here was a frontal clash between the juridical regime of commerce and the primal interests of the colonial populations. Small wonder that there was a very real tug at the leash-strings of legality, which, by a subtle psychological metamorphosis, soon became a pull away from the ties of loyalty.

Finally, historically and, in a sense, geopolitically, the civilized world was essentially European; at all events its diplomacy polarized there. But even the conception of a self-contained Continent was breaking down. It was becoming increasingly difficult to view the world as consisting chiefly of maritime powers with huge overseas dependencies to which they alone had access, while the other land-locked or land-centered states permanently played a subsidiary, client role. Consequently Europe was itself beginning to burst at the seams in the quest for wider empire and overland communications to trade marts. It is in this sense that one must recognize the efforts of Imperial Russia to reach out, in the preceding decades, and find windows on the West in the Baltic, a direct neighborly relation to Prussia and Austria over the body of a prostrate Poland, and nearer access to the markets of the Levant, at either end of the Black Sea, over the broad steppes of the Ukraine.

With the treaty of Kutchuk-Kainardji of 1774 Russia broke her previous, chiefly Muscovite, confines, and obtained an entering wedge among the Christian populaces of the Balkans, and thus gave to the Eastern Question a new degree of acuity. In the West there were bold endeavors to carry Continental civilization across the Mediterranean into North Africa and so to expand the economies of Spain and of the Italian States. The overland march of Russia, halted almost a century before at Nerchinsk, was being resumed to give the land of the Tsars various points of territorial contiguity with the Chinese Empire. In the heart of Europe, in the lands of the moribund Holy Roman Empire, latent change was also going on, marking the surrender of obsolescent feudal provincial privileges or the consensual fusion of dynastic domains. But everywhere the reduction of the number of existing state units was the rule. The peaceful annexation-by-partition formula was even then being applied to Poland and to the Ottoman Empire. But of the creation of new states, of the calling into being of new political entities, there was no thought. Existing states might add new provinces, but no new states were in gestation.

Indeed, the idea of a new commonwealth, of a new member of the Christian community of Europe, was almost totally lacking. Not since the rise of the Dutch Republic, not since the Peace of Westphalia, more than a century before, had members of the civilized community been called upon to greet a new candidate for membership or use the formulae for acknowledging the independence of a new state.[1]

[1] Into how much desuetude the practice of recognition had fallen may be noted by reference to the Treaty of Peace between Philip IV, King of Spain, and the United Provinces of the Low Countries, signed at Munster on January 30, 1648 which provided:

"I. In the first place the said Lord the King declares and acknowledges, That the said Lords the States General of the *Low Countries*, and all the respective Provinces thereof, together with all their associated Countries, Towns and Lands thereto belonging, are Free and Sovereign States, Provinces and Countries, upon which, or their associated Countries, Towns or Lands abovesaid, the said Lord the King has no manner of Pretensions; and that neither at this time, nor *in futurum*, he shall ever make any Pretensions to them for himself, or for his Heirs and Successors: and that in consequence hereof he is content to treat with the said Lords the States, even as he does at this present, and agree upon a perpetual Peace, on the Conditions afterwritten and declar'd, *viz.*

"II. That the said Peace shall be good, firm, faithful and inviolable; . . ." Stephen Whatley (ed.), *A General Collection of Treatys, Manifesto's, Contracts of Marriage, Renunciations, and other Publick Papers, from the Year 1495, to the Year 1712.* The Second Edition, II, 337. London, M.DCC.XXXII.

Similarly, the independence of Switzerland was only most grudgingly recognized by the Holy Roman Emperor, Ferdinand III, by Article VI of the Treaty of Osnabrug, of October 24, 1648, in the following terms:

"VI. And whereas His Imperial Majesty, upon the complaints made in presence of his Plenipotentiaries and Deputies in the present Assembly, *in the name of the City of Bazil and of all Switzerland*, touching certain procedures and executory Orders

Even the classic publicists and international lawyers of the seventeenth and eighteenth centuries were so busily engrossed with other matters that they made no mention of the process by which the existing international society could be theoretically expanded. And so the student encounters one of the many paradoxes of the world scene in the 1770's: the palpable dynamism of the economies, and the no less obvious staticity of the law. Clearly, here was a field of tension in which the antecedent law must be the loser.

From whatever perspective approached, the Law of Nations, as it then existed, was seriously defective and out of cadence with many of the trends of the times. Tending to be cast *en bloc* for all time by such of its expositors who premised it on an all-pervading Natural Law, which assertedly filled the juridical ether, it actually embalmed, in its postulates, many ancient abuses, such as human slavery, and did not give an affirmative answer to many of the current problems of the day. Manifestly it, too, was due and overdue for reform.

Indeed, in the third quarter of the eighteenth cen-

---

issu'd from the Imperial Chamber against the said City, *the other united Swiss Cantons and their Citizens and Subjects having asked the Counsel and Advice of the States of the Empire, did, by a particular Decree of the 14th of May last past, declare the said City of Bazil, and the other Swiss Cantons to be in possession of a quasi-full Liberty and Exemption from the Empire, and so no way subject to the Tribunals and Sentences of the said Empire; it has been resolv'd that this same decree shall be held as included in this Treaty of Peace, that it shall remain firm and lasting*, and that therefore all those procedures and arrests executed upon this occasion in any Form whatsoever, ought to be of no validity or effect." *Ibid.*, 415. (Italics mine.)

tury the Law of Nations still bore a number of feudal inheritances which had outlived much of their usefulness, if not their color; some of the patristic hallmarks of canon law, the burden of which the Spanish Jesuits had seared into the conscience of rapacious kings, and an increasing share of usages and computations derived from the eras of the great trading companies. Far from being *moderne*, it was, in many of its parts, more than ready for renovation. The Law of Peace, as we now conceive it, had undergone little substantive change since the Peace of Westphalia; the Law of Neutrality had stagnated for a century with little practical or doctrinal development; the Law of War had changed only slightly on land, but at sea it had become more inexorable, and harsher in its general incidence, with the steady rise and unchallenged mastery of the Seas by Great Britain. Despite the *Ordonnance de la Marine* of 1681, enacted by Louis XIV at the height of his power, the Law of the Sea was British Law, as laid down by the Lords Commissioners of the Admiralty and enforced by the Admiralty Court and the Judicial Committee of the Privy Council. And nowhere was there a hardy neutral who was safe from the reach of His Majesty's men of war, who might take up the cudgels for a pragmatic reordering of the spheres of belligerent pretension and neutral right. Here, too, were old scores to be settled at Britain's expense at the opportune moment in the event of a large-scale maritime war.

But let us look at the other side of the historical ledger: The colonies, several approaching the sesquicentennial of their establishment, scarcely remembered in their individual history any other role than that of subjects of the British Crown. Not until very late in their struggle against parliamentary encroachment or administrative reprisals did they assert any conception other than that of an escape from the vexations and tyrannical practices of the British ministry into a condition of libertarian freedom, virtually independent of any other human agency. The pamphlets, brochures, broadsides, and tracts of the early Revolutionary period are extremely insistent on the "freedom from" aspect of recovered liberty, and almost silent on the far more significant aspect, the "freedom to" take their part in the international community. Perhaps it was the very insistence of the patriots on the rights they claimed from the immanent Law of Nature that made some of them assume, with a theological optimism, the existence of a regularized international system, deriving from that same law, into which they would automatically be carried by some superhuman conveyor belt. For most of the colonists, however, the Law of Nature operated only at constitutional levels, and they were left to affirm its existence at the international level only when they were caught *in extremis.*

Let us not overestimate the actual tangible knowledge of international law possessed by the Revolutionary leaders. Grotius was known to a fairly wide circle of lawyers and divines, but more as a classicist and an indicator of broad legal norms than as an immediate hornbook to which the ignorant might repair. Pufendorf was the chief source of colonial knowledge of international law, either directly, or, as mediatized by Burlamaqui,[2] many of whose chapters are lucid paraphrases, almost a century after the death of the principal luminary, of the main writings of Pufendorf.

Of far greater importance than either Grotius or Pufendorf or even Burlamaqui, was Vattel, with whose writings there was not only general familiarity among the intellectuals of the colonies, but particularly among the members of the Second Continental Congress, since they were supplied with a copy of the Amsterdam edition of 1775 by Charles William Frederick Dumas, who early became one of the chief sources of accurate foreign intelligence for the Committee of Correspondence. Because Vattel was a Swiss, because his country was one of the last states in Europe to receive recognition at the hands of the Powers, because he had achieved a practical familiarity with the workings of neutrality, his book exercised an inordinate, though by no means exclusive,

[2] Jean Jacques Burlamaqui (1694-1748) was known in the colonial period chiefly for his natural law doctrines, which assertedly influenced to a considerable degree the views of Revolutionary leaders (cf. Ray Forrest Harvey, *Jean Jacques Burlamaqui: A Liberal Tradition in American Constitutionalism.* Chapel Hill, University of North Carolina Press, 1937). The international implications of his doctrines do not appear to have been adequately traced hitherto. The international legal principles espoused by Burlamaqui first appeared in 1751 as *Les Principes du droit politique*, and quickly went through a number of editions in Switzerland, in Holland (in French, 1751), in England (1752, 1763) and in Ireland (1776) before the Revolution reached decisive proportions in America. The monumental edition of Burlamaqui's works was the *Principes du Droit de la Nature et des Gens* by Professor F. Felice of the Faculty of Law of the University of Paris (Yverdon, 1766-1768).

influence on the thinking of the Second Continental Congress.[3]

Of such elements, then, was the legal background, the " mental furniture " of the Revolutionary leaders, composed. It was not much to build on, and it is difficult, in the melange of views of extreme pietists, ardently religious patriots, and men of the widest ranges of rationalism, to posit anything like a general *Weltanschauung* which could apply to the situation confronting the colonies. Nevertheless, I venture to suggest that from the *marginalia* of the Fathers, often from their personal correspondence to friends and loved ones, one may develop a fairly accurate picture of what went on in their minds, because it is certain that few of the men who answered the summons to the First or Second Continental Congress, had clearly in mind when they left home how the long scroll of history would unfold. But they did

[3] That Vattel was, and had long been, known to individual members of the Continental Congresses is beyond question. To take, for example, two outstanding names, John Adams records, in his Diary under date of December 27, 1765, his extensive reading of Vattel on the Interpretation of Treaties (Book II, Chapter 17, Sections 282, 292, 297) probably from the London edition of 1758 (*Works*, II, 166), while his kinsman Samuel Adams, some six years later, cites Vattel under dates of October 28, 1771 and January 27, 1772. Cf. Harry A. Cushing, *The Writings of Samuel Adams* (New York, 1908), II, 258-9, 323.

The influence of Vattel was undoubtedly pervasive, and the particular edition which Dumas sent to the Congress for its use, was plainly sympathetic with the colonial cause. It includes in the Preface, cryptically signed by a " D," the gist of the Declaration made by the Congress as to the Causes for Taking Up Arms. Perhaps it was this very fact that especially commended it to the members of the Second Continental Congress. It is only fair to add that, if Burlamaqui drew heavily on Pufendorff, Vattel likewise derived his doctrine extensively from Wolff.

have certain fixed notions, sometimes of long standing, which contributed to their concepts of the world in which the United Colonies, rechristened the United States of America, should play a part.

The first group comprised those caught up in the resistance movement, who, having a very imperfect notion of the rest of the world, were content to work for a pragmatically independent status for the colonies, a clean-cut separation from Great Britain, with only the minimum of working contacts with neighboring peoples or states. Such were the backwoodsmen, the trappers, the marginal farmers, and the overwhelming part of the slave population. But this grouping undoubtedly also included the farmers and small merchants in the less literate parts of the country. Their opinion, however distributed, knew only of recurrent wars in Europe, the corresponding difficulties with the Indians, the scarcity of luxury commodities, and the uncertainties of communication that accompanied every war on the European continent. If the connection with Britain could be broken, these vexations would cease, there would probably be peace in the hinterlands, and our commerce would be reasonably secure. This point of view, which met only the immediate problems, was not concerned with politics, or strategy, or diplomacy; it wanted only to achieve the break and return to *laissez faire*, or normalcy, of the *ante-bellum* style. I am prone to regard it as the most pervasive pattern, and as the ancestor of all mere wishful-thinking isolationism.

The second group was made up of those with much wider horizons, those who saw not only the constitutional side of the struggle with the British monarchy, but also sensed its immediate international import, the necessity for foreign alliances, and the strategic imperatives of our own vastly extended position. Foremost among these in the Continental Congress was John Adams, whose formula,[4] INDE-

[4] In his *Autobiography*, written very much later, Adams recounts under 1775, September, his difficulties in Congress owing to the prevailing spirit of conciliation shown by the Middle Atlantic colonies. "I constantly insisted that all such measures, instead of having any tendency to produce a reconciliation, would only be considered as proofs of our timidity and want of confidence in the ground we stood on, and would only encourage our enemies to greater exertions against us; that we should be driven to the necessity of declaring ourselves independent States, and that we ought now to be employed in preparing a plan of confederation for the Colonies, and treaties to be proposed to foreign powers, particularly to France and Spain; that all these measures ought to be maturely considered and carefully prepared, together with a declaration of independence; that these three measures, independence, confederation, and negotiation with foreign powers, particularly France, ought to go hand in hand, and be adopted all together; that foreign powers could not be expected to acknowledge us till we had acknowledged ourselves, and taken our station among them as a sovereign power and independent nation; . . ." But the "alliance" aspect was later edited out by Adams himself, as will presently become apparent. However, when publishing the *Works*, Charles Francis Adams, the grandson, working in the early 1850's, did the objective task of historical scholarship a great service by including in a footnote a memorandum found among Adams' papers:

"Mem. The confederation to be taken up in paragraphs. An alliance to be formed with France and Spain. Ambassadors to be sent to both courts . . . Treaties of commerce with France, Spain, Holland, Denmark, etc." Of it Charles Francis Adams says: "The memorandum gives in brief the system probably dilated upon in the speeches of the writer at this time." How much at variance this scheme was with what Adams actually thought, either then or certainly later, is evidenced by the further reasons given in the *Autobiography* for anticipating French support, but accepting it with reserve: ". . . that our negotiations with France ought, however, to be conducted with great caution, and with all the

PENDENCE—CONFEDERATION—ALLIANCE (The sequence is worth noting) first enunciated in September, 1775, was predestined to become the pattern of national behavior and so of the elemental foreign policy of the Revolutionary period. When seen in its larger aspects, the view which Adams espoused and eloquently expounded, was tinctured with an

---

foresight we could possibly obtain; that we ought not to enter into any alliance with her, which should entangle us in any future wars in Europe; that we ought to lay it down, as a first principle and a maxim never to be forgotten, to maintain an entire neutrality in all future European wars; that it never could be our interest to unite with France in the destruction of England, or in any measures to break her spirit, or reduce her to a situation in which she could not support her independence. On the other hand, it could never be our duty to unite with Britain in too great a humiliation of France; that our real, if not our nominal independence, would consist in our neutrality." Writing as he did after the wars of the French Revolution, John Adams undoubtedly exaggerated to some extent the weaknesses of the American position nearly fifty years earlier: "If we united with either nation, in any future war, we must become too subordinate and dependent on that nation and should be involved in all European wars, as we had been hitherto; that foreign powers would find means to corrupt our people, to influence our councils and, in fine, we should be little better than puppets, danced on the wires of the cabinets of Europe. We should be the sport of European intrigues and politics; that, therefore, in preparing treaties to be proposed to foreign powers, and in the instructions to be given to our ministers, we ought to confine ourselves strictly to a treaty of commerce; that such a treaty would be ample compensation to France for all the aid we should want from her. The opening of American trade to her would be a vast resource for her commerce and naval power, and a great assistance to her in protecting her East and West India possessions, as well as her fisheries; but that the bare dismemberment of the British empire would be to her an incalculable security and benefit, worth more than all the exertions we should require of her, even if it should draw her into another eight or ten years' war. . . . These and such as these, were my constant and daily topics, sometimes of reasoning and no doubt often of declamation, from the meeting of Congress in the autumn of 1775, through the whole winter and spring of 1776." John Adams, *Works*, II, 503-506, *passim.*

uncritical acceptance of the inevitability of a balance of power in Europe, viewed primarily as a struggle between Britain and France, of which the colonies had seen one extended example. This situation, Adams confidently saw and expected, would be projected for a number of centuries into the future. He therefore appears to have concluded from the evidence of the antecedent colonial experience, without ever consciously recording this aspect in print, that since the colonies had enjoyed a condition of non-oppression while Britain was balanced by France, the United States of America would enjoy independence and freedom when, and while, holding the balance between England and France. The need of an alliance with France was to him one of immediate, but passing, expediency, and he was ultimately willing to ramify the alliance system during the Revolutionary War only to withdraw into a divinely foreordained neutrality the moment Britain should have been humbled sufficiently, but no further than, to acknowledge our independence. Even after the signing the Declaration of Independence Adams consistently fought in the Continental Congress against " warranties of possessions "—the eighteenth century equivalent of our modern " territorial guarantees." [5]

[5] Writing of the draft plan of treaties, which is discussed below, Adams states in his *Autobiography* that " Many motions were made to insert in it articles of entangling alliance, of exclusive privileges, *and of warranties of possessions*; and it was argued that the present plan reported by the committee held out no sufficient temptation to France, who would despise it and refuse to receive our Ambassador. It was chiefly left to me to defend my report, though I had some able assistance, and we did defend it with so much success that the treaty passed without one particle of alliance, exclusive privilege, or warranty." *Ibid.*, II, 517-518 (italics mine).

In short, the inarticulate major premise of Adams' reasoning was that the United States had merely to adjust the existing balance of power, and then, by an abstentive neutrality, to hold it so.[6] The openly expressed terms were short-term alliance, if alliance at all there must be, full freedom of commerce, and no territorial guarantees.

The third group among the membership of the Congress embraced those who believed that the United States, in leaving the outgrown shell of colonialism, must launch a very venturous bark indeed.[7] Given the power relationships in Europe, the need of alliances was obvious, but their duration was not predetermined. To such persons, there appeared to be both short-range and long-range policies which the alliance system would further. And alliances, many of them, and immediately, seemed to offer the most prompt answer to the military necessities of the moment, as they appeared also to be the firmest guarantee of independence. Small wonder that, as the plan exfoliated, the more impetuous of

[6] It must be conceded that Adams' major moves enlisted the support of most of the leadership in Congress, and that, with the support of great trading interests, particularly in New England and the Southern States, he brought to pass much of that program within his lifetime; that he enlisted the support of Washington for his system not only in 1776-7 but during Washington's second administration, and that, as President, Adams tenaciously stuck to a theory of world relationships he espoused even before the Revolution.

[7] Of these Benjamin Franklin, Arthur Lee, and Silas Deane were perhaps the most outspoken and so the protagonists. They shared, in varying nuances, the common view that foreign aid must be sought, differing only in their estimate of the extent and scope of the alliance pattern.

our envoys, such as Silas Deane, analyzing the political situation abroad, advocated more and more alliances, and the maximum diversion of British military forces and the scattering of British naval power over an enormously extended area. These hot-heads were, however, continually compelled by Franklin to act in relation to the dominant purpose of synchronizing American diplomacy with that of France and maintaining the geared interrelationship, the cog-to-cog, wheel-within-a-wheel character of our moves within the French alliance system.

This is not the time or the place to trace chronologically the interplay of the three groups of thinkers. It will suffice for our purposes if it is suggested that the first, pulling hard at the tether that bound them to Great Britain, tended to become better informed as the struggle entered its more acute phases, and that with the signing of the Declaration of Independence, they were impelled by the very momentum of the decision taken to proceed farther on the road to making that independence real, and so to take the concrete measures leading to confederation and foreign treaties. The number of those who favored the French alliance may not be counted; but those who were opposed to the alliance pattern were not nearly so numerous, though stubbornly influential. By the time that the Treaty of Alliance with France had been consummated in 1778, the believers in the alliance pattern were undoubtedly preponderant. It required the longer, slower process of computing a post-Revolutionary policy to bring to light the believers in neutrality and the balance of power. To a world where men's lives and fortunes were pledged by the bold stroke of declaring independence, the very idea of neutrality was alien. There is some reason for believing that the idea of Adams, of abstaining from alliances, was in the ascendant only until the delegation left Philadelphia for Europe, and steadily lost ground thereafter. There are few direct records to confirm this, but it is the inexorable impression etched across the pages of patriot letters written during the terrible months when American fortunes were in the balance. Few were cool and calculating in computing the long-range course of policy. And very few thought beyond the day of victory.

It is thus possible to see, to a certain extent, with what perspectives, what "mental furniture," the men who played significant roles in the First and Second Continental Congresses entered those bodies. By and large, they had no conception of the vast international consequences to which their acts would inevitably lead. In their first steps, to cut off, by the Articles of Agreement,[8] their commerce with the mother country, they were dominated by the conception that England would, or could, trade only in her own colonial orbit, and that, by cutting off all purchases from her, they could quickly bring her to her knees. When this consummation was not immediately achieved, a total interdiction of commerce briefly followed, with consequences which need no

[8] For the text of the Articles see the Library of Congress Edition of the *Journals of the Continental Congress,* I (1774), 75-80 (hereafter cited as *JCC*).

elaboration here. The trade of the colonies languished, produce piled high or else rotted in the fields; the bases for a viable economy were undermined. That is why the Second Continental Congress soon had to occupy itself with the problem of trade, as well as that of conducting a limited land and maritime war. In default of a centralized administration empowered to formulate and carry out a coherent policy, the issues of the war itself, and of foreign trade, were subjected to very acrimonious debate.[9] We owe to the recording pen of John Adams, whose meticulous notes have come down to posterity, the picture of that first debate on American foreign policy, officially focused on trade, but ramifying considerably into other subjects.[10] The initial division occurred over the possibility, once hostilities had begun, of holding fast to an air-tight non-importation agreement. Tight-lipped men with razor-sharp consciences argued vehemently that the obligation of contract—the Articles of Association—took unquestioned precedence over the material discomfitures of the individual colonies, whereas merchants and planters, and, above all, those who were in any way concerned with the conduct of military operations, clearly saw that without foreign trade and foreign imports, first of saltpeter, then gunpowder, then clothing and equipment, the colonies were done for. In the end the counsels of expediency and survival triumphed over cold and formalistic legalism, and decisions to trade with the colonies of other foreign

[9] *Ibid.*, II (1775), 445-452; 485-491.
[10] John Adams, *Works*, II, 452-457; 469-484.

powers, then with the metropolises themselves, were reached. But commerce needed protection, and so armor; and very swiftly it became necessary to establish a navy and issue extensively letters of marque. Within a half dozen months of its convening, the Second Continental Congress actually assumed authority for the logical consequences of belligerency, with little realization of the international legal results.

These were far more apparent to foreign powers than to the colonists. In swift succession after the first battles of the Revolution the principal powers declared their attitude and went so far as to interdict traffic in contraband, chiefly in keeping with the stipulations of their commercial treaties, although Portugal, owing to her alliance with England, apparently pursued, until her adhesion to the Family Compact, a role of non-belligerent comparable to that which she was to play in World War II. As the various governments saw the flag of the colonies—an utterly unrecognized one—appear at the masthead of a frigate, a privateer, or a prize, they were confronted with a large number of legal problems which, in the process of solution, forced their hand, since the admission of prizes to their ports, along with the captor ships, raised in an acute form the question of their relations to Great Britain on the one hand, or alternatively, posed in a new form a question of piracy. The "neutral" powers were accordingly forced to inform themselves of the situation in the colonies, and obtain all the political and military intelligence possible. This continued all through the war, the ambassadors of the neutrals in turn meeting first the British, then the French and Spanish and Dutch, then the Americans—although protocol was at times sacrificed for speedy information—and all pooling their information at the foreign ministry or secretariat of state in their national capitals.

Meanwhile the Continental Congress inexorably moved on to the taking of major decisions from which there was no retreat. Of these, the three deeply interrelated ones, having to do with a Declaration of Independence, the drawing up of Articles of Confederation, and the drafting of the Plan of Treaties were undoubtedly the most crucial. The first, which has received the most minute and reverent treatment at the hands of many and eminent personages, is of importance here only in so far as it served notice on all governments of the internationally irrevocable character of the decisions reached and the reasons for separating from the state of which the colonies formerly formed a part. The Plan of Confederation, which was extensively debated in public and in private alike, calls for only one comment: whatever their jural postulates, in fundamental reality the Articles considered the nation as one from the standpoint of foreign policy. The third, and very basic decision, the debates on which have virtually passed into oblivion, concerned the treaty system. Here we find problems of first-hand importance to this study.

By a resolution of the Second Continental Congress on June 12, 1776,[11] a committee of five was desig-

[11] 5 *JCC* 433.

nated to draw up a Plan of Treaties with foreign powers. The body was initially made up of John Adams, John Dickinson, Benjamin Franklin, Benjamin Harrison, and Robert Morris. Later on in the course of its deliberations, James Wilson and Richard Henry Lee were added to its membership. Of its deliberations as a Committee we know next to nothing, but there is a skeletal record of the debates on its report, which produced a draft treaty of a very high order of organization and draftsmanship.* In addition, there are sidelights from the writings of John Adams which show how he fought, at every stage of the drafting, against any conception of alliance, and, still more tenaciously, against the idea of territorial guarantees. In the end, the draft Plan of Treaties emerged as the fusion of ideas concerning liberty of commerce in general with those which were indicia to a widespread system of neutrality. Up to the time when the American Commissioners departed for Paris in December, 1776, they were agreed only on the need for swift military assistance and the desirability of a free regime for commerce.

The Committee they left behind them was hesitant about alliance and altogether reluctant to subscribe to the principle of territorial guarantees. Notwithstanding, the American Commissioners were predestined to discover that the government of France, while deeming their demands to be quite modest, imperatively demanded that any understanding between the colonies and France must fall into the alliance pat-

* See Appendix I.

tern and carry with it the clauses of territorial guarantee.

It is interesting to note how the territorial guarantee principle, which lies at the heart of virtually every instrument of international organization, has been a psychological stumbling-block in American thinking on the subject from 1776 to 1946. And it is rather paradoxical that the only global scheme of organization which the United States has ever accepted, namely, the United Nations, expressly discards the extreme territorial guarantees of the League of Nations, pinning its faith on the efficacy of procedure rather than on the explicitness of guarantees.

The foregoing pages have traced how the thirteen disunited entities on the Atlantic Seaboard emerged as much from colonial mentality as from colonial status to take their place in the Family of Nations. In the process the impulsive gestures of "militia diplomacy," seeking cataclysmic solutions of colonial grievances by dramatic strokes and colossal diversions, gave way by attrition to the slower and more painstaking processes of traditional diplomacy. In this process not Silas Deane but Benjamin Franklin was the victor. In short, by declaring independence, the United States challenged an empire, but did not basically assault the preexisting system of diplomacy. It was eventually accepted into that system without great ceremonial and without great enthusiasm or haste. An uncomfortable symbiosis with the members of the European community marked the periods of the Wars of the French Revolution and the Napoleonic Wars, during which we were impotent to change the world situation and practiced, if only for survival, an abstentive neutrality. We capitulated to stark realities in accepting all authorities which rose and fell on the international horizon, because we could not logically do otherwise and still admit the legality of our own origin. It was this, more than any other factor, in my opinion, which led the United States without demur to make its terms with the successive regimes which were established in revolutionary Europe.

The acceptance of the United States into the Family of Nations was not complete until the end of the Napoleonic Wars. The endeavors made to enter into diplomatic intercourse and establish conventional relations before the outbreak of the Wars of the French Revolution were at least perfunctorily received, it must be admitted, by the other European Powers. Yet once established, they were kept formally correct. But success in the transformation of the preexisting regime of commerce was not immediately forthcoming, and the strictures on maritime commerce developed during an exhausting war of well-nigh global proportions prevented the acceptance, on any wide scale, of the freer regime of international commerce blueprinted in the Plan of Treaties. That is why it is not necessary to enter into the vexed question of neutral rights and duties, which fills the massive volumes of the American State Papers, to understand the role we played. The difficult role of a neutral, in which we were cast during the protracted conflict, was predetermined, cut-and-dried, by the attitude taken by John Adams in the first major debate on American foreign policy in 1776. American neutrality was the logical consequence of thinking in terms of the European balance of power and of the assumed disconnectedness of America, by reason of her diverse commercial functions, from the quarrels of Europe. Whatever the practical factors, such as a bankrupt treasury and a rapidly deteriorating naval and military establishment, that militated in favor of neutrality, the ideological premises were already there, founded as much on the ill-concealed resentment at earlier involvements in the wars of the seventeenth and eighteenth centuries as on the iron framework of neutrality in which, with theological finality, America was cast by her founders almost at the moment of declaring independence.

The diplomacy of the revolutionary period begins as a protest against the dragooning tactics of England toward the rebellious—or, shall we say with Franklin, the *insurgent* colonies?—, rises to inflammatory philippics and clamorous appeals for alliance, and ends with an acceptance of the alliance system, the principles of the Armed Neutrality and the institution of a freer regime of commerce. The net result is of no one man's willing; rather is it, of necessity, a composite work to which many devoted persons, frequently of contrarient points of view, contribute the best and hardest years of their lives.

In its earliest stages the colonial struggle is narrow, confused, and full of intestine quarrels. It is haggling, meticulous, and "strict constructionist." It is myopic and views with too close a focus on Massachusetts or Virginia situations that are of far greater importance. It is gratifying, as one reviews the irrefutable evidence, to observe how that focus widens, how the scope of concern increases, under stinging adversity. First Boston, then New York, then Quebec becomes a touchstone to Continental feeling and solidarity. This reaches its highest moments when a suffering, dejected, and nearly defeated America identifies her cause with the elemental rights of free men everywhere.[12] It is only then that she realizes the moral significance of the struggle and its effect on the community of mankind.

---

[12] That this feeling was reciprocated on the other side of the water is evident from a letter penned by Benjamin Franklin to Samuel Cooper from Paris on May 1, 1777, in which he declared: "All Europe is on our side of the question, as far as applause and good wishes can carry them. Those who live under arbitrary power do nevertheless approve of liberty and wish for it; they almost despair of recovering it in Europe. . . . It is thought that to lessen or prevent migrations [to America], the tyrannies established [in Europe] must relax and allow more liberty to their people. Hence it is a common observation here that *our cause is the cause of all mankind, and that we are fighting for their liberty in defending our own.* It is a glorious task assigned us by Providence, which has, I trust, given us spirit and virtue equal to it, and will at last crown it with success." John Bigelow, *The Complete Works of Benjamin Franklin*, VI, 96-97.

APPENDIX I.

SOME SOURCES OF THE PLAN OF TREATIES

For the origins of the Plan of Treaties we must, in default of records of debates and proceedings, go back to two principal sources: (1) the minimal data left to posterity in the records of the Continental Congress, and (2) the writings of John Adams before 1777. It is no disparagement of the admirable work done by Worthington C. Ford and his associates in editing the *Journals of the Continental Congress* to suggest that their fine scholarship was almost entirely conceived in the spirit of *lower criticism* (i. e., perfect rendition in an official edition of an existing text) and not of the *higher* variety, which pushes its inquiry back of the sources. For that reason the *Journals of the Continental Congress* reveal only two things: (a) proposed emendations of the basic text, with the indicia of authorship, and (b) written sources on which the Committee indisputably relied. The former reveal very little by way of ideas, being largely confined to the niceties of arrangement, but the latter are, for our purposes, of a very high order of authority.

The footnotes contained in the draft plan of treaties refer to works which were available and at the disposal of the Committee. The first of these was cryptically referred to by the rapporteur, without further identification or elaboration, as "Coll. of State Tracts." A careful check for authorship revealed it to be a three-volume compendium of political pamphlets of the period of the Glorious Revolution and the ensuing decade.[1] A careful reading of all three volumes for material relevant to the purposes of the Committee discloses only one document that passes muster—the Treaty of Reswick of 1697, whose pertinence is further attested by direct page citation, the one and only reference made to the whole work.[2] We may therefore dismiss the *Collection of State Tracts* as having had only a marginal, or peripheral importance, although very real and significant, on the evolution of the Plan of Treaties: It provided, by almost integral borrowing from the Treaty of Reswick, the Preamble to the Plan of Treaties.

The second treatise specifically referred to in the draft is even more cryptically cited as " Coll. of Sea Laws," from which the borrowings were decidedly more heavy.[3] It required the services of experts to

[1] *A Collection of State Tracts, published on Occasion of the late Revolution in 1688, and during the Reign of King William III.* London, 1705-1707, 3 vols.

[2] " Coll. of State Tracts, [III,] 109," *Journals of the Continental Congress, 1774-1789, edited from the original records in the Library of Congress by Worthington Chauncey Ford, Chief, Division of Manuscripts*, V, 1776 (June 5–October 8), 576, n. 2.

[3] In the *Journals of the Continental Congress*, V, on the pages (576-589) where the draft plan is reported, references to the " Coll. of Sea Laws " occur at several points: to p. 541 in note 2 of page 576; to pages 544-549 generically, and to " Art. 19, and 24 in pa. 542, Art. 10, in pa. 520," and " Art. 5, in pa. 519, if proper," all in note 1 on p. 578 of Vol. V. Careful collation of the passages to which reference is made with the text of the Draft Plan of Treaties reveals numerous borrowings beyond those specified in the pages specifically cited. Noteworthily the " Form of the Passports and letters, which are to be given, to the Ships and Barks, which shall go according to the twenty-seventh Article of this Treaty " is taken almost bodily (with some modernization of the

identify the volume as the work of an early eighteenth century compilator, Alexander Justice,[4] who also prepared other works for public consumption, The specific points of reference involved, as indicated by the actual page numbers[5] given do not appear to have exhausted the usefulness of the volume to Adams, because a fairly large number of passages on adjacent pages reveal the very direct and pertinent borrowings from Justice's work. The form of sea-letter, to cite but one example, is for all practical purposes integrally borrowed from treaties of much older vintage. What is outstanding from even this cursory view of the borrowings is that the " Coll. of Sea Laws " was in point of fact, in the genesis of the Plan of Treaties, far more influential than is superficially apparent.

The *Journals of the Continental Congress* contain one more cryptic reference, in the handwriting of John Adams, to a work cited twice[6] simply as " Coll.

English to suit Adams' sense of proprieties) from pp. 550-551, not in any way referenced. This demonstrates from the internal evidence of the volume that far more extensive use was made of it than the footnotes would indicate. Quite obviously the tracing of the detailed stipulations of the Plan of Treaties to their historical sources is a task beyond the compass of this Appendix.

[4] [Alexander Justice] *A general treatise of the dominion of the sea: and a compleat body of the sea-laws.* London, printed by D. Leach for J. Nicholson, 1705.

[5] Following the first edition of 1705, Justice's work was reissued on at least three later occasions, in all of which the pagination remained the same (2d ed, London, Printed by D. Leach, for J. Nicholson, 1709, 684, 107; 3d ed. London, Printed for the executors of J. Nicholson, 1710; 3d ed. enl. London, Thomas Page, 1724. Because of the identity of pagination, it is impossible—and equally unimportant—to tell which edition was in the hands of the Committee.

[6] In reference to the draft of Art. 24, Adams cites in support of

Treaties." This proved even more difficult to identify, but has been ascertained to refer, by comparison with the pages noted, to the second volume of an early eighteenth century compilation, believed to be the first of its kind in the English language, in which an anonymous, then pseudonymous collator brought together a somewhat heterogeneous "General Collection of Treatys, declarations of war, Manifesto's and other publick Papers relating to Peace and War among the Potentates of Europe." [7] Careful reading of all four volumes of the *General Collection of Treatys* reveals, as was the case with Justice's work,

---

a prohibition against privateering by French subjects, a marginal notation: "comp. Coll. Treaties pa. 20." and in support of Article 25, prohibiting the outfitting of foreign privateers in the ports of either of the contracting parties: "pa. 4." *Journals of the Continental Congress*, V, 584n-585n.

[7] Stephen Whatley, *A general collection of treatys, declarations of war, manifestoes and other public papers, relating to peace and war among the potentates of Europe, from 1648 to the present time. To which is prefixed an historical account of the French king's breach of the most solemn Treatys.* London, Printed (in two volumes) for J. J. and P. Knapton, J. Darby, D. Midwinter and A. Ward, A. Bettesworth and C. Hitch, J. Pemberton, J. Osborn and T. Longman, C. Rivington, F. Clay, J. Batley, R. Hett, and T. Hatchett, 1710; second edition (in four volumes), 1732. The identity of the author as Stephen Whatley is established primarily on the ground that, in 1731, four volumes of the *Acta Regia* containing earlier English treaties, were published by the same publishers over the avowed signature of Stephen Whatley, whereas the *General Collection of Treatys*, published in 1732, printed on identic paper, type, format, etc. bears only the initials S. W. In 1731 Whatley inscribed the *Acta Regia* to William Benson, Esq. in a flourishing dedication; in 1732 "S. W." used virtually the same forms to dedicate the *General Collection of Treatys* to Sir Robert Walpole. Identity of subject matter, outlet, format, style, leaves no other alternative but to conclude that Stephen Whatley and "S. W." were one and the same person.

that the drafters of the Plan of Treaties consulted the Whatley volumes at numerous points, and happen to have left the record of the works they consulted only in the form of Adams' marginal notations. It seems clear that the second volume, embracing the diplomatic transactions running back as far as 1495 in the *Magnum Intercursum* agreed to by Henry VII and the Dukes of Burgundy, was the most used, because it included the period lying back of the Peace of Utrecht, when British sea-power, much less formidable than it was in 1775-6, had to come to terms with the other countries trading with England. From the limited number of treaties within the four-volume collection which it has thus far been possible to identify as those used in preparing the draft plan, it is possible to formulate a general hypothesis, for which a number of passages in Adams' diary before 1776 give support: that the framers of the Plan of Treaties, in their discussions, saw that their principal commercial troubles stemmed from the fact of the virtually unchallenged supremacy of Great Britain on the high seas after the Peace of Paris of 1763. Since the decline of French sea-power was the index to the situation, the framers tried to look back to the earlier stabilizations, in the form of treaties, of the power relationships between Great Britain and France, and, collaterally, between Great Britain and Spain. Relations of England to Holland, Denmark, Sweden, etc. also entered into consideration. Envisaging a considerable commercial future for the United States, the framers thought to safeguard it by establishing a nexus of *commercial* treaties extending as widely as possible the rights of the United States as a trading nation. From this to the formula of " free ships, free goods " was an easy step, hence the quest for the best statements of the principle in the treaties of earlier times to which Great Britain was a party. The greatest common denominator of agreement between Great Britain and France and Spain on these matters was found, particularly as regards contraband, in the stipulations of the Treaty of Utrecht, which, with virtually only the minimum of verbal retouching, became Articles 25-30 of the Plan of Treaties.[8]

It is impossible in this brief compass to go further into the borrowings from earlier treaties, but it is possible to affirm without hesitation that each of the successive adjustments in the relations of power between Great Britain and France or Great Britain and Holland received respectful attention. That the Peace of Reswick of 1697 received careful scrutiny is obvious, but it is possible to bring many earlier treaties to book, noteworthily those of Breda and Gertruydenburg. In matters of detail, as to specific phraseology, the quest antecedes Cromwell, stops for a moment to examine briefly the treaties of Westphalia, than goes back to the days of Elizabeth, and, in the instance already noted, to the reign of Henry VII. There was no caprice in this; it was the product of the most exacting search. For the period back of

[8] Thus Article 25 derives from Art. XV, Article 26 from Art. XVII, Article 27 from Arts, XVIII, XIX, and XX of the Treaty of Utrecht of March 31/April 11, 1713. Similarly Article 28 reproduces Art. XXI, Article 29 Arts. XXII and XXIII, while the first part of Article 30 textually borrows Art. XXIV of the same treaty.

1648, with few exceptions, the framers of the Plan went to Justice's book for the earlier practices in the maritime law of the North Sea and the Baltic.[9]

With the works known to be before the Committee now exhausted, it is necessary to turn to Adams' own writings for further help. Here we encounter one of the basic problems which every autobiography written in the later years of a long life eventually presents: How far may any one trust the accuracy of a writer with respect to events preserved only in the firmament of memory? At the outset of this inquiry it seemed as though Adams' statement that

> Franklin had made some marks with a pencil against some articles in a printed volume of treaties, which he put into my hand [10]

might indicate only that Franklin gave Adams one of the volumes we have already discussed, and that no new volume was involved. The description would easily fit either Justice's work or the Whatley opus. Nevertheless Adams' meticulous reference to "a printed volume of treaties" nearly forty years after the event, would seem to imply something else than the volumes already mentioned.

[9] Indeed, so valuable a repository of knowledge concerning the sea-law of the Northern Countries was Alexander Justice's work that in 1757 Pieter Le Clercq rendered the massive compilation into Dutch, in which it became available to a wider public. Cf. *Algemeene Verhandeling van de Heerschappy der Zee, en een compleet Lichaam van de Zee-rechten. . . .* Uit het Engels vertaald door Pieter LeClercq. Amsterdam, Dirk Onder den Linden, M.DCC. LVII.

[10] Charles Francis Adams (ed.), *The Works of John Adams*, II. 516 (Boston, 1850).

Some of these were judiciously selected, [he adds] and I took them, *with others which I found necessary*, into the draught, and made my report to the committee at large . . .

From the bent of the minds of the two men one may reasonably infer that whereas Franklin was looking out for the terms of alliance, Adams was seeking security for commerce in his additional quest. Whether the "others . . . found necessary" referred solely to the single book which Franklin gave him or permits the selection from other sources as well, may be determined by probability, conjecture, or inference and implication. I have adopted the wider frame of reference in the discussion which follows.

Was there such a volume as Adams indicates, independent of the works already discussed? I am inclined to believe that there was, and that the missing volume may contain still further clues, if it can be positively identified. I can only suggest that up to the present, my researches point to a curious little volume assertedly printed in London, but without the name of any publisher or printer, and containing nothing but selections of articles from treaties. The book was published in 1741, and was available to the *commerçants* of the British metropolis during the years in which Franklin was stationed in London, hence it is not inconceivable that he should have acquired conversancy with the volume, if not outright ownership. At all events, the discovery of such a volume, with passages (which appear *ipsissimis verbis* in the Plan of Treaties), heavily underscored in black ink, offers something of a clue to what the missing volume might be, or have been, like.[11] Facing the title page is an elaborate escutcheon or coat of arms, under which is written with a large, cursive hand, "Philip Crespigny." Possibly merely the sign of ownership, the signature may, however, when juxtaposed to the coat of arms, be indicative of authorship, a point on which it is impossible at this writing to throw any light. It is significant, however, that in the text of the Draft Plan of Treaties, Article 25 of the Plan followed the clauses of Article XV of the Treaty of Utrecht, which is given in the volume, to the extent of copying directly words which the Committee later decided to strike out. This heightens the probability that the *Extracts from the Several Treaties* was in fact the volume to which Adams refers in his *Autobiography.* Positive proof is, at this distance, somewhat difficult to establish, but it must be admitted that the parallelisms are extraordinarily striking.

Did Adams consult any other sources? Are any of the articles from "others which [he] found necessary" drawn from any other source? Adams' solici-

[11] The volume, which is found in the Rare Book Collection of the Foreign Law Department of the Los Angeles County Law Library, is entitled *Extracts / from / the Several / Treaties / Substisting between / Great-Britain / and other Kingdoms and States / of such / Articles and Clauses as relate to the / Duty / and Conduct of the Commanders / of the King of Great-Britain's / Ships of War / together with / Such Articles of Later Treaties as Revive / or Confirm any Former Treaties, / which bear / any Relation to the same. London, Printed in the Year MDCCXLI.* In particular, Art. X of the Anglo-Spanish Treaty of Madrid of July 6, 1670, bears strong resemblance to Article 21 of the Plan of Treaties, although there is also resemblance to Art. XVI of the Treaty of Utrecht.

tude for neutral rights, which is so obvious in the *Autobiography*, although not in the *Diary*, may have a bearing on the answer. The *Diary* is not of value in establishing the growth of Adams' ideas at this time, and there are virtually no evidences of his having thought about neutrality prior to the assignment to the Committee on the Plan of Treaties. However, a work published in London in 1772, again without an assignable or recognizable author, furnishes a clue.[12] Appended to Volume II of this interesting collection is a forty-seven page disquisition by Charles Jenkinson on Neutral Rights, which makes up pp. 101 to 148 of the Appendix. This discussion, made timely by its publication in the midst of the Seven Years' War, may have been the source of Adams' interest in neutral rights. Without attempting in any way to account for its presence in America, we may safely infer that it may have been sent to naval officers stationed on the Atlantic seaboard, or to judges of the Vice-Admiralty courts, with which Adams had numerous dealings, or may merely have been forwarded to booksellers in the normal course of book distribution, or may have been shipped across by some friend of the colonial cause.

[12] *A Collection of all the Treaties of Peace, Alliance, and Commerce, between Great-Britain and other Powers, from the Revolution in 1688, to the Present Time.* London, Printed for J. Almon, opposite Burlington House in Piccadilly, MDCCLXXII. This first, and apparently only edition, contained in Volume I the treaties published between 1688 and 1727, while Volume 2 covered the treaties from 1728 to 1772. It is not impossible to assign Adams' cryptic " Coll. Treaties " to this opus, although we have already demonstrated that his page references to the Whatley opus render significant meaning.

One final "source" may be mentioned: From 1758 to 1761, while the young John Adams was reading law, he came upon a volume into which he delved intermittently over a period of more than two years, reading and absorbing small portions. It, too, was a book with unknown authorship, but it intrigued him enough to cause him to put into his diary a complete rendition of its rather long title:

I borrowed yesterday of Quincy [he wrote under Thursday, October 19, 1758] . . . a "General Treatise of naval trade and commerce as founded on the laws and statutes of this realm, in which those" (laws and statutes, I suppose) "relating to his majesty's customs, merchants, masters of ships, mariners, letters of marque, privateers, prizes, convoys, cruisers, &c. are particularly considered and treated with due care under all the necessary heads, from the earliest times down to the present," second edition, in two volumes [and] studied carefully about a dozen pages in mercantile law.[13]

The first volume of this rather stiff treatise deals exclusively with marine matters which concern peace

[13] A GENERAL / TREATISE / OF / NAVAL TRADE / AND / COMMERCE, / AS FOUNDED IN THE LAWS AND STATUTES / OF THIS REALM, / in which / Those relating to his Majesty's Customs, Mer-/chants, Masters of Ships, Mariners, Letters of Marque, Privateers, Prizes, Convoys, / Cruizers, &c. are particularly considered and / treated with due care under all the necessary / Heads, from the earliest Time down to the / Present. / The Second Edition, with many considerable / ADDITIONS and a new PREFACE. / In Two Volumes. / In the SAVOY: Printed by Henry Lintot, Law-Printer to the King's / most excellent Majesty; for J. Brotherton, J. Walthoe, S. Birt, T. Osborn, D. Browne, T. and T. Long-/man, J. Schuchburgh, Edw. Cumming, J. Worral, / C. Hitch and L. Hawes, J. and J. Rivington, J. / Ward, and M. Cooper. (Vol. II:) MDCCLIII. The reference in the Diary is found in Adams' *Works*, II, 44.

time commercial relations; the second volume, after dealing with the great trading companies, turns, in its ninth chapter, to the matter "Of Imbargoes on Ships Quarantains," and for nearly three hundred pages, which young Adams absorbed during the closing stages of the French and Indian War, deals with Letters of Marque and Reprisal, Depradations, Restitution, Privateers and Capers, Prizes, Cruizers at Sea and Convoys, Piracies, Safe-Conducts and Protections, Passports, League and Truces, Treaties of Commerce, and other Alliances with Foreign States, and closes with a discussion "Of Factors Agents and Supercargoes, of Consuls and Embassadors, and of the Admiralty Court and its Jurisdiction, &c. in Sea Affairs." Here, indubitably, is the source and wellspring of most of the ideas which John Adams made his own in later years. For our purposes it is ultimately not too important whether the volume was actually in the Committee's meeting place in Philadelphia, for John Adams had absorbed the volume long before.[14]

[14] That Adams gnawed away at the "general treatise" is apparent from subsequent entries: Saturday, October 21, 1758: "Rose with the sun. I am now set down to the laws relating to naval trade and commerce. . . ." Sunday, October 22, 1758: "Conversed with Captain Thacher about commercial affairs," to which Charles Francis Adams adds that there was enclosed "a minute abstract of the conversation; of bills of lading, invoices, accounts, etc. (*Ibid.*, II, 45 and n.) Adams' thoughts thereafter turn extensively to admiralty matters (*Ibid.*, 46) and when he next records reading, it is October 31, 1758: "Sat down and recollected myself and read a little in Van Muyden, a little in Naval Trade and Commerce." (*Ibid.*, 48). After recording his admission to the bar, November 6, 1758, Adams, in an extensive footnote, written many years later, describes the "dreary ramble" of legal training in colonial days, then adds: "I was desirous of seeking the law as well as I could

It is extraordinarily difficult, after the lapse of one hundred and seventy years, to reconstruct adequately a hurried episode in the revolutionary annals of the United States. Yet, in default of any committee records, and with the aid of only such *marginalia* as the *Journals of the Continental Congress* afford us, it has been possible to put together something of the pattern of thought actuating the framers of the Plan of Treaties, and to indicate, with absolute certainty on some points, and with varying degrees of exactitude on others, the specific sources on which they drew. It is possible now, in a larger setting, to note how the young barrister in Braintree, Massachusetts, working on a ponderous treatise, was actually in preparation for the crucial hour; it is possible to visualize the omnivorous Franklin, picking up, in London, a treatise with selected articles from standard commercial treaties; it is possible to look

---

in its fountains, and I obtained as much knowledge as I could of Bracton, Britton, Fleta and Glanville; but I suffered very much for want of books, which determined me to furnish myself at any sacrifice with a proper library; and *accordingly, by degrees, I procured the best library of law in the State*." (*Ibid.*, 50 n.) A year and a half later, on May 31, 1760, a Saturday, Adams records: "Read in Naval Trade and Commerce, concerning factors, consuls, ambassadors, &c., and the South Sea Company, &c." (*Ibid.*, II, 86). Since these refer to Chapters XVIII, XIX, and VII of Volume II, it is clear that much of the intervening time had been spent on the other volume, and in getting through the major part of Vol. II. On June 26, 1760, Adams began to read Montesquieu (*Ibid.*, II, 93), indicating thereby that he had finished the *General Treatise.* Five months later, on the "night before Thanksgiving," Adams drew a balance sheet of his preceding five years and more of studying, and took inventory, listing, *inter alia,* "also a General Treatise of Naval Trade and Commerce, as founded on the laws and statutes." (*Ibid.*, II, 103.) (Italics mine.)

over the shoulders of the Committee in session in Philadelphia and see on the table eight specific volumes, practically discern two more, and sense, from the contexts of the men deliberating there the influence of still others. The Plan of Treaties was not born *in vacuo*; it emerged from well-thumbed books, methodical planning, and a keen sense of the structure of international relations in the world into which the United States was even then emerging.

LECTURE II

RECOGNITION OF THE LATIN AMERICAN REPUBLICS, 1810-1826

The end of the Napoleonic Wars marked the opening of a new phase in the external relations of the United States of America. It was an era of official return of the nations to good manners and good neighborliness. This was a universal tendency, which could not fail to be reflected in the psychology of this nation. Our sense of relief at the end of the long wars in Europe is accurately reflected in the conception of an Era of Good Feeling. It was an era in which for the first time we could afford the luxury of looking around at other horizons than the European, over which the war clouds had so long hovered. Small wonder that James Monroe, on taking the oath of Presidential office, could speak, out of his varied experiences as Minister and Secretary of State, and express, as no other President had done before him,[1]

[1] In his final, rather embittered, annual address to Congress, on November 22, 1800, John Adams did indicate a personal awareness of the changing international scene, and of the United States' relationship to it. "As one of the grand community of nations," he declared, "our attention is irresistibly drawn to the important scenes which surround us. If they have exhibited an uncommon portion of calamity, it is the province of humanity to deplore and of wisdom to avoid the causes which may have produced it." Adams' admonitions, in view of his manifest inability to interpret the significance of the scene, were to turn eyes homeward, fortify and cling to domestic institutions and to "resist with unabating perseverence the progress of those dangerous innovations which may diminish this influence." S. D. Richardson, *Messages and Papers of the Presidents*, I, 307-308.

full confidence in America's " strength and efficiency as a member of the great community of nations." [2] Monroe, who had witnessed in person the rebirth of France, and the dislocation of the old forms and norms of the Family of States, was the first to give utterance to this new, self-conscious and extremely perspicacious *Weltanschauung*. America, under Madison, had seen the reordering of the map of Europe at Vienna but had no part in any of it. The small corner of the European scene on which attention was focussed was not Vienna but Ghent, where we consummated our real peace with Great Britain. Hence, for all practical purposes, we were excluded, or rather self-excluded, from the general settlement. But we were genuinely concerned in the rebuilding which necessarily followed, and were as eager to hold wide the portals of international commerce as the late belligerents had been to close them. For we saw that only in a world which generally abandoned the closed system of colonial economies and mercantilistic trading did there lie major hope of our free economic development. Accordingly, beginning with the Anglo-American commercial treaty of July 3, 1815 [3] which reestablished trade and inaugurated " a reciprocal liberty of commerce " between the United States and Britain's possessions in Europe as well as with a few selected ports in India, the campaign to liberalize the regime of commerce got under way. It was not destined to be easy sailing, for the Cana-

[2] First Inaugural, March 4, 1817. 4 *American State Papers, Foreign Relations* (hereafter cited as *ASP-FR*), 127.

[3] *Ibid.*, 7-8.

dian and British West Indian ports were virtually barred to us and it was historically destined to be a long time before the closed door was finally opened.

In the rebuilding of world trade, the United States expressly disclaimed special privileges and avowed its willingness to enter only into commercial arrangements based upon the principles of equality and reciprocity.[4] It was this affirmation of status which actuated us in getting rid of the odious business of paying tribute or ransom to the Barbary States. Moreover, the humanitarian concern over slavery as practiced by the rulers of Tripoli, Tunis, Algiers, and Morocco actuated our diplomatic support of the vigorous efforts of the British Government to stop the slave trade, even though it was psychologically impossible, owing to " the feelings and recollections of this country," [5] to sanction and participate in the business of search, and though meticulous and hairsplitting interpretations of states' rights led to the conclusion that accession to the British proposals would be unconstitutional.[6] Notwithstanding these psycho-constitutional limitations, it was Monroe's conviction, and Adams' reasoning, that led us to declare that

> the motives for declining this overture are compatible with an earnest wish that the measures concerted by these treaties

[4] *Ibid.*, 397-398.

[5] John Quincy Adams, Secretary of State, to Albert Gallatin and Richard Rush, at London, November 2, 1818. *Ibid.*, 400.

[6] " You will therefore express the regret of the President that the stipulations in the treaties communicated by Lord Castlereagh are of a character to which the peculiar situation and institutions of the United States do not permit them to accede." *Ibid.*, 401.

may prove successful in extirpating that root of numberless evils—the traffic in human blood; and with the determination to cooperate, to the utmost extent of our powers, in this great vindication of the sacred rights of humanity.[7]

Espousal of human liberty was of necessity given in a very edulcorated form. The time for establishing any controls of a supranational character was still very far off.[7a]

The major event of the period is the emergence of the Latin American Republics into full-fledged independence. The anticipation that they would in fact become independent was entertained in high quarters of the American government at a very early date, certainly by 1810,[8] but it was not until

[7] *Ibid.*, 401.

[7a] See Appendix II, pp. 80-81.

[8] Perhaps the most elaborately grounded expose of the inevitable separation of the overseas colonies in the Americas from Spain and Portugal was given by Thomas Pownall in his *Memorial, Most Humbly Addressed to the Sovereigns of Europe on the Present State of Affairs between the Old and New World* (London, 1780) 18 f. See also John A. Schutz, *Thomas Pownall: Eighteenth-Century Imperialist* [unpublished dissertation, University of California at Los Angeles, 1945] especially chapter IX, "The Atlantic Federation." Further indications were given in the reports of Jefferson from Paris in 1785 of conversations with a young Mexican nationalist whose zeal for the independence of his native land was matched only by his eloquence. Cf. *The Diplomatic Correspondence of the United States of America from the signing of the definitive Treaty of Peace, 10th September 1783 to the Adoption of the Constitution, March 4, 1789* (Washington, 1837), II, 47-52 (Thomas Jefferson to John Jay from Marseilles May 4, 1787). Finally, Rufus King, while Minister to Great Britain, reported to Secretary of State Madison his conviction that, if war with France were renewed after the Peace of Amiens, Great Britain would "immediately attempt the emancipation and independence of South America." 2 *ASP-FR* 561. A few months later, on his return to the United States, King wrote Madison from New York that, at the very moment when the preliminaries of the Peace of Amiens were signed, "an expedition,

the European conflict was over and with it the shackling juridical neutrality to which we were precommitted, that we were relatively free to view the struggle objectively. So closely wedded to neutrality were we psychologically, however, that its legal framework predetermined the thinking of the times and so set the postulates of our policy. Only as the conception of complete disinterestedness was eroded by the trends of public opinion were we able to consider the beginnings of an independent policy toward the new states.

In default of any organized nucleus of the community of nations to which to turn, the United States was compelled to devise its own rules and procedures for dealing with a swiftly evolving situation. The only precedents it could invoke concerned the recognition of the United States itself. Would they suffice to cover the cases of the half dozen aspirants for membership in the international community, some widely disconnected from the rest? The problem was a genuine one and the value of our own experience, apart from certain precise points of form, was not high. After initial overtures from the Argentine

---

fully prepared, was in readiness to set sail for the purpose of assisting the inhabitants of the provinces of Caraccas (sic) in throwing off their obedience to Spain." Asserting that Trinidad was retained by England chiefly with the view of furthering the revolt, King foresaw a resumption of the plan if war recurred, it being " known to be the opinion of the first men of the nation that the secondary object of the . . . war . . . is the entire independence of South America." *Ibid.*, 504. It is thus evident that, quite apart from such information as was contained in intelligence from the Peninsula, the precarious hold of the Iberian countries on their overseas possessions in America was well known to key personages at the helm of American foreign policy.

Government to the United States, early in 1818, Secretary of State John Quincy Adams suggested what was indisputably true, that the use of a treaty to effect recognition was unexceptionable, and that it was in fact the mode used by the United States to obtain recognition from France.[9] Before the idea of

[9] On January 6, 1818, Don Manuel Hermenegildo Aguirre, agent of the United Provinces of South America in the United States, wrote to Secretary Adams:

> In the last interview with which you honored me a few days ago, you were pleased to state that the act of acknowledgement of the independence of the United Provinces in South America ought to be reduced to a formal treaty between the two independent governments, as was practiced in the case of the Treaty of Amity and Commerce between the United States and His Most Christian Majesty in 1778.

Adams, being asked by Monroe to report to the Congress the existing situation, did so in a document which endeavored to evade responsibility for the authorship of the recognition-by-treaty idea:

> In the conferences held with him [Aguirre] on the subject, among other questions which it naturally suggested were those of the manner in which the acknowledgment of his government, should it be deemed advisable, might be made; and what were the territories which he considered as forming the state or nation to be recognized. It was observed [by Adams] that the manner in which the United States had been acknowledged as an independent Power by France was by a treaty concluded with them, as an existing independent Power; and in which each one of the states then composing the Union was distinctly named; that something of the same kind seemed to be necessary in the first acknowledgement of a new Government, that some definite idea might be formed, not of the precise boundaries, but of the general extent of the country thus recognized . . . It was after this that Mr. Aguirre wrote the letter offering to enter into negotiation for concluding a treaty, though admitting that he had no authority to that effect from his Government. It may be proper to observe that the mode of recognition by concluding a treaty had not been suggested as the only one practical or usual, but merely as that which had been adopted by France with the United States and as offering the most convenient means of designating the

an actual treaty could be implemented, Monroe believed it desirable to institute a more formal, extensive inquiry with a view to determining the general contours of our recognition policy. That mission was entrusted, at the especial request of the President, to C. A. Rodney, John Graham, and Theodorick Bland, who actually investigated on the spot the conditions in the La Plata basin and in Chile, and made an exhaustive and voluminous report on their return in November and December, 1818. Further probing was done by endeavoring to find out the disposition of European courts on the matter; but despite inevitable delays, and some suggestions of concerted action by, and also along with, the European Powers, the United States ultimately pursued its own independent course without any commitment to anyone in the matter.

Disengaging the policy of the United States from the immediate political transactions, such as the effective transfer of the Floridas from Spain to the United States, which cut athwart the natural impulses of our citizenry by compelling the Government of

---

> extent of the territory acknowledged as a new dominion. . . . It should be added that these observations were connected with others, stating the reasons upon which the present acknowledgement of the Government of La Plata, in any mode, was deemed by the President inexpedient in regard as well to their interests as to those of the United States.

(4 *ASP-FR* 173-174, 182). It is clear from the foregoing that, after having suggested a treaty, which would have excluded the House of Representatives from a share in the proceedings, it became singularly inappropriate for Adams to divulge to the House his authorship of the treaty idea.

the United States to follow a dilatory course until the Floridas were actually in hand, what are the steps by which it ultimately came to the recognition of the American Republics? These are found, tersely and cogently stated, in the documents which, beginning with Monroe's inaugural in 1817, culminated in the messages which passed in the spring of 1822 from the Executive to Congress and back, and to the Government of Spain. They reveal the long-range effect of the fact-finding mission, but they also bring to light for the first time the *Leitmotifs* of new policy, which are still encased in the framework of the old. The documents, it may be explained in advance, bear signs of that dual authorship which is characteristic of many things with which both Monroe and Adams had to do, and there is every evidence that the references to neutrality are the work of Adams, while the new departures are more firmly, more obviously, the work of the President.

Starting with the inaugural, Monroe warned against the possibilities of the recurrence of war, in which event it might contingently "be the object of the adverse party to overset our government, to break our Union, and demolish us as a nation." Battling against the conception of isolation that had been regnant in the Jefferson and Madison Administrations, down to the war of 1812, Monroe declared: [10] "Our distance from Europe, and the just, moderate and pacific policy of our Government, may form some security against these dangers; but they

[10] 4 *ASP-FR* 127-128.

ought to be anticipated and guarded against." [11] It was to the development of political and diplomatic means for averting dangers that Monroe dedicated his Administration; nor did he fail to note, out of the fullness of his experience as Secretary of State, that "we must support our rights or lose our character, and with it, perhaps, our liberties." "A people who fail to do it," he added, trenchantly, "can scarcely be said to hold a place among independent nations." That is why he concluded his inaugural pronouncement with a programmatic statement that it was incumbent on the United States, "as a security against foreign dangers, to adopt such arrangements as are indispensable to the support of our independence, our rights and liberties."

A further move forward was evidenced in Monroe's first message to Congress,[12] in which he declared that, notwithstanding a formally correct attitude of neutrality toward the military conflict, it was anticipated at an early stage that the contest between Spain and the colonies would become "highly interesting" to the United States and that "it was natural that

[11] There are abundant evidences in the diplomatic correspondence concerning the independence of the Latin American nations that Monroe, as Secretary of State in the preceding administration, was fully *au courant* of the moves made to compel the Spanish colonies to return to their allegiance, and of every important international move in connection with the settling of their ultimate fate. There appears in the foregoing passage a clear-cut statement of the exposed position of the United States and of the necessity of vindicating national rights at all costs. Cf. W. R. Manning, *Diplomatic Correspondence of the United States concerning Independence of the Latin American Nations.* New York, Oxford University Press, 1925. I-III, *passim.*

[12] 4 *ASP-FR* 130, December 2, 1817.

our citizens should sympathize in events which affected their neighbors." This was the entering wedge against the false premises of a neutrality which was officially maintained but in which, by that time, the citizenry certainly did not share. A year passed, during which the fact-finding commission carried out its mission of inquiry, and on November 16, 1818, Monroe, in his second annual message, reviewed the situation in South America and in Europe, the principal object of his attention being the Congress of Aix-la-Chapelle:

> From the general policy and course of proceedings observed by the Allied Powers in regard to the contest, it is inferred that they will confine their interposition to the expression of their sentiments; abstaining from the application of force. I state this impression, that force is not to be applied, with the greater satisfaction, because it is a course more consistent with justice, and likewise authorizes a hope that the calamities of the war will be confined to the parties only, and will be of shorter duration.[13]

This was not merely an inference, as Monroe was gracious enough to put it; it was indeed a *caveat*—the first intimation of a steadily crystallizing attitude.

A year later, when Monroe addressed his third annual message to the Congress, December 7, 1819, he noted the steady progress of the war in a sense favorable to the colonies. Repeating his earlier statement of the peculiar interest which the United States attached to the outcome, he declared:

> A virtuous people may and will confine themselves within the limits of a strict neutrality; but it is not in their power

[13] 4 *ASP-FR* 215.

to behold a conflict so vitally important to their neighbors without the sensibility and sympathy which naturally belong to such a case.[14]

Admitting that the United States had little occasion to curb excesses of partisan feeling for the Americas' cause, he noted that the record of the Latin American republics gave them "a strong claim to the favorable consideration of other nations." "These sentiments on the part of the United States," he added, "have not been withheld from other Powers with whom it is desirable to act in concert." [14a] It is obvious from the message, as well as its contexts, that at this particular stage the United States was considering, in a number of ways, cooperative action of several Powers, acting, in a sense, as an executive committee of the international legal community. None of these proposed concerted measures, it will be recalled, was

[14] *Ibid.*, 628.

[14a] During this period there was little disposition on the part of the United States to act in concert with the European Powers, but on occasion, where it was deemed necessary, consultation did take place—witness the situation when Spain, after having ceded the Floridas by treaty, prolonged ratification unduly. The need for external pressure on the Spanish court was obvious, and Monroe did not hesitate to use it. Pillorying the action of Madrid, he declared to Congress on December 7, 1819:

> In the course which the Spanish Government have on this occasion thought proper to pursue, it is satisfactory to know that they have not been countenanced by any other European Power. On the contrary, the opinion and wishes both of France and Great Britain have not been withheld either from the United States or from Spain, and have been unequivocal in favor of the ratification. There is also reason to believe that the sentiments of the Imperial Government of Russia have been the same, and that they have also been made known to the cabinet of Madrid. 4 *ASP-FR* 627.

finally carried out with the United States, hence the outcome of such proposals is altogether lacking in American annals. But by the time that Monroe next addressed a general message to Congress, December 5, 1821, the time was very nearly ripe for a decision. Monroe, however, did not, as he might well have done, publicize the situation. Noting the "great success" of the colonies during 1821 in the struggle for their independence, he declared:

It has long been manifest that it would be impossible for Spain to reduce these colonies by force, and equally so that no conditions short of their independence would be satisfactory to them. It may, therefore, be presumed, and it is earnestly hoped, that the Government of Spain, guided by enlightened and liberal counsels, will find it to comport with its interests, and due to its magnanimity, to terminate this exhausting controversy on that basis. To promote this result, by friendly counsel with the Government of Spain, will be the object of the Government of the United States.[15]

It is evident that the solution which Spain was to accept was quietly but firmly indicated in this manner. But the time was not yet.

On January 30, 1822, the House of Representatives called upon Monroe to lay before it such documents as might be in his possession from the agents of the United States with the South American governments which had declared their independence, as also the relevant papers received from their agents in the United States. Naturally Adams saw to the compilation of papers, but Monroe wrote the major portion of the message which was communicated to Congress

[15] 4 *ASP-FR* 739.

on March 8, 1822. Apart from the treatment *en bloc* of the problems of all the countries, indicated by his first use of the term "the Spanish provinces *in this hemisphere*" at the outset of the message, the historical *précis* differed little from the utterances he had previously made except for the fullness of detail that accompanied it. Express reference to our previous neutrality and the possible return to it if the contest were renewed are contained in the first and last paragraphs, and bear the inspiration, if not the hand, of Adams.

Monroe, however, quickly moved to new ground:

> This contest has now reached such a stage, and has been attended with such decisive success on the part of the provinces, that it merits the most profound consideration whether their right to the rank of independent nations, with all the advantages incident to it in their intercourse with the United States, is not complete. . . . Thus it is manifest that all those provinces are not only in the full enjoyment of their independence, but, considering the state of the war and other circumstances, that there is not the most remote prospect of their being deprived of it.
>
> When the result of such a contest is manifestly settled, the new governments have a claim to recognition by other powers which ought not to be resisted. . . . *The provinces belonging to this hemisphere are our neighbors*, and have successively, as each portion of the country acquired its independence, pressed their recognition by an appeal to facts not to be contested, and which they thought gave them a just title to it. To motives of interest this Government has invariably disclaimed all pretension, being resolved to take no part in the controversy, or other measure in regard to it, which should not merit the sanction of the civilized world. To other claims a just sensibility has always been felt, and frankly acknowledged; but they, in

themselves, could never become an adequate cause of action. It was incumbent on this government to look to every important fact and circumstances on which a sound opinion could be formed, which has been done. When we regard, then, the great length of time which this war has been prosecuted, the complete success which has attended it in favor of the provinces, the present condition of the parties and the utter inability of Spain to produce any change in it, we are compelled to conclude that its fate is settled, and that *the provinces which have declared their independence, and are in the enjoyment of it, ought to be recognized.*

Spain, Monroe declared, had expressed no particular views on the subject; hence he believed that an accommodation with the colonies on the basis of their unqualified independence might be presumed. The United States had cherished the sincere desire to act in concert with other Powers in the proposed recognition, but it was understood, he added guardedly, that they were not prepared for it. Believing that " the immense space between those Powers, even those which border on the Atlantic, and these provinces, makes the movement an affair of less interest and excitement to them than to us " the President assumed less interest on their part in the outcome and presumed that " the late events will dispel all doubt of the result." [16]

Monroe's message instantly struck fire. On the following day the Spanish ambassador in Washington, Don Joaquin de Anduaga, filed a fiery and reproachful protest with Adams, declaring that Monroe's action could not then or at any time lessen or invalidate in the least the right of Spain to the

[16] *Ibid.*, 818-819.

provinces or to employ whatever means might be in her power to reunite them to the rest of her dominions.[17]

This gave Adams the opportunity to rebut the Spanish argument and advance the doctrinal viewpoint on which the whole American position and conception of the foundations of international relations then stood. In a carefully drafted note of April 6, 1822, which reassured Spain of our friendly solicitude, Adams laid down doctrine far in advance of that which we ourselves employed during the Revolution, yet far more restrained than the "alien ideas" which Genet brought to America in 1793:[18]

In every question relating to the independence of a nation, two principles are involved: one of *right*, and the other of *fact*; the former exclusively depending upon the determination of the nation itself, and the latter resulting from the successful execution of that determination. This right has been recently exercised, as well by the Spanish nation in Europe, as by several of those countries in the American hemisphere which had for two or three centuries been connected as colonies with Spain. In the conflicts which have attended these revolutions, the United States have carefully abstained from taking any part respecting the right of the nations concerned in them to maintain or

[17] 4 *ASP-FR* 845-846. It is interesting to note that, from the Spanish point of view, this was indeed the announcement of a doctrine of non-recognition such as would preserve intact the postulates of an old legality at the very moment when it had lost all semblance of correspondence with actual events. Perhaps it is the fact that almost all instances of formal non-recognition are of record in circumstances where public armed force has irreparably injured the situation that has tended to make of non-recognition not a weapon for the maintenance of the existing legal order, but a surly and unrepentant, *fin de non recevoir.*

[18] *Ibid.*, 846.

newly organize their own political constitutions, and observing, where it was a contest of arms, the most impartial neutrality. But the civil war in which Spain was for some years involved with the inhabitants of her colonies in America has, in substance, ceased to exist. Treaties equivalent to an acknowledgement of independence have been concluded by the commanders and viceroys of Spain herself with the Republic of Colombia, with Mexico and with Peru; while, in the provinces of La Plata and in Chili, no Spanish force has for several years existed to dispute the independence which the inhabitants of those countries had declared.

Under these circumstances, the Government of the United States, far from consulting the dictates of a policy questionable in its morality, has yielded to an obligation of duty of the highest order, by recognizing as independent states nations which, after deliberately asserting their right to that character, had maintained and established it against all the resistance which had been or could be brought to oppose it. This recognition is neither intended to invalidate any right of Spain, nor to affect the employment of any means which she may yet be disposed or enabled to use, with a view to reuniting those provinces with the rest of her dominions. It is the mere acknowledgement of existing facts with the view to the regular establishment with the nations newly formed of those relations, political and commercial, which it is the moral obligation of civilized and Christian nations to entertain reciprocally with one another.

Rejecting the aspersions cast upon the South American republics by the Spanish Minister, Adams continued:

It is not doubted that other and more correct views of the whole subject will very shortly be taken by your government, and that it, as well as the other European Governments will show that deference to the example of the United States which you urge it as the duty or the policy of the United States to show to theirs. The effect of the example of one independent nation upon the councils and measures of another can be just only so far as it is voluntary; and as the United States desire that their example should be followed, so it is their intention to follow that of others upon no other principle. They confidently rely that the time is at hand when all the Governments of Europe friendly to Spain, and Spain herself, will not only concur in the acknowledgement of the independence of the American nations, but in the sentiment that nothing will tend more effectually to the welfare and happiness of Spain that the universal concurrence in that recognition.

Here, then, was the formal and considered position of the United States: in default of a concerted arrangement with other powers, individual action by one, but not capriciously, or from subjective motives or complex predilections; a decision arrived at after careful gathering of data, and a meticulous appraisal of the situation in terms of fact—and strategy; in short, by a rough-hewn facsimile of due process. But the recognition was more than a mere acknowledgment of fact; once arrived at in this fashion, the American practice was exemplary and was intended to establish an international norm to be followed until it reached the point of universality.

The aggregate result of the deep-probing inquiries instituted by Monroe and Adams was to evolve, virtually independently of all other chancelleries, a formal procedure, basically valid for nearly a century, for determining the modes of admission to the community of nations. It may be said to have developed by the engrafting of principles of the Anglo-American legal system into the major layer of growth of international law. The idea of a full-fledged enquiry on the spot, with ample public knowledge and fair notice to everyone involved, including the right of those who are the objects of inquiry to give evidence of their worthiness or otherwise to be received into the international community, is at the very heart of our conception, not only of legality in the abstract, but of due process of law in particular. The ascertaining of the fundamental facts in the case before the granting of recognition; the unqualified and irrevocable result of the act—all these are qualities intrinsic in the procedure decided upon by Monroe and Adams. Their decision fixed the postulates of recognition policy, not, to be sure, beyond the occasional challenge of whim or caprice, but in a clear-cut way to which only the die-hard and the ultra-legitimist could take exception.

The position taken by the United States is not, however, complete without taking into account the extensive report made by the Committee of Foreign Affairs of the House of Representatives, which rendered its report on March 19, 1822—half-way between Monroe's action in extending recognition, and Adams' retort courteous to the protests of the Spanish envoy. After a careful factual survey of the background, and establishing to its complete satisfaction the fact of Latin American independence, the Committee examined " the right and expediency, on the part of the United States, of recognizing the independence which those nations have thus effectively achieved ": [19]

[19] *Ibid.*, 848-851.

In this examination, it cannot be necessary to inquire into the right of the people of Spanish America 'to dissolve the political bands which have connected them with another, and to assume among the Powers of the earth that separate and equal station to which the laws of nature and of nature's God entitle them.' The right to change the political institutions of the state has, indeed, been exercised equally by Spain and by her colonies; and for us to deny to the people of Spanish America the right to independence on the principles which alone sanction it here, would be virtually to renounce our own.

The political right of this nation to acknowledge their independence, without offending others, does not depend on its justice, but on its actual establishment. To justify such a recognition by us, it is necessary only to show, as is already sufficiently shown, that the people of Spanish America are, within their respective limits, exclusively sovereign, and thus, in fact, independent. With them as with every other Government possessing and exercising the power of making war, the United States, *in common with all nations*, have the right of concerting the terms of mutual peace and intercourse.

Who is the rightful sovereign of a country, is not an inquiry permitted to foreign nations, to whom it is competent only to treat with 'the powers that be.'

There is no difference of opinion on this point among the writers on public law; and no diversity, with respect to it, in the practice of civilized nations. It is not necessary here to cite authority for a doctrine familiar to all who have paid the slightest attention to the subject. . . .

The peace of the world and the independence of every member of the great political family require that each should be the exclusive judge of its own internal proceedings, and that the fact alone should be regarded by foreign nations. . . . For a nation to be entitled, in respect to foreign states, to the enjoyment of these attributes [of sovereignty] 'and to figure directly in the great political society, it is sufficient that it is really sovereign and independent; that is, that it governs itself by its own authority and laws.' The people of Spanish America do notoriously so govern themselves, and the right of the United States to recognize the Governments which they have instituted is incontestable. A doubt of the expediency of such a recognition can be suggested only by the apprehension that it may seriously affect our peaceful and friendly relations with the nations *of the other hemisphere.*

A review of the situation in some detail convinced the Committee that this was not the case:

Your committee, therefore, instead of seriously apprehending that the recognition by the United States of the independence of Spanish America will be unacceptable to these nations, are not without hope that they may practically approve it, by severally adopting a similar measure. It is not, indeed, unreasonable to suppose that those governments have, like this, waited only for the evidence of facts which might not only suffice to justify them, under the laws and usages of nations, but to satisfy Spain herself that nothing has been prematurely done, or which could justly offend her feelings, or be considered as inconsistent with her rights. As their motives for not having hitherto recognized the independence of Spanish America may thus be supposed to have been analogous to our own, it is permitted to presume that the facts and reasons which have prevailed on us no longer to hesitate will, confirmed as they are by our example, have a like influence on them.

The consequences were foregone. In justice to their own feelings and the feelings of their fellow citizens, the members of the Committee made an undisguised declaration:

Happy in our institutions, we claim no privilege; we indulge no ambition to extend them to other nations; we admit the equal rights of all nations to form their own governments and to administer their own internal affairs as they may judge proper; and however they may, in these respects, differ from us, we do not on that account regard with the less satisfaction their tranquillity and happiness.

Your Committee having thus considered the subject referred to them in all its aspects, are unanimously of opinion that it is just and expedient to acknowledge the independence of the several nations of Spanish America, without any reference to the diversity in the forms of their governments. . . .

Here was an operative meeting of minds between the Executive and Legislative branches of the government in one of the most fundamental issues that had come before the policy determiners of the United States. But it was wholly an intra-mural affair. A careful analysis of the policy pursued toward Latin America by the United States leads to the conclusion that it involved an overwhelmingly unilateral determination by the government in Washington, to the virtual exclusion of any direct external influence or the exercise of concerted action by two or more independent states.

The consequences of the procedure followed in effecting recognition were that the United States was ill prepared to face the immediate issue of defining our relations with the other American Republics—a problem first confronting the government in the invitation extended by the newly recognized states to participate in the Panama Congress of 1826. It was only as that invitation raised problems involving a wider association of the nations in the Atlantic basin, that the United States found itself compelled to cope with the problem of forms of international association going beyond the ordinary norms of our commercial treaties. So rigid had the policy of non-participation in the politics of Europe became in a third of a century, so deeply ingrained the idea of a neutrality-which-persists-through-peace, that the happy consensus of 1822 broke down. The American legislative mind could not grapple with the problem. It was too large, to protean in its forms, for the legislative technicians to envisage.

Nowhere is there a clearer instance of this than in the report of the Foreign Relations Committee in regard to the participation of the United States in the proposed Congress: "What cogent reasons," asked the Committee, "now existed for adopting this new and untried measure, so much in conflict with the whole course of policy uniformly and happily pursued by the United States . . . from almost the very creation of this government to the present hour?" After reviewing the case history of the recognition of the Spanish American Republics and the establishing of conventional relations with them, the Committee continued its queries: "What necessity has since arisen to do more? What cause exists now to prompt the United States to establish new and stronger relations with them, and so to abandon that rule of conduct which has hitherto been here so steadily and happily pursued?" [20]

The replies of the Committee to its self-propounded questions are illuminating. In an attitude of complete diffidence and also one of meticulous, states' rights-conscious, strict construction, they raised

[20] 5 *ASP-FR* 858.

the *question préalable.* Acting assertedly out of "jealousy inspired by an ardent attachment to our rights and privileges," they expressed doubts as to the completeness of agreement between the United States and the other participants as to means and ends, procedures and objectives, "before the destinies of the United States should be committed to the deliberation and decisions of a Congress composed not of our own citizens but of the representatives of many different nations." Failing to find a full answer in the documents presented, they expressed "much surprise and great regret" at Adams' willingness to take the venture.[21] Then, with querulous trepidation, they expressed misgivings as to the possible content of problems "to which the existence of the new States may give rise"—a description given to Clay by the Mexican Minister—to which the latter added, with commendable candor, "and which it is not easy to point out or enumerate." [22] There was further complaint by the Committee as to the failure of either Adams or Clay to make clear how the "ample powers" sought for our envoys, were, if granted, to be used and exercised. . . .

Is it "wise or expedient," asked the Committee, "that the United States should be represented at a Congress of American nations by agents endowed

[21] The probability that Henry Clay, then Secretary of State, was the deciding factor, seems to have been overlooked. The Senate's action in terms of votes carefully recorded, appears to have been almost entirely along party lines, the Jacksonian Democrats being steadfast in opposition to all favorable action.

[22] Pablo Obregon to Clay in Washington. November 3, 1825. 5 *ASP-FR* 836.

with undefined powers to accomplish undefined objects?" adding that "if ever it may be proper to adopt such a measure there is nothing known to them that requires or justifies it at this time"—an argument that is not unknown to contemporary statesmen!

Further possibilities appalled the members:

> If the measures to be accomplished by the proposed Congress, whatever . . . their object or character, should not meet the concurring opinion of all the parties there to be represented we need not the lights of history to inform us that many consequences, mischievous in themselves, and greatly to be deplored, not only may, but most probably will, result. And that a difference of opinion will exist in regard to measures so important in themselves, and so various and diversified in their effects upon nations differing from each other in almost every particular, is much to be apprehended.

Mere exercise by the Senate of its power to withhold assent ought not, the Committee concluded, to be regarded as furnishing sufficient assurance against the possible and probably dangerous effects of the proposed measure.

Reviewing the items specifically mentioned in diplomatic correspondence as objectives of the Congress, the Committee reported that it had been unable "to discover . . . a single subject concerning which the United States ought to enter into any negotiation with the States of America to be assembled at the contemplated Congress at Panama."[23] The Committee sedulously exploited the differences in purpose between those stated to this Government by the

[23] *Ibid.*, 859.

American Republics and those announced to the Senate by the President. It sensed primordially in the measures to be concerted by the American Republics in the event of "the interference of any neutral nation in the question and war of independence between the new powers of this continent and Spain," the formation of "an eventual alliance" by a secret treaty. This, notwithstanding explicit assurances by Adams that we would attend "neither to contract alliances nor to engage in any undertaking or project imparting hostility to any other nation." The contrast of viewpoints led the Committee to believe that there were essential differences which "must unavoidably excite doubts" and so "contribute not a little to defeat other objects" of the Congress.

The second major Committee objection dealt with the Mexican proposal for opposition to the colonization in America by the European powers—a topic which Colombia placed at the head of the list—not because the idea was itself debatable but because, in the eyes of the American Republics, the two propositions of resistance to resubjugation and resistance to colonization were viewed as one, and hence were "to be effected by the joint and united efforts of all the States to be represented at the Congress, who should be bound by a solemn convention to secure this end." Again disbelieving Adams, and pinning more faith on the statements of Mexico and Colombia, the Committee concluded that every commitment along this line would "violate all the well-settled principles of the policy of the United States, and put at hazard their best interests, without any adequate motive for so novel an experiment." Its members sought to impale Adams on the dilemma that if we disagreed with the other delegations, it would be fatal to the Congress, whereas if Adams and the conferees were to reach agreement, it would be "fatal to the best interests of the United States!"

A third major point of difference related to the African slave trade, the complete abolition of which was placed by Colombia on the agenda of the Congress. It is obvious that this and related topics touched very closely the dynamite-laden problem of slavery itself, and that the deep cleavages of opinion already existing in the country on the subject elicited the very positive assertion that

> The United States . . . have not certainly the right, and ought never to feel the inclination to dictate to others who may differ with them upon this subject, nor do the Committee see the expediency of insulting other States . . . by ascending the moral chair and proclaiming from thence mere abstract principles, of the rectitude of which *each nation enjoys the perfect right of deciding for itself.*

Manifestly the Senate, with an important part of its membership emanating from slave states, could not, at all hazards, allow the status of slavery to come under discussion at the international level. That is why the status of Haiti, Cuba, and Puerto Rico "and of other parts of our hemisphere that shall hereafter be in like circumstances," again put on the agenda of the Congress by Colombia, further aroused Senatorial ire.[24]

[24] *Ibid.*, 860. The italics are those of the Committee.

Surely, if there is any subject within the whole circle of political relations, as to which it is the interest and the duty of all States to keep themselves free and unshackled by any previous stipulation, it is that which regards their future connexions with any other people not parties to such an agreement. Of the propriety or impropriety of such connexions *each must ever be permitted to judge freely for itself*, because the benefit or disadvantage to result from them must be peculiar, and very different to each; and that relation which is highly desirable at one time may become hurtful at another. In the opinion of this Committee therefore, *the United States should never permit themselves to enter into discussion with any foreign State whatever, as to the relations they should be obliged to establish with any other people not parties to such discussions.* And the objections to such a course become infinitely stronger, when the discussions are intended to refer, not only to those who then exist, but also to others who may hereafter be considered as placed "in like circumstances."

A clearer example of atomistic reasoning, of the compartmentalization of all dealings with foreign powers, could hardly be conceived.

In addition to objections to the agenda, the Committee balked at the more general objectives of the Congress. Guatemala having suggested "that as Europe had formed a Continental System, and held a Congress whenever questions affecting its interests were to be discussed, America should also form a system for itself," the Committee members gratuitously identified the phrase "Continental System" with Holy Alliance. They inveighed against it and all its works, holding it as not "of a character to invite the States of this continent to take that system as a model or example fit for their imitation," and falsely ascribed to the proponents of an American system a desire to straight-jacket the Americas and estop all societal progress:

> No compact with other States can be necessary to bestow upon each the power it now possesses to effect any change which experience may hereafter show to be beneficial to itself; and a stipulation to make such changes as the good of any others may hereafter require would either be futile in itself or must inevitably lead to discord and to wars.[25]

A further frontal objection of the Committee to the whole Congress rested on their doubt as to " the authority of the Government of the United States to enter into any negotiation with foreign nations for the purpose of settling and promulgating either principles of internal polity or mere abstract propositions as parts of the public law." They opposed even a " summary negotiation relative to existing interests important to this Continent alone " on the ground that all other civilized nations would consider it " a confederacy of the States therein represented for purposes as prejudicial to the interests of the Old as they are supposed to be beneficial to those of the New World." Suspicion thus once created would have deplorable consequences, and no refusal by the Senate to ratify agreements reached would lay low such suspicions!

> The United States . . . must prepare to embark their future destinies upon an unknown and turbulent ocean, directed by little experience, and destined for no certain haven. In such a voyage, the dissimilitude existing between themselves and their associates in interest, character,

[25] *Ibid., loc. cit.*

language, religion, manners, customs, habits, laws and almost every other particular, and the rivalship these discrepancies must surely produce among them, would generate discords which, if they did not destroy all hope of its successful termination, would make even success itself the ultimate cause of new and direful conflicts between themselves.

To this picture of unmitigated woe the Committee added a pontifical clincher: " Such has been the issue of all such enterprises in past time, and we have therefore strong reasons to expect in the future similar results from similar causes."

Subsidiary fears obsessed the Committee: that other objectives would be ruled off the agenda, thus leaving the United States in a " degraded position "; that the adoption of " general principles " of commerce by all would inflict local specialized injuries, which could be avoided only by special agreements *à deux*; that " the consentaneous adoption of principles of maritime neutrality, favorable to the navigation of peace and commerce in time of war," as proposed by Adams, would be attended by grave risks; [26] and that the discussion of " the advancement

[26a] " There exists so much risk of compromising and destroying the relations of neutrality, which the United States are now maintaining, should they involve themselves, by any compact, relative to belligerent rights entered into with only one of the parties to the present war, during its continuance, that . . . it would be highly inexpedient to make such an experiment at this time. Any principle relating to the rights of war, which one of the parties in the existing contest might be willing to adopt, as promoting its interests, could scarcely be regarded with indifference by the other. And the great maritime States of Europe would most probably consider —[Shades of the Armed Neutrality!]—that the United States had seized the occasion of this war to enter into a con-

of religious liberty"—another Presidential proposal—would be most inopportune.[27]

In fine, the Committee felt that agreement on any "unfit subjects" "must impair that freedom of action which it is so necessary for the United States to preserve." Hence it believed that agreement on the remaining subjects was "either not of sufficient importance to require the adoption of this new and untried experiment of a Congress of Nations" or might better be settled with each than with all.

> While the United States retain the position which they have hitherto occupied, and manifest a constant determination not to mingle their interests with those of the other States of America, they may continue to employ the influence they possess and have already happily exerted with the nations of Europe in favor of these new Republics; but if ever the United States permit themselves to be associated with those nations in any general Congress assembled for the discussion of common plans in any way affecting European interests, they will, by such an act, not only deprive themselves of the ability they now possess of rendering useful assistance to the other American States but also produce other effects prejudicial to their own interests. . . .[28]

---

federacy with the other States of this Continent now actually engaged in it for the purpose of settling principles intended to affect materially their future interests." *Ibid.*, 862.

[27] "If there be any subject more sacred and delicate than another, it is that which concerns religious liberty. The most cruel and devastating wars have been produced by such interferences, the blood of man has been poured out in torrents, and, from the days of the Crusades to the present hour, no benefit has resulted to the human family from discussions carried on by nations upon such subjects." *Ibid., loc. cit.*

[28] *Ibid., loc. cit.*

The Committee's report in effect proposed disunity and inaction. In order to placate provincial domestic opinion, it failed wholly to square its course of action with existing political realities at the international level.

It is plain in the retrospect of more than a century that the recalcitrant attitude of the Senate was based in part on political pique, in part on great sensitivity to the slavery question, but perhaps most accountably on plain ignorance of the diplomatic process. A vast unacquaintance with the world situation pervaded its discussions, and its resoluteness in not surrendering an iota of privilege was matched by the barefaced assertion and stubborn defense of ideas of state sovereignty which had certainly lain dormant during the three decades of our exposure as a nation to every wind that blew during the Revolutionary and Napoleonic storms. It is my personal conviction, based on a careful review of the evidence, that no hope of a basic change in the outlook of the United States toward supra-national institutions of any character whatsoever could be expected until the politically centrifugal tendencies running from nullification to outright secession were surmounted.[29] Only when the unity of the country constitutionally confirmed its unity in the face of foreign powers was

[29] This is not to underestimate the constructive work of many solid and substantial, even zealous, groups among the citizenry, who thought otherwise, but to establish the fact of the existence, particularly in the national legislature, of a fanatical faction whose outlook on international affairs was so provincial as to lose sight of the national interest, not to mention the larger needs of the international community.

a coherent conception of relationships to other states made possible.

Once the Senate, despite all its blustering, confirmed the necessary nominations, President Adams found occasion, in a message to the House of Representatives on March 17, 1826, to defend his course and refute the critics of his attitude and conduct. In a state paper of eloquence and ability [30] he stressed his desire "to meet in the spirit of kindness and friendship an overture made in that spirit by the three sister Republics of this hemisphere":

> The great revolution in human affairs which has brought into existence, nearly at the same time, eight sovereign and independent nations in our own quarter of the globe, has placed the United States in a situation not less novel, and scarcely less interesting, than that in which they had found themselves by their own transition from a cluster of colonies to a nation of sovereign states. The deliverance of the South American Republics from the oppression under which they had been so long afflicted was hailed by the people [31] of this Union as among the most auspicious events of the age.

Monroe having already opened up diplomatic relations with the newly recognized States in 1822, under authorization of Congress "without exacting from these Republics, as by the ancient principles of political primogeniture he might have done, that the compliment of a plenipotentiary mission should have been paid first by them to the United States," Adams merely followed in the footsteps of his predecessor.

[30] 5 *ASP-FR* 882-886.

[31] As contrasted with the "plenipotentiaries" of the several "sovereign" States in the Senate.

The invitation to the Panama Congress, declared the President,

> had sprung from the urgent, immediate and momentous common interests of the great communities struggling for independence and, as it were, quickening into life. From them the invitation to us appeared respectful and friendly; from us to them it could scarcely have been made without exposing ourselves to suspicions of purposes of ambition, if not of domination, more suited to rouse resistance and excite distrust than to conciliate favor and friendship.
>
> The first and paramount principle upon which it was deemed wise and just to lay the cornerstone of all our future relations with them was *disinterestedness*; the next was cordial good will to them; the third was a claim of fair and equal reciprocity . . . The proposal itself implied that the Republics by whom it was made *believed* that important interests of ours or of theirs rendered our attendence there desirable. They had given us notice that, in the novelty of their situation, and in the spirit of deference to our experience, they would be pleased to have the benefit of our friendly counsel. . . .

In further statements the President indicated the inescapable necessity of being represented, not merely for the protection of American interests, but because of the need of being on the ground even to decline their proposals, and, in other contingencies, give them advice in their own interest. Neither sullen repulses nor aspiring pretensions would be welcome at Panama. But

> objects of the highest importance, not only to the future welfare of the whole human race, but bearing directly upon the special interests of this Union, *will* engage the deliberations of the Congress of Panama whether we are represented there or not. Others, if we are represented, may be

offered by our plenipotentiaries for consideration, having in view both these great results—our own interests and the improvement of the condition of man upon earth.

Then, with a prospective look and rare intuition, the President concluded:

> It may be that, in the lapse of many centuries, no other opportunity so favorable will be presented to the Government of the United States to subserve the benevolent purposes of Divine Providence, to dispense the promised blessings of the Redeemer of mankind, to promote the prevalence in future ages of peace on earth and good will to man, as will now be placed in their power by participating in the deliberations of this Congress.

Without attributing to Adams Messianic powers of perspicacity, it is distinctly noteworthy to put of record that the periods in which the United States has been most potentially influential in shaping the institutions and mores of the Great Community have been at the moments when protracted wars are drawing to a close and the fundamental principles of reconstruction are at stake. Even Adams saw the analogy with the situation prevailing at the close of our War of Independence, and drew the moral:

> Now, at this propitious moment, the new-born nations of this hemisphere, assembling by their representatives at the isthmus between its two continents, to settle the principles of their future international intercourse with other nations and with us, ask, in this great exigency, for our advice upon those very fundamental maxims which we from our cradle at first proclaimed, and partially succeeded to introduce into the code of national law.

Adverting to the numerous causes of friction in commerce, inflicting irreparable injuries for which payment of claims after the fact afforded no great satisfaction, Adams disclosed the real remedy:

> The settlement of general principles, pervading with equal efficacy all the American States, can alone put an end to these evils, and can alone be accomplished at the proposed assembly.

It is superfluous to discuss here the project which Adams had most at heart, that of abolishing private war upon the ocean, for the time was not yet ripe in 1826 for a Declaration of Paris. Of greater importance is the collaborative basis which he sought to put under the Monroe Doctrine, in terms more reminiscent of Havana in 1940 than of Panama—or Washington—in 1826. The non-colonization principle, he declared,

> rested upon a course of reasoning equally simple and conclusive. With the exception of the existing European colonies, which it was in nowise intended to disturb, the two continents consisted of several sovereign and independent nations whose territories covered their whole surface. By this, their independent condition, the United States enjoyed the right of commercial intercourse with every part of their possessions. To attempt the establishment of a colony in these possessions would be to usurp, to the exclusion of others, a commercial intercourse, which was the common possession of all. It could not be done without encroaching on the existing rights of the United States. . . . *Most of the new American Republics have declared their entire assent to them* [the positions taken by Monroe]; *and they now propose, among the subjects of consultation at Panama, to take into consideration the means of making effectual the assertion of that principle, as well as the means of resisting interference from abroad with the domestic concerns of the American Governments.* . . . Should it be

deemed advisable to contract a conventional engagement on this topic, our views would extend no further than to a mutual pledge of the parties to the compact to maintain the principle in application to its own territory, and to permit no colonial lodgments or establishments of European jurisdiction upon its own soil; and, with respect to the obtrusive interference from abroad, if its future character may be inferred from that which has been and perhaps still is exercised in more than one of the new States, *a joint declaration of its character, and exposure of it to the world, may be probably all that the occasion would require.* Whether the United States should or should not be parties to such a declaration may justly form a part of the deliberation. That there is an evil to be remedied needs little insight into the secret history of late years to know, and that this remedy may best be concerted at Panama meeting deserves at least the experiment of consideration. [Italics mine.]

It is clear that Adams was willing to commit this nation, at the Panama Congress, to reciprocal pledges of a negative character—not to allow foreign colonization—coupled with contingent promises of a joint course of action which would create in the world a deterrent climate of opinion. Beyond that it was, in the given circumstances, impossible for him to go. Paradoxically, John Quincy Adams, who had spent years reaffirming the isolationist position taken by his distinguished father, was now forced to cope with the irrationality with which it was held by the new generation who had come to reverence it, accepting it out of its context and utterly uncritically: Repeating to the House the gist of Washington's admonitions, he was forced to recall also that the counsel of Washington was founded upon the circumstances in the country and the world at the time when it was given; that whatever the humble position in the hour of our beginnings, "the period was not far distant when we might defy material injury from external annoyance—when we might take such an attitude as would cause our neutrality to be respected, and with reference to belligerent nations, might choose peace or war, as our interests, guided by justice, should counsel." Like Woodrow Wilson and Franklin Roosevelt at much later dates, he was forced to distinguish the historical contexts of the Age of the Great Pronouncements from those of his own day, and so find the implications of the situation. To Adams it was necessary to admit the factor of geographical distance as isolating us from Europe; but the situation with regard to the New World was vastly different:

> We were then the only independent nation of this hemisphere; and we were surrounded by European colonies, with the greater part of which we had no more intercourse than with the inhabitants of another planet. Those colonies have now been transformed into eight independent nations, extending to our very borders. Seven of them Republics like ourselves, with whom we have an immensely growing commercial, and *must* have, and have already, important political, connections; with reference to whom our situation is neither distant nor detached; whose political principles and systems of Government, congenial with our own, must and will have an action and counteraction upon us and ours to which we cannot be indifferent if we would.

There was, in Adams' message, a final plea "for urging upon all the new nations of the South the just and liberal principles of religious liberty." Already conceded to our citizens by two treaties, there was hope that the "existing prejudices which are struggling against it . . . may perhaps be more successfully combatted at this general meeting than at the separate seats of government of each Republic." In the last analysis, Adams sought to commit this Government to a cooperative policy with our new neighbors in the nascent hemisphere community on the basis of a fundamental identification of the tasks of the Panama Congress with the historic purposes of the United States:

> That the Congress at Panama will accomplish all or even any of the transcendent benefits to the human race which warmed the conceptions of its first proposer, it were, perhaps, indulging too sanguine a forecast of events to promise. It is, in its nature, a measure speculative and experimental. The blessing of heaven may turn it to the account of human improvement. Accidents unforseen and mischances not to be anticipated may baffle all its high purposes and disappoint its fairest expectations. But the design is great, is benevolent, is humane.
>
> It looks to the melioration of the condition of man. It is congenial with that spirit which prompted the Declaration of Independence; which inspired the preamble of our first treaty with France; which dictated our first treaty with Prussia, and the instructions under which it was negotiated; which filled the hearts and fired the souls of the immortal founders of our Revolution.

Let us keep the record of actual accomplishments, however unpleasant, clearly before us and recall that, in the utterly de-institutionalized setting of the existing community of American States all the advantages which should have accrued to us from our primogeniture, our primacy, and our potential leadership were allowed to lapse. In 1826, as again in 1919, the heaviest battalions were on the side of provincialism, particularism, and ignorance. The divinely appointed, or fortuitous, opportunity for cooperative action was indeed lost and did not recur. After aiding so conspicuously in the introduction of the American Republics to the older, European, Society of States, the chance for our forefathers to bring forth on these continents a new confederacy of states espousing a common political faith was lost, and the process of organic understanding was abruptly halted. For nearly sixty years thereafter we wandered in the political wilderness because we refused, in the golden hour of opportunity, to aid in giving institutional form and mold to the aspirations for an organized community of states in the New World. In the end it was Blaine, not Monroe, who planted; Wilson, not Adams, who watered; and Hull, not Clay, who gathered the increase. In the long retrospect of history it is not the brilliant coup, the dramatic stroke, but the consistent perspicacity transcending any momentary political advantage, that sets the seal of statesmanship upon a man, a policy, and, eventually, a tradition. Let it stand of record that, though we had miniscule personalities, certainly the post-Napoleonic generation did not lack its own leonine figures who could see the distant scene.

APPENDIX II

Opinion of the Russian Cabinet upon the Slave Trade

The execution of the law should be confided to an institution, the seat of which should be in a central point on the coast of Africa, and in the formation of which all Christian States should take a part.

Declared forever neutral, to be estranged from all political and local interests, like the fraternal and Christian alliance, of which it would be a practical manifestation, this institution would follow the single object of strictly maintaining the execution of the law. It would consist of a maritime force, composed of a sufficient number of ships-of-war, appropriated to the service assigned to them.

Of a judicial power, which should judge all crimes relating to the trade, according to a legislation established upon the subject by the common law.

Of a supreme council, in which would reside the authority of the institution; which would regulate the operations of the maritime force, would revise the sentences of the tribunals, would put them in execution, would inspect all the details, and would render an account of its administration to the future European conferences.

The right of visit and of detention would be granted to this institution as the means of fulfilling its end; and perhaps no maritime nation would refuse to submit its flag to this police, exerted in a limited and clearly defined manner, and by a power too feeble to allow of vexations, too disinterested on all maritime and commercial questions, and above all, too widely combined in its elements not to observe a severe but impartial justice towards all.

Would it not be possible to compose this institution of such different elements as to give it no other tendency, as long as it remained united, but that of doing its duty? [1]

The expense which it would occasion, divided amongst all the Christian States, could not be very burdensome, and its duration would be regulated according to the time required for the development of African civilization, which it would protect, and it might also bring about a happy change in the system of civilization in the colonies.[2]

[1] Every endeavor to curb the slave trade necessarily entailed some form of supervision of the area frequented by the slave ships. It was implicit in all the British proposals, which envisaged a visitation and search of every suspect ship. The fact of British power at sea enabled the British government to suggest the patrol in a routine manner. Naturally American opinion, so soon after our military and naval contest, was exasperated at the thought of visit and search in time of peace. The Russian government, not to be outdistanced, even on paper, by the British, promptly brought forward the proposal given below, which went very far in the direction of establishing a full-fledged super-government, albeit for strictly defined purposes. How far from ready the world then was for such a series of international agencies scarcely requires comment. The project is not, however, without interest, inasmuch as it acquainted the United States Government with the minimum of governmental apparatus: a Control Council, a judiciary, and a maritime force representing the funded power of all the participating states. It is hardly necessary to comment that the cross-reference, in the Russian proposal, to the " fraternal and Christian alliance " was sufficient to prevent its being realized politically. Nevertheless, it represents a singularly bold idea in what is probably the earliest of diplomatic blueprints in our archives relating to supranational agencies.

[2] 5 *ASP-FR* 118-119.

LECTURE III

THE UNITED STATES AND THE EUROPEAN STATE SYSTEM, 1826-1914

The core of our thinking in the two preceding lectures has dealt with the United States itself, and its coming into being; then with the expansion of the American system to include the other American Republics. Our present task is to trace the attitude of the United States toward the European State System and to endeavor to integrate and to differentiate the views expressed in that regard for nearly nine decades before 1914. The task is not easy and the trends are not all in the same direction. But so engaging is the interest in the subject, so great, in my opinion, the light that it sheds alike on our history and our collective mentality, that it is well worth the emprise.

It will be recalled that the attitude of the revolutionary leaders toward the countries of Europe was not uniform. Too many of our citizens, whether Puritan or Cavalier, Catholic or Protestant, free-born or indentured servants, had, in coming to America, fled from an oppressive social order in the Old World, to make Europe an inviting partner in democratic freedom. And yet the dualistic trend initially noted, to appeal, on the one hand, to the enemies of England upon the Continent for immediate assistance and alliance, even if it involved a disregard for all the conventional proprieties of diplomacy, and, on the other, to seek, at a slower tempo and with infinite punctilio, the formal recognition from European sovereigns which would give us leverage in the international community, did not outlast the Revolutionary War. Our pleas for assistance were not immediately heeded, even by France, and we were ultimately accepted only when the heady wine of our Revolutionary days had cooled to the point where it could be contained by the old bottles of ordinary diplomacy. Our peace was made with the aid of two powerful monarchs, and it was from George III, and not from some new Cromwell at the head of an English Republic, that we received the final acknowledgment of our independence. Thereafter, our desire for commerce led us to conclude treaties indifferently with both monarchies and republics. In the Critical Period and even after, we could not afford to be squeamish!

With the coming of the French Revolution, however, a major schism was created in the minds of the American citizenry, according as the concept of solidarity with popular movements in other lands was made the determinant factor in the thinking of many, or the straight-jacket of political neutrality was invoked as the norm of our aggregate behavior. It is superfluous to establish the fact that the policy of neutrality formally triumphed, but its successful consummation was made possible only by the passage of the Alien and Sedition Acts which, to this day, are still regarded as odious. The causal correlation between the two deserves to be noted, for it reveals the existence in the country of an anti-isolationist, anti-neutrality movement of very extensive proportions and obtaining so localized an ascendancy as to tug very hard at the leashstrings of legality. This sense of solidarity with free men everywhere, but particularly in Europe, was presently extended, after the lapse of two decades, to the New World, and it proved far harder to repress, particularly as no odium arising from unpleasant memories of historical origins or social relationships extended to that " quarter of the foreign world."

Notwithstanding, the neutrality legislation of the period presupposed a corporate popular abstention from dealings with the defenders of public liberties in the New World which was in flagrant contravention of the facts. The application of the isolationist neutrality devised for Europe to the affairs of the Western Hemisphere was largely the work of John Quincy Adams, not of Monroe. And it will be recalled that the anomalous position of the average American citizen in this period was not pretty. For months and years, running into decades, he was prohibited by a neutrality declared by one of its advocates to inhere in the moral order of the universe, from doing any substantial thing in behalf of those with whom he felt in ideological kinship.[1] More-

[1] It is noteworthy that juridically neutrality is, first and foremost, a territorial conception—a means of withdrawing an area from a war. Perhaps it was because the United States Government had been so recently engaged in a protracted struggle with Great Britain to become master in its own domain that there was an insidious appeal to the ranks of officialdom in the idea of making neutrality apply throughout the territorial area of the new nation. It is clear that solidarity, precisely because it implied co-action with groups

over, certain acts which would under other circumstances seem magnificently humanitarian, were proscribed under criminal penalties—all in relation to a finding by a single individual that a war, which had been over for perhaps a decade, still theoretically existed! Yet once recognition was accorded, the acts in question ceased to be morally odious and there could be a return, corporately and individually, to the ordinary ways of human decency and behavior.

The United States and the Greek Independence Movement

Small wonder that very shortly after the recognition of the American Republics, the same argument which was used in their behalf was applied by the protagonists of Greece in America with added force and a special appeal on the grounds of religion, to the struggle of the Greek people for liberation from Ottoman rule. The factual background is not difficult to relate. As early as December, 1822, a memorial was laid before the House of Representatives on behalf of the Greeks by Henry Dwight, of Massachusetts. The sentiment of the House being "against meddling with the subject" according to J. C. Bancroft Davis' account in the official Treaty Notes to

---

outside a given territorial jurisdiction, was frontally at variance with the concept of neutrality; not less so because it also implied an obedient response of some of our citizenry, for whatever reason, to appeals originating outside that territorial jurisdiction. It is beyond question that formal legal neutrality was a fundamental weapon in traverse of any pleas—racial, religious, economic, or ideological—originating outside the United States.

his edition of the *Treaties of the United States*, the memorial was ordered to lie on the table. A year later, however, the special mention of the Greeks by President Monroe in the celebrated message by which he enunciated the doctrine that bears his name, gave new impetus to the cause of the Hellenes:

> A strong hope has long been entertained, founded on the heroic struggle of the Greeks, that they would succeed in their contest and resume their equal station among the nations of the earth. It is believed that the whole civilized world take a deep interest in their welfare. Although no Power has declared in their favor, yet none, according to our information, has taken part against them. Their cause and their name have protected them from dangers which might ere this have overwhelmed any other people. The ordinary calculations of interest and of acquisition with a view to aggrandizement, which mingles so much in the transactions of nations, seems to have had no effect in regard to them. From the facts which have come to our knowledge, there is good cause to believe that their enemy has lost forever all dominion over them; that Greece will become again an independent nation. That she may obtain that rank is the object of our most ardent wishes.

It is of singular significance that the expression of an interest and sympathy with the Greek liberation movement came in almost the same breath as the promulgation of a *ne plus ultra* to Europe in the New World. Instead of proclaiming a genuine isolation, President Monroe's message breathed a moral solidarity with *two other* "quarters of the foreign world." Whatever the extent of our withdrawal from the scene in days of our military and economic impotence, here was an assertion of an interest and concern in what went on elsewhere in the civilized world. The failure of the Adams Administration, as will be noted below, to follow up the gesture by Monroe reveals the fundamental fact that the momentary focus point of our national emotions, eliciting our sympathy for some particular cause abroad, was never large enough, or sustained enough, to overcome the contrarient force of the *los von Europa* tradition.

The particular significance of the Greek liberation case seems to me to lie in the fact that it was the first in a series of test situations in which a powerful dynamic—the sense of solidarity with a people seeking political liberation, reinforced by a sense of cultural and religious solidarity—was set in motion against the prevailing drive away from European entanglements. A fuller analysis of the situation gives rise to what seems to me a tenable hypothesis: that if ever the degree of solicitude for the European situation should become great enough, for whatever reason, the isolationist point of view would, sooner or later, give way, exactly in proportion to the duration of the strain and the directness of the impact upon us. The Greek Revolution was an event on a small scale by comparison with the Spanish-American revolutions, yet in a microcosmic sort of way, it became a touchstone, as the following pages will show, to fundamental popular feeling and the deeper, more powerful trends in national policy.

The pronouncement by Monroe was, however, little more than an expression of a pious hope, for the President, despite the accuracy of his analysis, and his emphasis on the low risk to be run in extending recognition then, did not follow up his generous plea and recognition did not actually take place until 1833, after Jackson had entered office.

The mention of the Greeks in the Presidential message, however, touched off a vigorous affirmative reaction both in the Congress and among the people. Every opportunity was given Monroe to proceed, as Daniel Webster, on December 8, 1823, introduced into the House a resolution for the appointment of an agent or commissioner to Greece—a move which shortly resulted in a call for papers by the House. In the ensuing weeks Monroe submitted the correspondence,[2] and a week's debate in the House occurred. Moreover, extensive memorials were presented to it from leading personalities in Boston and New York, as well as from the Legislature of South Carolina. Of the discussion as a whole J. C. Bancroft Davis writes tersely that " it took a wide range, developed great diversity of sentiment, and produced no result." This statement covers up the arguments adduced, ignores the entire trend of public opinion and buries it under official silence. Let us look at the record, because it is far, far more enlightening.

The problem of the Greek liberation movement, although first noted by the American Legation in Madrid late in 1822, was officially posed to President Monroe by Richard Rush in a despatch of February 23, 1823, from London, recounting to Secretary of State Adams conversations with Andreas Luriottis, the first Greek emissary in London:

[2] 5 *ASP-FR* 251-262.

I assured him that the fortunes of his country were dear to the people of the United States, who, cherishing the freedom which they themselves inherited and enjoyed, looked with the warmest sympathy upon the struggle of the Greeks for their national liberties, and that the Government of the United States participated in this feeling.

To the inquiries of Luriottis as to whether the United States would open political or diplomatic relations with his government, Rush returned an evasive answer, leaving it to the President to decide the matter:

All that I could say was to reiterate the assurance of the friendly interest that was felt amongst us for the success of the cause in which his country was embarked; and I adverted to the part which my Government had acted in relation to the South American struggle—a part so much in advance of that of any other government—as a sure indication that it could feel no backwardness in welcoming, when the proper day arrived, the new-born freedom of Greece into the family of nations.

As far as official policy was concerned, the only legitimate impression which the Greek Government, in its hour of extremity, could have formed from the foregoing, was that the attitude of the United States would be friendly, affirmative and prompt. However, after "mature consideration" with Monroe, Adams replied, noting the official pronouncements of the President, and adding:

They are cordially felt by the people of this Union, who, *sympathizing with the cause of freedom and independence wherever its standard is unfurled*, behold with peculiar interest the display of Grecian energy in defence of Grecian liberties. . . . But while cheering with their best wishes the cause of the Greeks, the United States are forbidden by the duties of their situation from taking part in the war, to which their relation is that of neutrality. At peace themselves with all the world, their established policy and the obligations of the law of nations preclude them from becoming voluntary auxiliaries to a cause which would involve them in *war*.

This perfectly expresses the position in which Adams believed with religious fervor.

If in the progress of events, the Greeks should be enabled to establish and organize themselves as an independent nation, the United States will be among the first to welcome them in that capacity into the general family, to establish diplomatic and commercial relations with them suited to the mutual interests of the two countries, and to recognize with special satisfaction their constituted state *in the character of a sister republic.* [Italics are Adams'.]

Here was a doctrine of measured risks and limited liabilities—the United States undertaking not to be the first to recognize—linked to an explicit assumption that the only form that a liberated state could adopt would be republican. It was in keeping with the policy adopted toward Latin America; it projected into the European world the conception that the United States would have an *a priori* regard for republican institutions.

Such was the reply to Luriottis. In the accompanying instructions to Rush, Adams emphasized that " in declining the proposal of giving active aid to the cause of Grecian emancipation," our Government was governed " not by its inclinations or a sentiment of indifference to the cause, but by its constitutional duties, clear and unequivocal." These Adams went on to explain. Governmental assistance could be only financial or military, and might involve the United States in war with the Ottoman Porte and perhaps with all the Barbary Powers.

To make this disposal either of force or treasure . . . is, by our constitution, not within the competency of the Executive. It could be determined only by an Act of Congress, which would assuredly not be adopted should it even be recommended by the Executive.

This was the practical argument of a President with an uncertain Congress. But the real argument was assertedly on higher grounds:

The policy of the United States with reference to foreign nations has always been founded upon the moral principle of natural law—*peace* with all mankind. From whatever cause war between other nations, whether foreign or domestic, has arisen, the unvarying law of the United States has been *peace* with both belligerents. From the first war of the French Revolution to the recent invasion of Spain, there has been a succession of wars, national and civil, in almost every one of which *one* of the parties was contending for liberty or independence. [The italics are Adams'.]

Notwithstanding the "strong impulse of feeling" actuating "the people of the United States to take side with the party which, at its commencement, was *contending* apparently at least, for both," and despite the fact that "a stronger case to claim their interference could scarcely have been presented," the United States nevertheless "declared themselves neutral, and the principle then deliberately settled has," declared Adams, "been invariably adhered to ever since." On closer examination, the argument yields nothing more than a stubborn case of *stare decisis*, which, coupled with the granitic tenacity of the Adams family and the assumption of an invisible connection with a higher law, meant standing pat.

On the more formal side of recognition, Adams also drew on the thirty-year-old tradition of the United States:

> Precluded by their neutral position from interfering in the question of right, the United States have recognized the fact of foreign sovereignty only when it was undisputed, or disputed without any rational prospect of success. In this manner the successive changes of government in many of the European states, and the revolutionary governments of South America have been acknowledged. The condition of the Greeks is not yet such as will admit of the recognition upon these principles.

Despite reassurances of friendly feeling and a sincere disposition to render the Greeks any service compatible with American neutrality, this marked the end of the discussion. This was official policy.

What actuated Congressional discussion was the powerful force of mobilized public opinion operating outside of all legal institutions. The mass meeting in Boston, first of those which have embalmed their resolutions in the *American State Papers*, literally glowed with convincing doctrine in an appeal to the principles of the American Revolution:

> The contest of an oppressed and enslaved people for the invaluable blessings of self-government, and of a Christian people for the enjoyment of religious liberty, has a claim to the best wishes of this nation for its eventual success, and to whatever aid and encouragement, consistently with the primary duty of self-preservation, it may have the ability to afford.

So far this was an echo of Monroe's pronouncement, with the addition of a religious note. There follows the identification of American interest with the Greek cause, and the raising of the question above the level of Congressional caprice to the plane of world significance:

No one who has duly reflected upon the consequences which have resulted from our own successful struggle in the cause of civil liberty, not as respects the interests of our nation only, but as it has affected also the condition of the whole civilized world, can hesitate to admit that the question of the erection of a new independent Christian State is the most momentous that can occur in the progress of human affairs, and especially deserving the attention of the representatives of a free people. . . . The emancipation from a barbarous despotism of a gallant and enterprising and intelligent people must be followed by the most propitious consequences, and cannot fail to add to the security of all free governments, by increasing the number of those who are devoted to their common defense.

To this clear, quantitative statement of the values of solidarity, is added the strategic and geo-political finishing touch:

The extermination of the Turkish despotism on the coasts and islands of the Mediterranean Sea has justly been regarded as a more worthy object of concert and coalition among civilized Powers than any which ever engaged their united attention. . . . It is quite obvious that the erection of a new and free state in the Mediterranean, possessing not only the coasts of Southern Greece, but the islands, particularly of Candia and Cyprus, would form a powerful check upon the barbarous dependencies of the Porte in those seas, and give facility to that commercial enterprise which now finds its way to one port of European or Asiatic Turkey.

While not suggesting a specific course for the United States to follow, the memorialists felt, "in common with their fellow citizens generally," the just weight and obligation of the non-intervention doctrine, and contented themselves with expressing their assurance that, "if the peculiar and unprecedented condition of the Greeks should, in the opinion of the Government of the United States, form a case of exception to the general rule of policy," the measures adopted would receive their cordial support. This was inoffensive enough even in the home state of the Secretary of State.

Finally the memorialists adduced special considerations to actuate American official policy:

But your memorialists at any rate cannot refrain from the expression of their earnest wish that the indignation and abhorrence which they are satisfied is universal throughout the United States at the mode in which the Turkish Government is carrying on the war against Greece should be distinctly avowed in the face of the world, and that other civilized and Christian nations should be invited to join in a solemn remonstrance against such barbarous and inhuman depravity.

The sale of forty thousand Christian women and children (after the massacre of their husbands and fathers) in open market, in the presence of Christian Europe, and without one word of remonstrance from the surrounding nations, is a circumstance discreditable to the age in which we live. If older and nearer nations are silent on such a subject, there is the greater reason and the more honor in giving utterance to the feelings which are excited on this side of the Atlantic, and of endeavoring to obtain the interference and combining the sentiment of all civilized nations to put an end to such horrible scenes.

The just indignation of the world has recently been

manifested by a simultaneous effort to humble and restrain the Barbary Powers. Every year has witnessed some new exertion to abolish the horrible traffic in African slaves; an amelioration of the ancient laws of war with regard to private property has recently been propounded as a subject worthy the consideration of nations; and yet no remonstrance has been made in behalf of Christian brotherhood and suffering humanity."

What gives special significance to this plea is its organic relationship to the other great liberal reform movements of the nineteenth century, and the obviously consciously felt bearing of one on all the others. The proposal of a grand remonstrance is not the only measure envisaged: obtaining the interference of all civilized nations, and the development of a common sentiment among them " to put an end to " continuing abuses is the goal.

The memorial from the South Carolina Legislature, which was passed the same day as the Boston resolutions, was infinitely briefer. It merely put of record the interest of South Carolina in " the noble and patriotic struggle of the modern Greeks " and declared that the State would " hail with pleasure the recognition by the American Government of the independence of Greece."

The memorial from an assemblage of notables in New York was by all means the most forthright and direct in its demands. Viewing with " lively sensibility " the Greek cause, the Gotham memorialists declared it " not only entitled to the good wishes of this country, but as far as might be done consistently with the views of the Government, to every possible assistance." Declaring Greek independence to be "of the highest concern to the interests of the human race" and to be supported by the most powerful considerations that could possibly be addressed either to the judgment or the sympathy of mankind, the petition asked Congress

> that the independence of the Greek nation might be recognized by the Government of this country . . . either that the independence of the Greeks may be speedily and formally recognized, or such steps preparatory thereto taken as may, in the opinion of the Government, be consistent with its interests, its policy and its honor.

The supporting argument endeavored to prove from the behavior of the Greeks in the contest that "they have sufficiently vindicated their title to assume a separate and equal station among the nations of the world." To clinch the argument, the memorialists left to the Congress the decision as to how far "the case of the South American Governments, whose national existence was admitted by the United States sometime since, [might] be deemed analogous," not neglecting to note "that there are peculiar circumstances connected with the cause of the Greeks which ought to awaken the most active concern for their welfare, and which require the application of every just precedent in support of their independence."

Into the Congressional debate, which was entirely in the House of Representatives,[3] it is of course impossible to enter in detail. Under the visible inspiration of Webster, ably supported by Clay, the discussion proceeded in Committee of the Whole, with

[3] 41 *Annals of Congress*, 18th Congress, 1st Session, cols. 1085-1214, *passim.*

much of the mentality which revealed itself in the Panama Congress affair two years later already in evidence.

Taking the lead in a keynote speech of January 19, 1824, Webster approached the problem from the standpoint of the total world situation and the specific part of the United States in it. Declaring that the United States must "take a part, honorable or dishonorable, in all that is done in the civilized world," he affirmed the vital interest of the country in the "general tendency" towards constitutional self-government, as also in the "antagonistic principle" tending to "prostrate the liberties of the entire civilized world" under the Holy Alliance. The magisterial address was directed chiefly against the doctrines of legitimism, and the self-asserted "undoubted right" of the Alliance "to take a hostile attitude in regard to those states in which an overthrow of the government may operate as an example"—including Greece. Because the doctrines of the Holy Alliance undermined the mutual independence of nations and legitimated arbitrary intervention, they might, Webster held, ultimately be directed against the United States. That is why Greece became a test case, involving the moral solidarity of all free peoples. Since the United States owed its existence to the successful assertion of the right of lawful resistance, Webster favored giving the Greeks, in their struggle for identical principles, the cheering aid of American opinion and example. The remaining argument was based on the identification of Greek and American interests, which

Webster's opponents took great pains to challenge and dispute.

The fundamental identification of the United States with the cause of human freedom was the crux of much of the debate which followed. Joel R. Poinsett of South Carolina, later to serve outstandingly in our diplomatic service, feared the Holy Alliance and urged absolute non-intervention; [4] John Randolph of Virginia, expressing ultra-isolationist views, warned of disaster if any interventory steps, however mild, were taken; [5] at least they might upset the projects for roads and canals he was then actively sponsoring. George Cary of Georgia questioned whether the Greek cause called on us "to step out of our character and mingle again in the turmoil of European politics," [6] and feared that even a commercial connection with Greece would be dangerous. While countenancing individual action, he pled: "As a nation, as a government, let us not mingle ourselves with the embroiled policy and endless disputes of Europe."

The most myopic view was that of Silas Wood of New York, who argued:

> The duties of every nation are limited to the prosperity and security of its own citizens; it owes nothing to other nations but the duties of humanity. This is more particularly the case with a government like ours, which is only entrusted with certain specific powers.[7]

This ultra-strict constructionism plus an argument

[4] *Ibid.*, cols. 1104-1111.
[5] *Ibid.*, cols. 1111-1112.
[6] *Ibid.*, cols. 1127-1132.
[7] *Ibid.*, cols. 1132-1138.

that non-intervention was implicit in " the law of moral order " closed his case.

The supporters of the Greek cause were not wanting. Henry Clay vied with Webster in eloquence, if not in erudition, demanding immediate and affirmative action, and denouncing what he termed " shivering, contracted but mistaken policy—cold, unfeeling, pence-calculating . . . which shrinks before it is menaced . . . for fear of some remote possible consequence of conceivable danger." [8] On the whole, the weight of historical argument came from Northern representatives, such as Henry Dwight of Massachusetts, who articulated the antithetical moralities,[9] and Francis Baylies, of the same State, who pled for the cause of the Greeks in terms of the advance of the Christian religion,[10] Daniel Cook, of Illinois, in an able legal argument,[11] contrasted with great irony the folly of trying to suppress the slave trade, but not the enslavement of free human beings. To him and to Patrick Farrelly of Pennsylvania [12] the Greek cause was merely one for prompt *de facto* recognition, in keeping with our established tradition. This view was shared by Sam Houston of Tennessee,[13] who felt the proposed resolution would inform Greece that " although our own policy interdicts us from acting in her behalf, yet we recognize her among the nations of the earth."

In the later rounds of discussion, Ichabod Bartlett of New Hampshire, opposing the resolution, de-

[8] *Ibid.*, cols. 1113-1114.
[9] *Ibid.*, cols. 1116-1126.
[10] *Ibid.*, cols. 1139-1144.
[11] *Ibid.*, cols. 1143-1150.
[12] *Ibid.*, cols. 1155-1158.
[13] *Ibid.*, cols. 1160-1163.

plored any departure, however merited, from the principle of non-intervention, because thereby non-intervention would cease to be a principle[14]—an argument that convinced a number of members. Only Alfred Cuthbert of Georgia deliberately assumed that the innocuous resolution under discussion—to provide for the salary of an agent to Greece—was actually a declaration of war on the Ottoman Porte, perchance on the Holy Alliance and even other states.[15]

The House of Representative, as is well known, actually took no action. But the debates revealed, even better than the discussions of 1826 regarding the Panama Congress, the fundamental cleavages in public opinion. Here the issue was more clearly posed in respect to Europe, but the weight of sentiment, in a cause vividly realized though actually disembodied, was overwhelmingly on the Greek side. What deterred action was in fact the preoccupation with domestic concerns, the sense that political action for moral reform could safely be left to England, the feeling that it would be a transgression of the moral order between states for us to protest, and lastly the belief that we could accomplish more by individual effort than by corporate protest or representation. On the other hand, as admitted even by John Randolph, the zeal shown for the propagation of liberty in other lands reached a new high and would not be denied. In short, the United States having achieved her own national independence and espoused the cause of liberty in the New World, our

[14] *Ibid.*, cols. 1150-1155.

[15] *Ibid.*, cols. 1165-1170.

nationals could hardly be blamed for giving of their treasure, and extending their moral support to, the principles that gave America birth, when they were instinctively discovered to be at stake in another quarter of the not-so-foreign world.

After the lapse of a century and a quarter, this initial sparring between government and public looks strangely mild and inconsequential, yet it reveals that even with very little material power on which to rely, the United States was increasingly disposed to look ever more diligently into conditions elsewhere in the world which outraged its moral sense. That this ran counter to the doctrine of non-intervention, which, by 1824, had become a political dogma, must be fully admitted; but it is also evident that new conceptions were already in the air, and that moral compunctions of a very respectable segment of society were hardening into convictions which no verbal formula, such as neutrality, could inhibit. Finally, the Greek incident revealed that the public reaction was no adventitious paroxysm but bore a very definite relationship to three other very significant movements affecting the international community: (1) the cooperative endeavor then in process to stamp out the slave trade; (2) the movement to secure additional immunities for private property at sea, and (3) the calling of a Congress of Nations for a variety of purposes, ranging from the advancement of arbitration or mediation to the codification of international law. Far from being a fitful, impulsive gesture to be perfunctorily dismissed as irrational, the first plea on a concerted scale for what later came to be termed "humanitarian intervention" was symptomatic of a vague and amorphous movement to reform the law of the community of nations, even if it were necessary to give that community institutions in order to reform its law.

It will be freely conceded that the movement gained no further momentum. It was left to Britain and to Russia to intervene where we feared to tread.[16] The conclusion of an important commercial convention between the United States and the Ottoman Porte, at the moment when Turkey was particularly hard pressed, gained important political and stra-

[16] Adams, as President, tried to propitiate American opinion in his message to Congress on December 4, 1827, by touching the Greek question tangentially, in connection with the accession of Nicholas I to the throne of Russia: "From the interest taken by this Sovereign in behalf of the suffering Greeks," he wrote, "and from the spirit with which others of the great European Powers are cooperating with him, *the friends of freedom and humanity may indulge the hope that they will obtain relief from that most unequal of conflicts, which they have so long and so gallantly sustained; that they will enjoy the blessings of self-government, which, by their sufferings in the cause of liberty, they have richly earned; and that their independence will be secured by those liberal institutions of which their country furnished the earliest examples in the history of mankind, and which have consecrated to immortal remembrance the very soil for which they are now again profusely pouring forth their blood.*" Somehow this lyrical passage is not the old Adams, but seems to bear the hallmarks of the influence of Henry Clay. "The sympathies which the people and Government of the United States have so warmly indulged with their cause," Adams continued, "have been acknowledged by their Government in a letter of thanks which I have received from their illustrious President, a translation of which is now communicated to Congress, the representatives of that nation to whom this tribute of gratitude was intended to be paid, and to whom it was justly due." Notwithstanding this beaming, effervescent attitude, Adams and Clay did nothing to recognize Greece! Cf. 6 *ASP-FR* 627 (Italics mine).

tegic leverages, some of which, such as the right of navigation through the Straits by American ships, are of peculiar diplomatic significance in our day. Granted that these removed any risks which a policy of intervention might have run, it is nevertheless clear that an important momentum was given by the episode to contrarient tendencies, utterly hostile to the principle of non-intervention. It will presently be seen that the failure of the Monroe-Adams administration to go further did not divert or dissipate the impounded moral and political forces involved. When recognition was ultimately given to Greece, in 1833, the immediate crisis was settled, but the public attitude on such matters was not abated. That is why the mid-century crisis over the fate of the Hungarian Republic, involved in the Kossuth episode, merely revealed the widened basis, the increased intensity and fervor of the American public, in challenging the right of annihilation of a small state by a combination of Great Powers, and affirming as never before in our history, the right of self-determination.

The Hungarian Crisis, 1849-1852

The factual foundation behind the episode which, while it lasted, brought sharply into relief popular and governmental opinion, is relatively simple. For our purposes we need not go back of the endeavor of Louis Kossuth, in 1848, to rebel against the centralization of political power by the Habsburgs, and to proclaim an independent Hungarian State, of which he assumed the title of Governor. That the anti-dynastic character of his move involved a penchant for republicanism is generally acknowledged but that the regime Kossuth sought to bring into being in his country was wholly democratic is perhaps more debatable. Suffice it to say that enough democracy and liberalism attached to the Kossuthian reforms to make them utterly unpalatable to Francis Joseph. However, having been defeated by the Hungarians in the field, the Austrian monarch was not in a position to save the Hungarian half of his kingdom, without external assistance. Hence, appealing to Nicholas I of Russia for aid, he elicited an intervention which overthrew the first Hungarian Republic, dragooned and slaughtered its votaries, and forced Kossuth into exile in Turkey.

It was from Turkish hands that the U. S. S. *Mississippi* received Kossuth and a limited group of friends, and brought them to the straits of Gibraltar, whence Kossuth left for a stay in Britain, where he was most enthusiastically received. But the type of triumphal tour which he made in the United States vastly exceeded the warmth of his reception in England. Public debate took place in the Senate and in the House over the method of officially receiving him, and it was in the course of these deliberations that the contrarient viewpoints of Americans, favoring an exclusive and aloof non-intervention, or sympathizing with liberal movements in other lands, came most forcefully to general attention.

Of very particular significance here are the public attitudes taken, governmentally and by outstanding citizens, on the issue presented, to be sure, in the person of Kossuth, but most importantly by the fact of the rise and existence, however brief, of a republic in the heart of monarchical Europe. That this presaged an eventual transformation of the Continent was a widely held belief in 1851 and 1852, and conviction quickly crystallized about the utterances of the orotund Hungarian exile, and elicited further pronouncements on the issue. I should like to venture the opinion that for all practical purposes, the attitude which the United States was to take toward the nationalities of the Habsburg Empire in the hour of its dissolution basically stems from the situation of 1848-1852, and that the die was cast by Kossuth himself, some seventy years before the fact. Let us now examine the evidence in the case.

It is important to differentiate the legal position taken by both President Taylor and Secretary of State Webster to the effect that, had the Hungarian Government given evidences of viability, we would have recognized it as a *de facto* government, from the much more involved and important political question as to whether the actions of Imperial Russia, in overwhelming the country and so terminating the existence of the Hungarian Republic, were sufficiently flagrant violations of the rights of other nations to have warranted—the use of the pluperfect is necessary, since nothing was in fact done about it by other Powers—counter-intervention. It is the latter question that formed the subject of acrimonious discussion in various parts of the country as well as in the halls of Congress.

The problem beset the chief executive, President Fillmore, with peculiar difficulties. The issue of human freedom was always apt to be contrasted, in the public mind, with human slavery. And the Hungarian question, dramatized in the person and utterances of Kossuth, came so close on the heels of the Compromise of 1850 that he made every endeavor to avoid reopening so recently settled a controversy. Though counselling the observance of traditional neutrality in international contests and preferring that the United States should effect the moral conquest of world opinion by the sheer force of virtuous example, President Fillmore could not refrain from expressing to the Congress, on December 2, 1851, "the deep interest which we feel in the spread of liberal principles and the establishment of free governments," declaring that

> the sympathy with which we witness every struggle against oppression forbids that we should be indifferent to those in which the strong arm of a foreign Power is invoked to stifle public sentiment and repress the spirit of freedom in any country.[17]

That the Senate, at least, understood the issue, is not in doubt. According to Senator Samuel A. Foote of Mississippi, it was "a great struggle between the principles of freedom and the principles of slavery." At such a moment, he asked,

> does it behoove the American people to join the side of despotism or to stand by the cause of freedom? We must

[17] *Congressional Globe*, Volume 24, Part 1 (Thirty-Second Congress, First Session), 15; hereinafter cited as *CG*, thus: *CG*, 24: 1, 15 (*32:1*).

do one or the other. We cannot avoid the solemn alternative presented. . . . Those who are not for freedom are for slavery.[18]

In this manner the " third alternative " of neutrality was excluded.

Senator Lewis Cass of Michigan beheld in " the exiled Governor of Hungary "

not merely . . . the champion of his country's independence (though in that character he was entitled to the sympathy and regard of every lover of liberty), but . . . the representative of a sacred cause—of a great and glorious cause, involving human rights in every nation of the globe.[19]

The dramatic figure of Kossuth, eloquent, fervent and inspiring, galvanized Senatorial and public opinion on the whole issue of intervention. It was this personal equation which differentiated the pleas for Hungary from the no less earnest but far less vivid pleas made on behalf of Greece a quarter of a century before. To those in America who had been reared on the juridical dichotomy of one into two worlds, the voice of the zealous Hungarian was beguiling. We were being asked to depart from long-standing principle. All the old doubts of 1826 were multiplied and magnified a thousand fold. But to those who premised their societal outlook on the moral unity of the universe, Kossuth possessed a peculiar symbolism:

I feel, [declared Senator James Shields of Illinois] that if there is one man who will carry out . . . the concentration of the moral force of this age against despotism, that man

[18] *Ibid.*, 23. [19] *Ibid.*, 25.

is Louis Kossuth. . . . I think that is his mission—not to involve us in war, not to force us into intervention, but to combine, unite and concentrate the moral force of the civilized world against the power of the oppression of the world.[20]

The lengths to which the United States should go in behalf of other nations were set forth in a keynote address by Senator William H. Seward of New York, whose views are entitled to special consideration in view of his subsequent service as Secretary of State. Urging official welcome to the Hungarian Governor, he declared that adverse action would be most unfortunate:

It would have the effect to encourage the advocates of oppression throughout Europe in their efforts to prevent the transition of the nations of Europe from under the system of force to the voluntary system of government which we have established and commended to their adoption.[21]

Then, warming to his theme, Seward proceeded:

Sir, in the course of human events we see the nations of Europe struggling to throw off the despotic systems of government, and to establish governments upon the principle of republicanism or of constitutional monarchy. Whenever such efforts are made we see it invariably happen that the existing despotisms of Europe combine to repress those struggles, combine to subdue the people. The consequence is, that despotism is a common cause and it results also that the cause of constitutional liberty has become one common cause—the cause of mankind against despotism. Now *whatever people leads the way at any time in any crisis in this contest for civil liberty becomes*

[20] *Ibid.*, 34.

[21] *Ibid.*, 42.

the representative of the nations of the earth. We once occupied that proud and interesting position, and we engaged the sympathies of civilized men throughout the world. No one can deny that recently Hungary assumed that same position, and the records of our own Legislature show that *we, in common with the friends of civil liberty in Europe, hold Hungary to be the representative of the nations of the earth in this great cause.* We had a messenger on the verge of the battlefield ready to acknowledge her independence.

It happens, in the Providence of God, that whenever a nation thus assumes to open this controversy for liberty, in behalf of the nations of the earth, some one man more than another becomes identified with the struggle by his virtues, by his valor, by his wisdom, or by his sufferings, until he eclipses others who may be associated with him, and comes to be regarded by the country itself, in whose behalf he labors and struggles, and by mankind, as the representative of that nation, and of that cause. . . . We honor those who serve the common cause of civil liberty throughout the world. *That cause is our own cause.*[22]

This was no mere passing flight of oratory, for it crystallized a feeling and conviction fiercely held by a large number of senators, primarily from the Northeast to the Northwest. Once again, it was the traditionalists, the states' rights advocates, who besought the country in no wise to depart from its noninterventionist doctrine, though here and there was found an isolationist from New England, and an interventionist from the deep South.

As the debate continued in both houses, it became thickly entangled with particularism, and in the House of Representatives it was not specially

[22] *Ibid.*, 42. (Italics mine.)

lucid. In the midst of those seeking to clarify the situation, the voice of Senator Robert F. Stockton of New Jersey boomed self-reliantly:

> Europe will discern an emphatic moral in the event. The despots . . . will see that on all suitable occasions we will speak out our abhorrence of their atrocious systems of government, and our sympathy with those gallant men, whether successful or unsuccessful, who strike a blow in defence of national independence and free government . . .

Then, introducing an element of flexibility into the rather tradition-bound atmosphere in which he was speaking, he continued:

> I am not one of those who think that no change will ever be made in the principles of national policy which govern our foreign relations; on the contrary, I feel assured that the wonderful growth and development of the United States . . . will demand a modification of our national policy, in various respects different from that which prevailed in the infancy of the country. . . . I will hazard the assertion that the rigid neutrality of the Washington administration, wise and just as it then was, would not now (if a similar belligerent state of the world existed) be possible . . . I have adverted to [it] only to show the change which has taken place in these principles which will no doubt hereafter govern our foreign relations.[23]

It is only fair to note that, given the temper of the times, Senator Stockton tended to become an "interventionist-imperialist." What is of major import to our generation is the realization today that in 1851 the unilateral official abstention of the United States from the main currents of world affairs was already

[23] *Ibid.*, 51.

subject to question, not only by the public at large, but by the members of the Upper House, so responsibly entrusted with a share in the treaty-making power.

In the House of Representatives William Churchwell of Tennessee saw the changing situation, but could not adjust to it, declaring he was not prepared to sponsor intervention or even interference, in European affairs, and that certainly the American people were likewise unprepared.[24] In this he undoubtedly spoke for the populace of the hinterland south of the Ohio, but not north or east. Thus David T. Disney of the Buckeye State understood more clearly than many others when he proclaimed:

> We are a living antagonism to the despotic governments of Europe, and they can never have peace and quiet there so long as this country exists. . . . And when our institutions are having this constant effect upon Europe, it is all idle for you to shrink back and say that because your immediate, peculiar and personal interests are not directly and immediately concerned, that you will not interfere. Such is not the Law of Nature; it is not the Law of God; it is not the Law which God Himself has stamped upon Humanity.[25]

Manifestly, in popular esteem, the immutable Law of Nature had changed sides! Neutrality and nonintervention at least were not, as they had been, in John Quincy Adams' day, under its immediate protection. This time there could be no doubt that the people themselves constituted the heaviest battalions.

It was not at the seat of government of the United States, however, that the issue was subjected to its

[24] *Ibid.*, 174-5.
[25] *Ibid.*, 173.

most probing debate. It was when Kossuth morally "invaded" New England that he struck the most responsive chords in minds and hearts. To plead, deep in abolitionist territory, for the cause of Hungary, was to identify his cause with that of free men everywhere. That is why his sojourn in New England has, as no other, left us with a fully etched picture of the public mind. It elicited from the Legislature of the Commonwealth of Massachusetts one of the ablest documents on foreign policy ever penned in such quarters—the Hazewell Report,[26] under date of March 13, 1852, which frontally challenged the idea of non-intervention.

Affirming the right of the States through their policy-making bodies to crystallize and channel opinion when national leadership was diffuse or lethargic, the Report laboriously and philosophically established the doctrine of international solidarity, thus avoiding an ethical dualism between the code of conduct binding on states and that binding on men. It was the belief of the Hazewell Committee that the States of our Union could clearly draw to the attention of the national government cases where diplomatic interposition, or even military interference, might be necessary.

Turning specifically to the case of Hungary, the Report justified recognition of Hungarian independence, which, by any criterion previously followed by the United States, would have been warranted, either

[26] The text of the Hazewell Report is appended to a compilation of Kossuth's addresses, published under the title, *Kossuth in New England* (Boston: John P. Jewett and Company, 1852, 287-306).

de facto or *de jure.* The Habsburgs having thus been dismissed from the historical scene, Russia's role in the destruction of Hungary was subjected to keen scrutiny. In the opinion of the Committee,

Russia was determined upon not allowing any nation to live under free institutions in her vicinity. . . . There is nothing too high for them not to strike, when the blow is also aimed against human rights; nothing so humble that they will refrain from placing their feet upon it, when the act is also a trampling on the hopes of mankind. The only hope that the world has of being saved from lasting slavery beneath the same yoke that now weighs so heavily on Poland and Hungary, and which threatens both Italy and Germany is to be found in the union of nations which are both strong and free. . . . It is the want of union among constitutionally governed countries that has given so much weight to a Power like Russia—far more than her victories, the extension of her territory, and the skill of her diplomacy.[27]

In this terse analysis a committee of the legislature of one of our commonwealths found the answer to the problem posed by the destruction of Hungarian independence—not in unilateral intervention or declamatory judgments against specific nations, but in international organization, by states wedded to love of freedom, in short, by " peace-loving nations." To reach this concert of opinion Massachusetts was willing to abandon sixty years of an antithetical tradition. In this spirit the Committee recommended that it was

the duty and the interest of all constitutionally governed nations to cultivate the most intimate relations with each

[27] *Ibid.*, 297-298.

other, to the end that, should the emergency arise, [they might] the more easily combine their powers to repel the acts of despots.

Warning that Pilgrim tradition had been made obsolete by the Revolution, and that the ideas of the Revolutionary period itself were already outmoded, the rapporteur, Charles C. Hazewell, added a finishing touch:

We should not insist upon waiting for the appearance of another generation before we take our proper place among the leading nations of the world. We have the power at this moment to perform a great part in the transaction of important affairs; and the recollection of the manner in which their country was redeemed from a condition of colonial vassalage cannot fail to cause Americans to consider themselves bound, so far as they honestly can, to aid peoples who are engaged in contending for their rights.[28]

Unhappily it was not given to the ideas of the Hazewell Committee to bear fruit immediately. The mills of the gods ground with more than their usual *lenteur*, and the immediate day of reckoning on which Louis Kossuth and his associates counted was exceedingly slow in coming. In the seventy years between the Liberal Revolution of 1848 and the Republican Revolution of 1918, the cup of European suffering was drained to the dregs by many peoples—the Poles and Lithuanians, for example, whose ill-starred rebellion in 1863 was expected to elicit the heartiest sympathy from the United States. But the United States itself was in the throes of civil war at the time and the same Seward who spoke eloquently in behalf

[28] *Ibid.*, 306.

of oppressed peoples in 1851, was forced, little more than a decade later, to have no traffic with revolutionary secession, whether in Warsaw or Montgomery, in Vilna or in Virginia, at Radom or on the Rappahannock. Hence the appeals of France and Great Britain for aid to the distressed Poles and Lithuanians were rejected,[29] and the United States stood solidly with Imperial Russia.

The same was true when Armenians were massacred in Turkey: there was minor remonstrance but no major demonstration. In 1899 the case of the Finns offered another opportunity, and this time the Michigan Legislature came to their rescue, mildly petitioning President McKinley in their behalf,[30] but

[29] See Appendix III.

[30] On June 12, 1899, Julius S. Stearns, Secretary of State of the State of Michigan, transmitted to Senator McMillan of Michigan, an authenticated copy of a concurrent resolution of the legislature, signed by Governor H. S. Pingree on June 7, 1899, declaring that "WHEREAS the American people remain unalterably and uncompromisingly opposed to all forms of oppression and political usurpation and

WHEREAS the American people have always entertained the most profound sympathy for every people of whatever race, nationality or creed, in their efforts to secure and preserve self-government and to maintain inviolate all their civil, political and religious liberties," the Michigan Legislature "respectfully but urgently requested President McKinley to instruct our commissioners to the Peace Conference [at The Hague] to express, in case the opportunity presents itself, the disapproval of the people of the United States of the policy of the Russian Government in its present administration of civil and military affairs in Finland." It likewise besought the President "through our duly accredited representative at the Court of Saint Petersburgh, if not inconsistent with the public interest, to express to the Government of the Czar the serious concern of the Government of the United States because of the abrogation of the Act of Assurance, etc. . . . *CR* 33: 81 (*56: 1*) Senate, Dec. 6, 1899.

to no avail. The South African war offered another occasion, and the memorials from racially interested kinsmen swamped Congress. But official policy held that we were not interested in Europe, in Africa, or in the Near East generally, and only modestly in Asia! At the Hague Conferences of 1899 and 1907 it was explicitly understood that

> all questions concerning the political relations of states and the order of things established by treaties, as in general all the questions . . . not included directly in the program adopted [were to] be absolutely excluded from the deliberations of the Conference,[31]

notwithstanding which we signed with explicit reservations, or else defined our position so that

> Nothing contained [in the conventions signed] shall be so construed as to require the United States of America to depart from its traditional policy of not intruding upon, interfering with, or entangling itself in, the political questions or policy or internal administration of any foreign State; nor shall anything contained in the said convention be construed to imply a relinquishment by the United States of America of its traditional attitude toward purely American questions.[32]

To the Hazewells of pre-1914 days the entire picture was maddening. The prospect of averting major political catastrophes by deciding, at The Hague, what annuities the Pious Fund of the Californias should yield, or the proper rates of taxation on foreign-owned houses in Japan, or the allegiance

[31] James Brown Scott, *The Hague Peace Conferences: American Instructions and Reports*, 7.

[32] *Ibid.*, 57 (1899), 98 (1907).

of deserters from Casablanca, or the future of the Muscat dhows—all this ignored the trenchant reality, the reckoning in Europe between the largely outworn dynastic system and the thwarted, but dynamic popular movements of the 1848 variety.

> When we take the banner of freedom once more in Europe [declared Kossuth in one of his addresses in America], when the turning point in the fate of Europe arrives, we shall look for active support from the United States—for such support as we have the right to claim. We hope that the United States may be pleased to recognize those principles which are the common property of all humanity, and, by being common property, are your own—the principle that every nation has a right to stand by itself, frame and establish its own institutions and that no foreign power has a right to interfere. That is the principle for which we contend and on which we claim the people of the United States should insist.[33]

Here was set down a rendezvous of the American people with destiny. It is a matter of historic record that, in 1918, we did not fail that rendezvous.

[30] *Kossuth in New England*, 17.

APPENDIX III

America and the Polish Insurrection

No. 342.]

Department of State
Washington, May 11, 1863.

SIR: Mr. Mercier has read to me, and at my request has left with me, a copy of an instruction under the date of the 23d of April last, which he has received from Mr. Drouyn de l'Huys, and which relates to exciting and interesting events in Poland that are now engaging the serious attention of the principal States in Western Europe.

Mr. Mercier has, at the same time, favored me with a copy of an instruction relating to the same events which has been transmitted by Mr. Drouyn de l'Huys to the ambassador of France at St. Petersburgh.

We learn from the first of these papers that the proceeding which has thus been adopted at Paris with a view to the exercise of a moral influence with the Emperor of Russia, has received the approbation and concurrence of the court of Vienna and the cabinet at London, and that the Emperor of the French, justly appreciating at one and the same time our historical sympathy with the Poles, and our ancient friendship with Russia, would be gratified with a cooperation in that important proceeding by the government of the United States.

Having taken the instructions of the President, I am now to communicate our views upon the subject, for the information of Mr. Drouyn de l'Huys.

This government is profoundly and agreeably impressed with the consideration which the Emperor has manifested towards the United States by inviting their concurrence in a proceeding having for its object the double interests of public order and humanity. Nor is it less favorably impressed with the sentiments and the prudential considerations which the Emperor has in so becoming a manner expressed to the court of St. Petersburgh. They are such only as appeal to the just emotions and best sympathies of mankind. The enlightened and humane character of the Emperor of Russia, so recently illustrated by the enfranchisement of a large mass of the Russian people from inherited bondage, and the establishment of an impartial and effective administration of justice throughout his dominions, warrant a belief that the appeal will be received and responded to by him with all the favor that is consistent with the general welfare of the great state over which he presides with such eminent wisdom and moderation.

Notwithstanding, however, the favor with which we thus regard the suggestion of the Emperor of the French, this government finds an insurmountable difficulty in the way of any active co-operation with the governments of France, Austria, and Great Britain, to which it is thus invited.

Founding our institutions upon the basis of the rights of man, the builders of our republic came all at once to be regarded as political reformers, and it soon became manifest that revolutionists in every country hailed them in that character, and looked to the United States for effective sympathy, if not for active support and patronage. Our invaluable Constitution had hardly been established when it became necessary for the government of the United States to consider to what extent we could, with propriety, safety, and beneficence, intervene, either by alliance or concerted action with friendly powers or otherwise, in the political affairs of foreign states. An urgent appeal for such aid and sympathy was made in behalf of France, and the appeal was sanctioned and enforced by the treaty then existing of mutual alliance and defence, a treaty without which it may even now be confessed, to the honor of France, our own sovereignty and independence could not have been so early secured. So deeply did this appeal touch the heart of the American people, that only the deference they cherished to the counsels of the Father of our Country, who then was at the fullness of his unapproachable moral greatness, reconciled them to the stern decision that, in view of the location of this republic, the characters, habits, and sentiments of its constituent parts, and especially its complex yet unique and very popular Constitution, the American people must be content to recommend the cause of human progress by the wisdom with which they should exercise the powers of self-government, forbearing at all times, and in every way, from foreign alliances, intervention, and interference.

It is true that Washington thought a time might come when, our institutions being firmly consolidated and working with complete success, we might safely and perhaps beneficially take part in the consultations held by foreign states for the common advantage of the nations. Since that period occasions have frequently happened which presented seductions to a departure from what, superficially viewed, seemed a course of isolation and indifference. It is scarcely necessary to recur to them. One was an invitation to a congress of newly emancipated Spanish American states; another an urgent appeal to aid Hungary in a revolution aiming at the restoration of her ancient and illustrious independence; another, the project of a joint guarantee of Cuba to Spain in concurrence with France and Great Britain; and more recently, an invitation to a co-operative demonstration with Spain, France, and Great Britain in Mexico; and, later still, suggestions by some of the Spanish American states for a common council of the republican states situated upon the American continent. These suggestions were successively disallowed by the government, and its decision was approved in each case by the deliberate judgment of the American people. Our policy of nonintervention, straight, absolute, and peculiar as it may seem to other nations, has thus become a traditional one, which could not be abandoned without the most urgent occasion, amounting to a manifest necessity. Certainly it could not be wisely departed from at this moment, when the existence of a local, although as we trust only a transient disturbance, deprives the government of the counsel of a portion of the American people, to whom so wide a departure from the settled policy of the country must in any case be deeply interesting.

The President will not allow himself to think for a single moment that the Emperor of the French will see anything but respect and friendship for himself and the people of France, with good wishes for the preservation of peace and order, and the progress of humanity in Europe, in the adherence of the United States on this occasion to the policy which they have thus far pursued with safety, and not without advantage, as they think, to the interests of mankind.

I am, sir, your obedient servant,

WILLIAM H. SEWARD.[1]

WILLIAM L. DAYTON, ESQ., &C, &C., &C.

[1] *Papers relating to Foreign Affairs, accompanying the Annual Message of the President to the First Session of the Thirty-Eighth Congress.* Part I, pp. 667-668. Washington, Government Printing Office, 1864.

LECTURE IV

The Reconstruction of the International Order, 1914-1919

It is peculiarly difficult for this generation to come to an adequate understanding of the world before 1914. The double tempest that has raged over the world has obliterated so many of the old landmarks, eroded the old channels of thought, and exposed so much that is intractable in the streambed of history that it is difficult for men who were not adult when the first storms broke to recall the contours, the rather soft and otiose contours of that world. And yet it is the world from which we have sprung, the matrix in which much of the present world was finally molded. To get back to, and understand that world is as difficult an intellectual process at times as renascence, physical or spiritual, was to that nocturnal visitor, Nicodemus, two thousand years ago. Notwithstanding the enormous difficulties, chiefly psychological in character, let us make the endeavor, for it is possible to us only by recapitulation, by an intellectual rather than an emotional process, to recover 1914.

That a great reckoning was imminent in the political order of Europe, of Asia, and of other portions of the world into which a new tempo was being introduced by the coming of the machine age will be readily granted today, as it was a third of a century ago. But that the general international order would also require reconstitution, that the lush days of exploitative empire were on their way out, was not so easily realized. There was a mystic normalcy about the world that had been, for the most part, allowed to *evolve* for nearly a century in Western Europe that gave it every appearance of endurance. How pervasive this was may be seen from the words used by Woodrow Wilson, in his first annual message to Congress on December 2, 1913, when he declared:

> Many happy manifestations multiply about us of a growing cordiality and sense of community of interest among the nations, foreshadowing an age of settled peace and good will. More and more readily each decade do the nations manifest their willingness to bind themselves by solemn treaty to the processes of peace, the processes of frankness and fair concession. So far the United States has stood at the front of such negotiations.[1]

Yet less than eight months after so optimistic an utterance, the whole edifice of Europe was tottering, and nearly a billion people in the world were at war. What were the reactions of the United States of America? How did it meet, and with what resources, the crisis of 1914?

The published records of our diplomacy of the period afford little help except in one quarter—Latin America; by the fast moving processes of history, the initiative was swiftly taken out of our hands. While the United States was privileged to offer its

[1] *Congressional Record, 63rd Congress, 2nd session*, 51, 43-45; *The Public Papers of Woodrow Wilson*, II, Part 1, 70-71, hereinafter cited as *CR and PPWW*.

good offices in the earliest phase of the struggle, they were firmly declined and the war thereafter pursued its own inevitable course. From a juridical standpoint, the efforts of the Department of State were not concerned with any attempts to return to the *status quo ante*; rather was every effort bent to put into force and effect the conventional laws of war, carefully prepared at The Hague for just such an eventuality. Indeed, as one looks back at the sad scene in retrospect, the most important struggle diplomatically ventured by the United States was to attempt to place all belligerents in a common straight-jacket by obtaining their belated adhesion, for practical working purposes, to the rules of naval warfare as laid down *in vacuo* by the Declaration of London of 1909.

The enormous duties suddenly imposed on our diplomatic service in caring for the official representation of the interests of one belligerent in the territory of his adversary quickly swamped all our facilities and taxed the resources of our diplomatic officers in the field. There was not a shadow of an effort, despite overtures from half a dozen neighbors, to concert with other neutrals upon a common course of conduct, and any strong initiative at the domestic end was precluded by the very temper of the President and the Secretary of State, and the apathetic feeling of most of the Cabinet—at least at the outset. It was not long before the country and the world discovered that, with the coming of war, the directing hands of wider policy in the United States became those of Woodrow Wilson personally, influenced by both his official family and by a number of unofficial advisers, among whom Colonel Edward M. House was by all odds the most important. In consequence, the evolution of policy in the United States can without difficulty be traced on the surface—in the official utterances of the President, either to foreign governments directly, or through the public addresses and papers of the President, although the hinterlands are more difficult to reach. For our purposes it will be of value initially to trace the President's own thoughts as to the nature of impending changes, and get the contexts in time and place and circumstance by which policy and formula and contribution came to be made.

For an incredibly long period President Wilson followed without deviation the traditional conception of America as furnishing to other nations an example of the actuating purposes, the fundamental principles and the long term practices which would have international value and advance peace. It was nothing new as a general statement, but the pre-war utterances of the President materially sharpened and pointed up the expressions by his predecessors which had grown weary in well doing and had ceased to have clear-cut meaning. One of his earliest addresses after he took office stressed the principle of custodianship as a new function of American foreign policy, although still in an exemplary stage:

Every day I . . . ask myself the question, How are you going to assist in some small part to give the American people, *and, by example, the peoples of the world*, more liberty, more happiness, more substanial prosperity? . . . We are the custodians, in some degree, of the principles which have made men free and governments just.[2]

And on the same day, in another address intended to be heard below the Rio Grande, he declared:

I would like to believe that all this hemisphere is devoted to the same sacred purpose and that nowhere can any government endure which is stained by blood or supported by anything but the consent of the governed.[2a]

Here are found, in close juxtaposition, two ideas which were destined to shape much of the Wilsonian view of international cooperation, at least in the Western Hemisphere: first, the idea that the Americas constitute a community devoted to the development of a common system of political ideas, and second, a passionate belief in the right of every people to be governed by a regime of its own choice. To these germinal ideas Wilson presently added a third, quite casually removing any territorial limits on its application when he declared at Mobile

. . . there is a reason and a compulsion lying behind all this which is dearer than anything else to the thoughtful men of America. I mean the development of constitutional liberty in the world. Human rights, national integrity, and opportunity as against material interests—that is the issue which we now have to face . . . our relationship with the rest of America is . . . the relationship of a family of mankind devoted to the development of true constitutional liberty.[3]

[2] Address at Congress Hall, October 25, 1913 *CR* Vol. 50, 5809-5810.

[2a] Addresses at Swarthmore College, October 25, 1913 *CR* Vol. 50, 5861-5862.

[3] Address at Mobile, Alabama, October 27, 1913. *PPWW* II, Pt. 1, 64-69.

Too much emphasis cannot be placed on this triad of ideas, because they are fundamental to the later exfoliation of the Wilsonian system.[4] Taken together with the self-denying ordinance enunciated at Mobile, that the United States would never seek another foot of territory by conquest, the elements propounded by Wilson as a basis of international policy proved to be mutually compatible and could be accepted as a working basis for a closer integration of the Americas.

Further evidences of the consistency with which Wilson would hold to these premises of action came in connection with the difficult Mexican situation. In informing Congress of the crisis at Tampico, Wilson, on April 20, 1914, expressly repudiated any thought of aggression or aggrandizement, and emphasized his wish "always to keep our great influence unimpaired for the uses of liberty, both in the United States and wherever else it may be employed for the benefit of mankind."[5] The same ideas, in slightly

[4] I am carefully separating the use of the word custodian or custodianship, which Wilson employed in the sense of guardianship of a cultural heritage, from trusteeship which Wilson, following the Democratic party platform of 1912, applied in his discussions of Philippine affairs to refer to responsibility for the tutelage of colonial areas. Cf. his message of December 2, 1913, to Congress. *Ibid.*, 76.

[5] Special Address to Congress, April 20, 1914. *CR* Vol. 51, 6908-6909. Wilson further confirmed this viewpoint in an interview with Samuel G. Blythe on April 27, 1914, indicating that "the Monroe Doctrine means an unselfish friendship for our neighbors—a disinterested friendship, in the sense of not being interested in our aggrandizement—and that our motives are only the motives inspired by a higher humanity, by our sense of duty and responsibility, and by our determination that human liberty shall prevail in our hemisphere." *CR* Vol. 51, 9095-9096. Also in the *Saturday Evening Post*, May 23, 1914.

different language, were employed on half a dozen other occasions before the outbreak of World War I. On only one of these, however, did Wilson specifically refer to Washington's Farewell Address—the Bible of non-interventionists—in a note of national pride which was unquestionable:

> It was not merely because of passing and transient circumstances that Washington said we must keep free of entangling alliances. It was because he saw that no country had yet set its face in the same direction in which America had set her face. We cannot form alliances with those who are not going our way; and in our might and majesty and in the confidence and definiteness of our own purpose we need not and we should not form alliances with any nation in the world.[6]

From this unequivocal adherence to the no alliance pattern it was less than three months before Wilson saw it his duty to plead for neutrality in thought and in action on the part of every American.

The first year of war produced no great clarification. There was a studied insistence on reservation of judgment, coolness of thinking, steadiness of balance, that characterized the public utterances of the President. The immediate impacts, political and economic, of the great struggle, forced him almost exclusively to a vindication of the neutral position which the United States took in keeping with its long historic tradition. Only as the conflict sharpened in the spring of 1915 came did the President speak out, this time to reemphasize the cult of human

[6] *PPWW* II, Pt. 1, 109. Address at Unveiling of Statue to the Memory of Commodore Barry, May 16, 1914.

liberty,[7] the "disengaged," rather than the "neutral," character of the United States; its mediatory role in world finance, yet its detached and distant position in the politics of the world.[8] In a number of addresses during April and May he developed the thesis that neutrality gave to the United States the opportunity to give counsel at the close of hostilities; it was this that was "something so much greater to do than fight";[9] the moral force of righteous example, even if an interim role, was preeminently praiseworthy,[10] and it gave the United States a vicarious opportunity to speak for others, for the whole of humanity: "It is not pretension on our part," Wilson declared, "to say that we are privileged to stand for what every nation would wish to stand for, and speak for those things which all humanity must desire."[11]

By autumn of 1915 Wilson first began to question the adequacies of neutrality, more, to be sure, as a formula for the policy of the United States than as a status in the community of nations: "Neutrality" he declared, "is a negative word. It is a word that does not express what America ought to feel." Then, enlarging on his theme, he began to let the public in on his inmost thoughts:

[7] Address to the Daughters of the American Revolution, Washington, April 19, 1915. *PPWW*, II, pt. 1, 300.

[8] Address to the Associated Press, New York, April 20, 1915. *Ibid.*, 302-307.

[9] *Ibid.*, 305.

[10] Address at Philadelphia, May 10, 1915, the so-called "Too Proud to Fight" speech. *Ibid.*, 321.

[11] Address on "The Ideals of the Navy," New York City, May 17, 1915. *Ibid.*, 330.

America has a heart and that heart throbs with all sorts of intense sympathies, but America has schooled its heart to love the things that America believes in and it ought to devote itself only to the things that America believes in; and, believing that America stands apart in its ideals, it ought not to allow itself to be drawn, as far as its heart is concerned, into anybody's quarrel.

So far this was an indication of transcendent emotions and fixed beliefs. But the long nights of reasoning in the White House had begun to show their cumulative effect:

Not because it does not understand the quarrel,[12] not because it does not in its head assess the merits of the controversy, but because America has promised the world to stand apart and maintain certain principles of action which are grounded in law and justice. We are not trying to keep out of trouble; we are trying to preserve the foundations upon which peace can be rebuilt.[13] Peace can only be rebuilt up on the ancient and accepted principles of international law, only upon those things which remind nations of their duties to each other, and, deeper than that, of their duties to mankind and to humanity. America has a great cause which is not confined to the American continent. It is the cause of humanity itself.[14]

[12] On a number of later occasions President Wilson disclaimed interest in the causes of the quarrel, or declared that it would take historians of future decades to assess the responsibility. I am convinced for my own part that Wilson knew the issues from the outset, and for long intervals lapsed into silence because he feared his inability personally to withhold his judgment.

[13] In keeping with the larger thesis in these lectures, that for at least the major part of the war most statesmen were thinking backward to the Hague Conferences, it would appear that Wilson at this particular stage, when the issues with Great Britain were at their tensest, was still thinking in terms of the Declaration of London and the Hague Conventions.

[14] Address to the Daughters of the American Revolution, Washington, October 11, 1915. *PPWW*, II, pt. 1, 376.

By the beginning of November, 1915, as if sounding out public opinion in advance of the preparedness program, Wilson turned from passive acquiescence and nostalgic memories of the past and its traditions, to new goals and objectives. In a ringing speech at the Manhattan Club in New York, November 4, 1915, he uttered the *credo* which was to become more clear as the months went by:

Our principles are well known. . . . We believe in the liberty of men and of peoples—of men to choose their own lives and of peoples to choose their own allegiance. Our ambition, too, all the world has knowledge of. It is not only to be free and prosperous ourselves, but also to be the friend and thoughtful partisan of those who are free or who desire freedom the world over. If we have had aggressive purposes and covetous ambitions, they were the fruit of our thoughtless youth as a nation and we have put them aside. We shall, I confidently believe, never again take another foot of territory by conquest. We shall never in any circumstances seek to make an independent people subject to our dominion; because we believe, we passionately believe, in the right of every people to choose their own allegiance and be free of masters altogether. For ourselves we wish nothing but the full liberty of self-development; and with ourselves in this great matter we associate all the peoples of our hemisphere. We wish not only for the United States but for them the fullest freedom of independent growth and action, for we know that throughout this hemisphere the same aspirations are everywhere being worked out, under diverse conditions but with the same impulse and ultimate object.[15]

[15] *Ibid.*, 384-392. (Italics mine.) This address is also noteworthy for the forthright declaration that "We are the champions of religious right here *and everywhere* that it may be our privilege to give it our countenance and support." It is a touchstone to the conception of minority guarantees to which Wilson later freely subscribed.

There was a reprise of this theme in the annual message to Congress on December 7, 1915, Wilson declaring that " the whole face of international affairs . . . now presents a prospect of reorganization and reconstruction such as statesmen and peoples have never been called upon to attempt before." Particularizing, Wilson referred to the states of the new world, noting that

> the states of America have become conscious of a new and more vital community of interest and moral partnership in affairs, more clearly conscious of the many common sympathies and interests and duties which bid them stand together. . . . All the governments of America stand, so far as we are concerned, upon a footing of genuine equality and unquestioned independence . . . the states of America are not hostile rivals but cooperating friends, . . . their growing sense of community, alike in matters political and matters economic, is likely to give them a new significance as factors in international affairs and in the political history of the world. It presents them as in a very deep and true sense a unit in world affairs, spiritual partners, standing together because thinking together, quick with common sympathies and common ideals. This is Pan-Americanism. It has none of the spirit of empire in it. It is the embodiment . . . of the spirit of law and independence and liberty and mutual service.[16]

This was not merely disavowal of aggressive intentions; it was the beginning of constructive statesmanship. Wilson saw that the historical moment for cementing together an American community of nations was at hand, and he sought to utilize it, fearing that if the unparalleled opportunity should pass,

[16] *CR* 53:95-100; *PPWW*, II, Pt. 1, 405-409 *passim*.

it might never return.[17] For that reason he disclosed, in a programmatic address to the Second Pan-American Scientific Congress, on January 6, 1916, the core ideas that had actuated a very pertinent diplomatic negotiation for more than a year preceding:

> Latterly there has been a very frank interchange of views between the authorities in Washington and those who represented the other States of this hemisphere. . . . These gentlemen have seen that if America is to come into her own, into her legitimate own, in a world of peace and order, she must establish the foundations of amity so that no one will hereafter doubt them. . . . It will be accomplished in the first place, by the States of America uniting in guaranteeing to each other absolutely political independence and territorial integrity. In the second place, and as a necessary corollary to that, guaranteeing the agreement to settle all pending boundary disputes as soon as possible and by amicable process; by agreeing that all disputes among themselves, should they unhappily arise, will be handled by patient, impartial investigation, and settled by arbitration; and the agreement necessary to the peace of the Americas, that no State of either continent will permit revolutionary expeditions against another State to be fitted out on its territory, and that they will prohibit the exportation of the munitions of war for the purpose of supplying revolutionists against neighboring Governments.[18]

Certainly, as a programmatic utterance, this crystallized concretely into express stipulations the "vital community of interest" expressed to Congress only a month before. Actually, at a moment of stalemate in the negotiations, when there was very little prospect of gaining the objective merely *inter partes*, it

[17] *Ibid.*, 418.
[18] *PPWW*, II, Pt. 1, 439-445, at 444.

was something like political genius to disclose to the public gaze propositions on the verge of being rejected, and have their disclosure transform the ideological impact and moral force into a well-nigh irresistible appeal:

These are very practical suggestions which have sprung up in the minds of thoughtful men, and I, for my part, believe that they are going to lead the way to something that America has prayed for for many a generation. For they are based, in the first place, so far as the stronger states are concerned, upon the handsome principle of self-restraint and respect for the rights of everybody. They are based upon the principles of absolute political equality among the States, equality of right, not equality of indulgence. They are based, in short, upon the solid, eternal foundations of justice and humanity. No man can turn away from these things without turning away from the hope of the world.[19]

I think it safe to conclude that, without abandoning the possibility of coming to an agreement with the other American Republics with regard to the proposed guarantee treaty, President Wilson from this point on pinned greater hope on securing the objectives in question on a world-wide, rather than a hemispheric, basis. The evidence for this becomes increasingly clear in any study of his utterances and public papers during 1916, and it is buttressed by the Lansing Papers, published after the death of the wartime Secretary of State, covering data not dis-

[19] *Ibid.*, 444. The zeal which Wilson felt for the cause is evidenced in the " hope of the world " phrase, which was to stay with him in all his advocacy of the League.

closed in the official *Foreign Relations of the United States.*[20]

The trend is most obvious in the series of addresses on preparedness made by the President in a week-long tour of speeches at the end of January and in the beginning of February, 1916. These repeated the theme of American support for "the right of every people to determine its own destiny and its own affairs" [21]—a proposition which lay at the heart of the reorganization of the defeated empires at the close of World War I—and dwelt heavily on the fact that America was outgrowing her provincial status,[22] and must assume a world outlook and world responsibilities,[23] without ceasing to be an

[20] *Lansing Papers*, II, 496-500, hereafter referred to as *LP*. See Appendix IV below.

[21] Aeolian Hall, New York, January 27, 1916. *PPWW*, II, Pt. 2, 2-4.

[22] Speaking in a keynote address in New York, also on January 27, 1916, Wilson said: "We live in a world which we did not make, which we cannot alter, which we cannot think into a different condition from that which actually exists. . . . America has been reluctant to match her wits with the rest of the world. . . . We cannot any longer be a provincial nation . . . It [America] has been willing to fight for the liberty of others as well as for its own liberty. . . . We have made ourselves in some sort the champions of free government and national sovereignty in both continents of this hemisphere; so that there are certain obligations which every American knows we have undertaken. . . . *We must all of us think from this time out in terms of the world*, and must learn what it is that America has set out to maintain as a standard-bearer for all those who love liberty and justice and righteousness in political action." *Ibid.*, 5-10. (Italics mine.)

[23] "We want to maintain the equal right of this nation as against the action of all other nations," the President declared at Pittsburgh, January 29, 1916, "and we wish to maintain the peace and unity of the Western Hemisphere. Those are great things to defend, and in their defense sometimes our thought must take a great sweep, even beyond our borders. . . . The most necessary

example to other nations. Slowly, as the addresses piled up, there was an almost imperceptible shift in emphasis, from things definitely stated in domestic terms to positions taken in international ones, always with the principle of trusteeship for the silent, the inarticulate, populations of the world in mind.[24] Gradually, too, the obligations assumed toward the Western Hemisphere were widened, the trammels removed, and the ethical issues involved carefully restated.[25] Skilfully the President built out from the formal juridical postulates of neutrality and separate action, to the need for joint responsibility and cooperative action with other countries. There were lapses, as at Cleveland and Milwaukee, into the old

---

thing to do now is to make America acquainted with her own situation in the world and acquainted with the fact that not all the processes of conduct are within her own control; that, on the contrary, they are daily and hourly affected by things which she cannot govern or direct." *Ibid.*, 17-30.

[24] In another address at Pittsburgh on January 29, 1916, he declared: "the thing that is hard is to fight for the things that do not immediately touch us in order that others may live whom we do not love and do not even know, in order that the great tides of the national life might flow free and unobstructed, in order that the great ideals and purposes of the people we never see might be realized. . . . The flag stands for something for which we are all trustees, the great part that America is to play in the world." *Ibid.*, 29-30.

[25] "America stands for the right of men to determine whom they will obey and whom they will serve; for the right of political freedom and a people's sovereignty. . . . America has not only to assert her right to her own life within her own borders, she has also to assert her right to the just and equal treatment of her citizens wherever they go. And she has something even more than that to insist upon, because she made up her mind long ago that she was going to stand up, so far as this Western Hemisphere is concerned, for the right of peoples to choose their own politics without foreign influence or interference. So she has a gigantic task which she cannot shirk without disgrace." *Ibid.*, 30.

neutrality and non-interventionism,[26] perhaps due to the local political climate, perhaps—and to my view more probably—because it was impossible for Wilson to extricate himself all at once from the nexus of inherited ideas regarding our relations with the rest of the world.

In ensuing addresses President Wilson moved from the position that we were, because of our very aloofness from the struggle, able " to maintain our position as the trustees of the moral judgment of the world,[27] to the stand that we might at any time have " to assert the principles of law in a world in which the principles of law have broken down," instancing our obligations to the Western Hemisphere in particular to vindicate these by force. Speaking at Des Moines, where he sought to uproot the tradition of isolationism, Wilson for the first time since the outbreak of the war broached indirectly the problem of a post-war organization:

America is looked upon to sit in a sort of moral judgment upon the processes of war. . . . What is America expected

[26] Cleveland, January 29, 1916; Milwaukee, January 31, 1916. *Ibid.*, 36-39; 47-55.

[27] Address at Chicago, January 31, 1916. *PPWW*, II, Pt. 2, 56-70. Here Wilson, though yielding to Lansing's insistence, as elsewhere noted, on matters of covenanting to maintain republican institutions in the New World, declared, *inter alia*: " What of the great trusteeship we have set up for liberty of government and national independence in the whole Western Hemisphere? . . . We stand pledged to see that both the continents of America are left free to be used by their people as those people choose to use them, under a principle of national popular sovereignty as absolute and unchallenged as our own. And at this very moment, as I am speaking to you, the Americas are drawing together upon that handsome principle of *reciprocal respect and reciprocal defense* "—the latter certainly a new note in Pan-Americanism.

to do? She is expected to do nothing less than keep law alive while the rest of the world burns. You know that there is no international tribunal, my fellow citizens. I pray God that if this contest have no other result, it will at least have the result of creating an international tribune and producing some sort of joint guarantee of peace on the part of the great nations of the world.[28]

Reiterating this theme at Topeka, Wilson pushed still further his earlier statements, declaring that "The flag stands for the rights of mankind, no matter where they be, no matter what their antecedents, no matter what the race involved; it stands for the absolute right to political liberty and free self-government, . . ." [38] In the third year of a world conflict, Wilson was, consciously or otherwise, following in the steps of Samuel Adams and others in sensing as universal values, the timeless, non-space-conditioned, or otherwise contingent rights of men to political liberty and self-government. That is why when the *Sussex* crisis came in April, 1916, Wilson averred

We cannot forget that we are in some sort and by the force of circumstances the responsible spokesmen for the rights of humanity, and that we cannot remain silent while those rights seem in process of being swept away. . . . We owe it to a due regard for our own rights as a nation, to our sense of duty as a representative of the rights of neutrals the world over, and to a just conception of the rights of mankind to take this stand now with the utmost solemnity and firmness.[30]

[28] *Ibid.*, 70-82, at 75.
[29] *Ibid.*, 82-94 at 92.
[30] *Ibid.*, 158.

While other counselors were offering specific solutions of many kinds, Wilson thought through the problem of adopting an advocacy of international organization. It took courage and conviction to arrive at the far-reaching change. Ray Stannard Baker, who probably knew more of Wilson than any other biographer, dates the change-over to a decision arrived at by Wilson about May 9 or 10, 1916. With the *Sussex* crisis out of the way, it was necessary to formulate an objective toward which American policy might move. Wilson sternly determined to make the cause of the reorganization of the international community his own. This he did in a historic address to the First Annual Assemblage of The League to Enforce Peace in Washington on May 27, 1916.[31] By a fluke of historical circumstance, the

[31] Just when Wilson absorbed, or developed, the idea he here decided to further, is highly controversial. Baker endeavors to trace the ideology of world federation back as far as 1887 (*Woodrow Wilson: Life and Letters*, hereinafter cited as *WWLL*, VI, 204) with special emphasis on earlier statements in letters to private individuals as far back as August, 1914 (*Ibid.*, V, 74-75), envisaging "an association of the nations all bound together for the protection of the integrity of each, so that any one nation breaking from this bond will bring upon herself war; that is to say, punishment, automatically." This statement is intrinsically of interest chiefly for the use of the word "association," which Wilson employed in the first public declaration on May 27, and for the idea of guaranteed integrity, which is thus seen to be inseparable from the Wilsonian ideological complex from the beginning. The idea of giving and breaking bond has already been discussed in connection with the Pan-American treaty.

A second stage in Wilson's position with regard to the reorganization of the international community came when, on Christmas Eve, 1915, he penned the instructions for Colonel House to follow in his conversation with British leaders: "The only possible guarantees, that is, the only guarantees that any rational man could accept, are (a) military and naval disarmament and

attitude of the British Foreign Office at the moment precluded the discussing of any mediatory enterprises. Wilson was therefore left quite free to analyze the world scene, and America's obligations to it, and thereafter to propound the constructive steps forward. Perhaps it was this very freedom that led Wilson to dissever the program from the

---

(b) a league of nations to secure each nation against aggression and maintain the absolute freedom of the seas" (*Ibid.*, VI, 138). This was followed by the famous cable of January 9, 1916, in which Wilson indicated that he would be "willing and glad when the opportunity comes to cooperate in a policy seeking to bring about and maintain permanent peace among civilized nations." (*Ibid.*, 142).

A third stage in the evolution of Wilson's attitude came during the round of preparedness speeches in late January and early February, 1916, when, having at least in principle offered a territorial guarantee to the other American nations, he wished to use it as the basis for the further projection of the idea into a larger setting. Undoubtedly the Sussex crisis was a deterrent to the fuller development of this theme, but once it was passed, there was no longer need for furtive consultations and secret cables. Wilson had decided to take his stand publicly and openly. By May 10, 1916, House was able to tell Sir Edward Grey: "I believe the President would now be willing to publicly commit the United States to joining with the other powers in a convention looking to the maintenance of peace after the war . . ." (*Ibid.*, 204). At this time only two elements of a league plan were clear to Wilson: "the signatory nations were to 'pledge themselves to side against any power breaking a treaty,' and 'against any nation refusing in case of dispute to adopt some other method of settlement than that of war.' Rules were to be formulated for 'limiting armaments both on land and sea' and for making warfare 'more humane to those actually engaged and safe-guarding the lives and property of neutrals and non-combatants'" (*Ibid.*, 204). It was at this stage that Wilson decided to open up the discussion to public channels and make his historic pronouncement.

The genesis of the speech itself is exhaustively given by Baker, *op. cit.*, 212-226 and by Seymour, *IPCH*, II, 293-338, *passim.* It should be noted that House claims a very great deal of credit for the May 27 speech, Seymour giving his suggestions in columns parallel to those of the President's final text. (*Ibid.*, 337-338).

circumstances and the antecedents of the war, although in the program he enunciated, there was really very little that was entirely new. It was because the speech had integrative value in enunciating the concern the United States would feel about the future peace that it was peculiarly impressive:

. . . we shall be as much concerned as the nations at war to see peace assume an aspect of permanence, give promise of days from which the anxiety of uncertainty shall be lifted, bring some assurance that peace and war shall always hereafter be reckoned part of the common interest of mankind. We are participants, whether we would or not, in the life of the world. The interests of all nations are our own also. We are partners with the rest. What affects mankind is inevitably our affair as well as the affair of the nations of Europe and of Asia.[32]

Looking back upon the circumstances attending the outbreak of the war, the President felt that if it had been possible to substitute conference for force, the conflict itself might not have occurred. The lesson which Wilson drew pointedly was " that the peace of the world must henceforth depend upon a new and more wholesome diplomacy." His was a quest for an international consensus upon which to

[32] This doctrine of common concern Wilson had been building up and gradually expanding over a number of years, and most particularly, ever since the start of the preparedness addresses. This utterance must be regarded as containing, in nuclear form, the fundamental premises underlying Article 11 of the Covenant, and, to a lesser extent, the concept of situations which are of concern to the peace of the world, which is found in Art. 3, par. 3; Art. 4, par. 4; Art. 17, par. 4 and Art. 19 of the Covenant. The text of the address itself is given in *PPWW* II, Pt. 2, 184-188, and in *Enforced Peace*, the Proceedings of the First Annual National Assemblage of the League to Enforce Peace, 159-164.

build an institutional superstructure—a point virtually lost to most of the critics and commentators on the momentous address:

Only when the great nations of the world have reached some sort of agreement as to what they hold to be fundamental to their common interest, and as to some feasible method of acting in concert when any nation or group of nations seeks to disturb those fundamental things, can we feel that civilization is at last in a way of justifying its existence and claiming to be finally established.[33]

Buttressing this point by an appeal to the principles of Gladstone and Asquith, that the principle of public right must henceforth take precedence over the individual interests of particular nations, and that the nations of the world must in some way band themselves together to see that the right prevails against any sort of selfish aggression, Wilson sought to make a bid for the public opinion of the English-speaking world, and enlist support in that quarter politically. Declaring that henceforth alliance must not be set up against alliance, understanding against understanding—a direct thrust at the pre-war system of the balance of power, as between alliances and ententes—Wilson came to the positive affirmation "that there must be a common agreement for a common object, and that at the heart of that common object must lie the inviolable rights of peoples and of mankind." International understanding was possible only through cooperation-in-a-common-cause; the guiding principle of such a common cause must

[33] *PPWW*, II, Pt. 2, at 186.

be even-handed and impartial justice. In this *abregé* of the essential argument, Wilson's plea for the creation of an international consensus stands out above all other things. Believing that a system rejecting the arbitrary use of force was essential to peace, he appraised it as embodying the passionate conviction of America. Then came the *credo*:

We believe these fundamental things: First, that every people has a right to choose the sovereignty under which they shall live. . . . Second, that the small states of the world have a right to enjoy the same integrity that great and powerful nations expect and insist upon, and third, that the world has a right to be free from every disturbance of its peace that has its origin in aggression and disregard of the rights of peoples and nations. So sincerely do we believe in these things that I am sure that I speak the mind and wish of the people of America when I say that the United States is willing to become a partner in any feasible association of nations formed in order to realize these objects and make them secure against violation.[34]

Of the original design of Colonel House to extort a statement of war objectives from the belligerents there remains only a trace. Wilson proposed

First, such a settlement with regard to their own immediate interests as the belligerents may agree upon. . . .[35] Our interest is only in peace and its future guarantees. Second, an universal association of the nations to maintain the inviolate security of the highway of the seas for the com-

[34] *Ibid.*, 187.

[35] This, according to Seymour (*IPCH*, II, 299) and Baker (*WWLL*, VI, 213n) was the residue of the idea of a negotiated peace and a forerunner, if one may infer it from their exposés, of the "peace without victory" phrase of the President's famous address to the Senate on January 22, 1917.

mon and unhindered use of all the nations of the world, and to prevent any war begun either contrary to treaty covenants or without warning and full submission of the causes to the opinion of the world—a virtual guarantee of territorial integrity and political independence.[36]

Here was a rather revolutionary statement, when compressed, although every element in it had been set forth on one occasion or another by the President. He came, he told his audience, not "to discuss a programme" but "to avow a creed." That single sentence is perhaps the touchstone to much that followed, for Wilson sought to keep amorphous and unrigidified the skeletal structure of the League for as long as possible, certainly until the eve of the convening of the Peace Conference, meanwhile devoting his efforts to the utmost to gain acceptance for the underlying postulates or the express principles of the future organization; in short, to create and foster the maximum area of agreement upon purposes, before the structure should have solidified too much:

I feel that the world is even now upon the eve of a great consummation, when some *common* force will be brought into existence which shall safeguard right as the first and most fundamental interest of all peoples and all govern-

[36] Seymour pertinently points out (*loc. cit.*, 297 n.) that at the very last moment "Wilson changed *alliance* to read *association of nations*; *freedom of the seas* to read *the inviolate security of the highway of the seas for the common and unhindered use of all the nations of the world* (in order to assure the British that the suggestion was not directed against their restrictions on trade as much as against the submarine) *full inquiry* to read *full submission of the causes to the opinion of the world.* (Italics Seymour's.)

ments, when coercion shall be summoned not to the service of political ambition or selfish hostility, but to the service of a *common* order, a *common* justice and a *common* peace (Italics mine).[37]

There is a general belief that because he failed to give his affirmative support to the working out of the League mechanism, Wilson neglected the objectives and purposes. This is far from the case. The ideas were not thrust upon the American public mind integrally, rather were they given in homeopathic doses—perhaps too small, given the emotional drives of a wartime era, to be either intellectually or emotionally effective. Yet seen in the calm retrospect of thirty years, their cumulative trend is irresistible. Thus he declared at West Point, June 13, 1916:

We stand here with the glorious power of this country, ready to swing it out into the field of action whenever liberty and independence and political integrity are threatened anywhere in the Western Hemisphere. And we are ready—nobody has authorized me to say this, but I am sure of it—we are ready to join with the other nations of the world in seeing that the kind of justice prevails everywhere that we believe in.[38]

[37] Wilson reiterated this theme three days later in a Memorial Day address at Arlington when he declared, *inter alia*, "The United States has again to work out by spiritual process a new union, when *men shall not think of what divides them but . . . what unites them* . . . because we are made up, and consciously made up, out of all the great family of mankind, we are champions of the rights of mankind." Wilson concluded "*We are not only ready to cooperate, but we are ready to fight against any aggression, whether from without or from within.*" This was clearly inching along a bit further in committing the government of the United States towards the type of international organizaion which he had just officially championed. *PPWW*, II, Pt. 2, 193-194.

[38] *Ibid.*, 205-206.

Steadily Wilson infiltrated the idea, consciously, purposefully, non-contentiously. It is true that he was unable to procure for the idea of international organization the unequivocal endorsement of the Democratic National Convention, but in his speech of acceptance Wilson pushed the idea further:

There must be a just and settled peace, and we here in America must contribute the full force of our enthusiasm and of our authority as a nation to the organization of that peace upon world-wide foundations that cannot easily be shaken. No nation should be forced to take sides in any quarrel in which its own honor and integrity and the fortunes of its people are not involved; but *no nation can any longer remain neutral as against any wilful disturbance of the peace of the world* . . . when peace comes again, a new atmosphere of justice and friendship must be generated by means the world has never tried before. *The nations of the world must unite in joint guarantees that whatever is done to disturb the whole world's life must first be tested in the court of the whole world's opinion before it is attempted.*[39]

The significance of this pronouncement lies in the fact that for the first time in any public utterance, and by no means in mere metaphor, Wilson implied the creation of an agency, a special instrument, to

[39] *PPWW*, II, Pt. 2, 287-288. This speech is important for its formal avowal of the limited role of neutrality in the world of the future, because with the giving of joint guarantees, the possibility of a separate course of action would be excluded. The general tenor of Wilson's speeches from this point forward was that neutrality was a desirable but untenable position; that the United States must be continuously on the alert to the possibility that it might not cover the contingencies the country might have to face. Cf. Address at Cincinnati, October 26, 1916. *Ibid.*, 376-382.

act as "the court of the whole world's opinion." For all his rejection of mechanism and emphasis upon objectives, the particular parts of the mechanism began to be revealed. But the drive for the formulation of objectives continued.

In one of the major addresses of the Presidential campaign, at Omaha, on October 5, 1916, Wilson broke cleanly with the non-intervention tradition. Because such a fundamental reconsideration of the postulates of policy toward the rest of the world was in the balance, Wilson declared: "We have never yet sufficiently formulated our program for America with regard to the part she is going to play in the world, and it is imperative that she should formulate it at once." This position, which Wilson followed through relentlessly in his dealings with the opposing belligerents, is the clue to the very heart of American diplomacy from then on to the moment when America entered the war and defined her own objectives in the full.

. . . when we exert the force of this Nation we want to know what we are exerting it for . . . we have always remembered and revered the advice of the great Washington, who advised us to avoid foreign entanglements. By that I understand him to mean avoid being entangled in the ambitions and the national purposes of other nations. It does not mean—if I may be permitted to venture an interpretation of the meaning of that great man—that we are to avoid the entanglements of the world, for we are part of the world, and nothing that concerns the whole world can be indifferent to us. . . . Nothing that concerns humanity, nothing that concerns the essential rights of mankind can be foreign or indifferent to us.

It was indispensable for Wilson, the humanist, to establish this premise, if he were to break the provincialism, the parochial trammels, that held in the United States:

We want all the world to know, [he continued,] that we are ready to lend our force without stint to the preservation of peace in the interest of mankind. The world is no longer divided into little circles of interest. The world no longer consists of neighborhoods. The world is linked together in a common life and interest such as humanity never saw before, and *the starting of wars can never again be a private and individual matter for the nations.*

What disturbs the life of the whole world is the concern of the whole world, and it is our duty to lend the full force of this nation, moral and physical, to a league of nations which shall see to it that nobody disturbs the peace of the world without submitting his case first to the opinion of mankind.[40]

Consciously or unconsciously, the President uttered in his Omaha address the cardinal principles which later, with every right by primogeniture, became his principal contribution to the Covenant in the words of Article 11.[41] A full twenty-four years before

[40] *PPWW*, II, Pt. 2, 346-348. Speech delivered at Omaha, October 5, 1916. (Italics mine.)

[41] Any war or threat of war, whether immediately affecting any of the Members of the League or not, is hereby declared a matter of concern to the whole League, [It will be remembered that Wilson's May 27 pronouncement was for "an universal association of nations], and the League shall take any action that may be deemed wise and effectual to safeguard the peace of nations. . . . It is also declared to be the friendly right of each Member of the League to bring to the attention of the Assembly or of the Council any circumstance whatever affecting international relations which threatens to disturb international peace or the good understanding between nations upon which peace depends.

another presidential candidate reached the inexorable conception of "one world," Wilson ascertained and proclaimed its underlying unity, and the need of organizing its power.

Thus matters stood at the time of the Presidential election of 1916. Once it was over, Wilson turned to the task of endeavoring to end the conflict in Europe before it should have engulfed the United States. Into the ensuing negotiations, as conducted through Lansing, whose sympathies with the movement were open to serious question and who sabotaged by deliberate indiscretions the work of his chief, we need not enter, as they have been fully documented many times over. What is of very real interest, however, is the key document discovered by Baker in the "bulky folder" containing the documents lying back of the peace offer. This "proposed draft" was prepared about November 27, 1916, and then discussed with House. Because it reveals the whole scope of Wilson's thought, "before it had been whittled down by the fears and sympathies of his advisers," it is perhaps the most revealing document of the period,[42] certainly from the point of view of these lectures.

In it Wilson summarized the reasons for his position: the difficulties of every country; the intolerable position of neutrals; the attritional war and its dangers for the future; the immense urgency of immediate action. Summing up the professions on each side, Wilson emphasized that they did not envision

[42] *WWLL*, VI, 379-388.

"conquest or destruction" of antagonists; that they wished "to safeguard the rights of small nations and of peoples" and that they desired to end war, which, the President interpolated, "cannot be done by conquest or destruction of nationalities." This marked his initial endeavor to find the common ground between belligerents.

In the next section of the document, Wilson essayed to find common ground between the belligerents and the United States: "A common object," he declared, "has been professed by the leaders of the governments at war, viz., such a league to enforce peace as will make its future secure." To clinch this he added: "The United States is willing to lend its whole force of every kind to that end, with equal resolution and enthusiasm." This was certainly a position far, far in advance of any previously taken by the President. To clinch it all, the President in a final section wrote down his objects:

> To stop the war before it is too late to remedy what it has done;
>
> To reconsider peace on the basis of *the rights of the weak along with the rights of the strong, the rights of peoples as well as the rights of governments;*
>
> To effect a league of nations based upon a peace which shall be guaranteed against breach by the common force *and an intelligent organization of the common interest.*[43]

This certainly introduced several new elements into the ideological complex Wilson had already built up. The emphasis on the rights of peoples as contrasted with those of governments can only have

[43] *Ibid.*, 381. (Italics mine.)

been a subtle plea for revolution in polyglot states, while the " intelligent organization of the common interests " is a novel feature, to which the President had previously given no articulate expression.[44]

On further scrutiny, Baker's remarkable document, which is printed solidly, is easily discernible to have been two—the " thumb-nail sketch " of a long diplomatic note, or little more than an outline with topic sentences, and the formal note itself, couched in infinitely more sensitive language, and conveying many nuances which the outline does not yield. It is therefore necessary to observe the exfoliation of Wilson's thought in the amplified passages:

Leaders on both sides have declared very earnestly and in terms whose sincerity no one can justly doubt that it was no part of their wish or purpose to crush their antagonists, make conquest of their territories or possessions, deprive them of their equal place and opportunity among the great peoples of the world. They have declared also that they are fighting no less for the rights of small and weak nations and peoples than for those of the great and powerful states immediately involved. They have declared their desire for peace, but for a peace that will last, a peace based, not upon the uncertain balance of powerful alliances offset against one another, but upon guarantees in which the whole civilized world would join, that the rights and privi-

[44] It should be remembered that the President was being daily bombarded during 1916 by the advocates of the liberation of this or that nationality. That Wilson ultimately felt the collective impact is more than clearly in evidence here. The " intelligent organization of the common interest " is remarkably like the ideas set forth in 1916 by Dr. Alfred Fried. Indeed the Baker document bears strong resemblances to passages on pp. 102-133 of Dr. Fried's *The Restoration of Europe*, the American edition of which was published early in 1916.

> leges of every nation and people should be the common and definite obligation of all governments.
>
> With these objects the people and government of the United States whole-heartedly sympathize. . . . We are ready to join a league of nations that will pledge itself to their accomplishment and definitely unite in an organization not only of purpose but of force as well that will be adequate to assure their realization. They are ready to lend their every resource, whether of men or money or substance to such a combination, so purposed and so organized.[45]

This, to say the least, considerably filled out the skeleton outline. In the concluding paragraph of the expanded version, Wilson felt confident that "the very great and substantial guarantee" of the peace would be supplied by "a league of nations formed to unite their force in active cooperation for the preservation of the world's peace." In another passage, he hailed the "opportunity to form such a league of nations as all now desire, a league united and powerful enough in force and purpose to guarantee the peace of the world against further breach by injustice or aggression—guarantee it by the sheer force of an intelligent and irresistible organization of the major force of mankind in the common interest of civilization."[46]

It is plain that, under the terrific pressures of the belligerents, and in the hope of sparing the United States from participation in the conflict, Wilson thought through, faster and farther than he had ever done before, the general implications of his May pronouncement for a new form of organization of the international community.

[45] *WWLL*, VI, 384. [46] *Ibid.*, 386.

The note finally despatched to the belligerent governments was considerably watered down, hence much that Wilson sought to include in this final grandiose effort to build up a consensus was lost.[47] When the replies of the belligerents were in hand, Wilson resolved to make an appeal to world opinion, by stating the problem in his own way, where the belligerents had been reluctant, and by delineating the kind of peace to which the United States could bring itself to subscribe.

In an address to the Senate of the United States on January 22, 1917, he disclosed without reserve the blueprint for the position which the United States

[47] "Each side," declared the note, "desires to make the rights and privileges of weak peoples and small states as secure against aggression or denial in the future as the rights and privileges of the great and powerful states now at war." This was to a large degree wish-thinking, as the situation in Austria-Hungary was certainly known to President Wilson, and was depicted in the news which came to him as quite different from this fine generalization. "Each wishes itself to be made secure in the future, along with all other nations and peoples, against the recurrence of wars like this and against aggression or selfish interference of any kind." Here the President was on much firmer ground. "Each would be jealous of the formation of any more rival leagues to preserve an uncertain balance of power amidst multiplying suspicions"—this was a thesis which Wilson produced by interpretation of the numerous appeals that reached him from every side—"but each is ready to consider the formation of a league of nations to insure peace and justice throughout the world." This universalized the President's own feelings. "Before that final step can be taken, however, each deems it necessary first to settle the issues of the present war upon terms which will certainly safeguard the independence, the territorial integrity, and the political and commercial freedom of the nations involved." Here Wilson, defeated in the effort to stress the objectives of the league idea, reinserts the objectives as those of the preliminary peace. The mention of "commercial freedom" appears to have been a concession to well-known State Department views. *PPWW*, II, Pt. 2, 404.

would take "in the days to come when it will be necessary to lay afresh and upon a new plan the foundations of peace among the nations." This called for adding "their authority and their power to the authority and force of other nations to guarantee peace and justice throughout the world." Since such a settlement could not be postponed, the President endeavored to state the conditions on which the American people could be asked to approve formal and solemn adherence to a League for Peace. Carefully eschewing for the United States any participation in the actual terms of peace, Wilson nevertheless sought to indicate the kinds of terms acceptable for guarantee. "We shall . . . have a voice in determining whether they shall be made lasting or not by the guarantees of a universal covenant, and our judgment upon what is fundamental and essential as a condition precedent to permanency should be spoken now, not afterwards, when it may be too late."

Wilson's first plea was for the inclusion of the entire New World in any arrangements for a guaranteed peace.[48] To do this the elements of that peace must satisfy the principles of the American governments, and be consistent with their political faith and with the practical convictions "which the peo-

[48] It will be recalled that it was President Theodore Roosevelt who insisted on the inclusion of the Latin American Governments in the Second Hague Conference, thus giving them *locus standi* with respect to the nuclear institutions of an international judiciary. Wilson was merely endeavoring here to write large, for the whole structure of international relationships, the procedure confined and circumscribed to a great degree in 1907.

ples of America have once and for all embraced and undertaken to defend." With striking consistency, the President carried over integrally into his wider plans the *res iudicata* of the Pan-American pact, and of Pan-American cooperation generally.

The second foundation for the new international order was the creation of paramount force:

It will be absolutely necessary that a force be created as a guarantor of the permanency of the settlement so much greater than the force of any nation now engaged or any alliance hitherto formed or projected that no nation, no probable combination of nations, could face or withstand it. If the peace presently to be made is to endure, it must be a peace made secure by the organized major force of mankind.

Wilson's third major conviction was that "there must be, not a balance of power but a community of power; not organized rivalries, but an organized common peace." While succinctly stated here, it became a point on which the President was later both insistent and incessant. "Mankind," he declared elsewhere in this same message, "is looking now for freedom of life, not for equipoises in power."

In his quest for large areas of agreement, Wilson was convinced that only a peace between equals could last. That is why he called for "peace without victory"—a phrase predestined to become immortal—where "peace without conquest" is what he actually desired. "The equality of nations upon which peace must be founded if it is to last must be an equality of rights." Here Wilson was striding in the seven-league boots of John Marshall: "Russia and Geneva have equal rights." This went far beyond the scope of any League of Nations, and sought fundamental agreement on the general terms of the peace. "Right," he continued, "must be based on the common strength . . . of the nations upon whose concert peace must depend."[49]

The keystone of Wilson's political thinking was next disclosed as the cornerstone of the new international edifice. "No peace can last, or ought to last," he declared "which does not recognize and accept the principle that governments derive all their just powers from the consent of the governed, and that no right anywhere exists to hand peoples about from sovereignty to sovereignty as if they were property." This was the logical corollary to the abandonment of the principle of the balance of power—the military principle of equilibrium applied to diplomacy—for if the principle was abandoned, then the practice of throwing peoples about as makeweights in the scales of the balance must be discarded also. While the President referred to Poland as an example—the only instance of a concrete peace term in his whole address—he went on to give voice to the fundamental principle lying back of the minority guarantee treaties later concluded at Paris and incorporated into the constitutions of several countries, both victorious and defeated: "that henceforth inviolable security of life, of worship, and of industrial and social development should be guaranteed to all peoples who have lived hitherto under the

[49] All quoted matter is from *PPWW*, II, Pt. 2, 407-414.

power of governments devoted to a faith and purpose hostile to their own." This too was a corollary, for if people were not to be bandied about on territory, they must, while staying put, be treated as humans.

When compared with the foregoing principles, the remaining points of which Wilson spoke—freedom of access to the sea, freedom of the seas itself, and the limitation of armaments—seem procedurally trivial, contrasting strongly with the fundamental human importance of his earlier principles. They conduced to the conclusion that henceforth "The statesmen of the world must plan for peace and nations must adjust and accommodate their policy to it as they have planned for war and made ready for pitiless contest and rivalry."

In conclusion, Wilson endeavored to demonstrate the congruity of the program thus outlined with the historical American tradition:

> In holding out the expectation that the people and Government of the United States will join the other civilized nations of the world in guaranteeing the permanence of peace upon such terms as I have named, I speak with the greater boldness and confidence because it is clear to every man who can think that there is in this promise no breach in either our traditions or our policy as a nation, but a fulfilment, rather, of all that we have professed or striven for. I am proposing . . . that the nations should with one accord adopt the doctrine of President Monroe as the doctrine of the world: that no nation should seek to extend its polity over any other nation or people, but that every people should be left free to determine its own polity, its own way of development, unhindered, unthreatened, unafraid, the little along with the great and powerful.

I am proposing that henceforth all nations avoid entangling alliances which would draw them into competitions of power; catch them in a net of intrigue and selfish rivalry, and disturb their own affairs with influences intruded from without. There is no entangling alliance in a concert of power. When all unite to act in the same sense and with the same purpose all act in the common interest and are free to live their own lives under a common protection.

I am proposing government by the consent of the governed. . . . These are American principles, American policies. We could stand for no others. . . .

It was not difficult for him to see the line of continuity: according to his principal biographer, the President had been deeply communing with the writings, if not the spirit, of James Monroe.

This was the last opportunity vouchsafed Wilson, in what must be universally admitted as a great state-paper, to suggest the fundamentals on which there must be agreement. It was virtually the last time he spoke as a neutral, for when the next major ideological and programmatic utterance came it was on the threshhold of war. War had in fact begun against us when Woodrow Wilson took the oath of office for the second time. It was on the cold windswept steps of the Capitol that he pledged to the visible audience and to the myriads of his countrymen who were present only in spirit, the things for which America would stand, either in peace or in war:

That all nations are equally interested in the peace of the world and in the political stability of free peoples, and equally responsible for their maintenance;

That the essential principle of peace is the actual equality of nations in all matters of right or privilege;

That peace cannot securely or justly rest upon an armed balance of power;

That governments derive all their just powers from the consent of the governed and that no other powers should be supported by the common thought, purpose, or power of the family of nations;

That the seas should be equally free and safe for the use of all peoples, under rules set up by common agreement and consent, and that, so far as practicable, they should be accessible to all upon equal terms;

That national armaments should be limited to the necessities of national order and domestic safety;

That the community of interest and of power upon which peace must henceforth depend imposes upon each nation the duty of seeing to it that all influences proceeding from its own citizens meant to encourage or assist revolution in other states should be sternly and effectually suppressed and prevented.[50]

In this ultra-condensed form may be noted many of the principles of the Senate address with a strange throw-back at the end to Bryan's munitions control program for the prevention of revolution, but also with a new, crisp, clear-cut statement as to the limitation of armament which was predestined to pass, with its phraseology almost unchanged, into the first part of Article 8 of the League of Nations Covenant. It is clear that by the time that the United States entered the war, the major ideas which were involved in the international reorganization were already articulated and of record. In his great war message Wilson emphasized the continuity of ideas and objectives:

[50] *PPWW*, III, Pt. 1, 3-4.

> . . . let us be very clear, and make very clear to all the world what our motives and our objects are. My own thought has not been driven from its habitual and normal course by the unhappy events of the last two months, and I do not believe that the thought of the Nation has been altered or clouded by them. I have exactly the same things in mind now that I had in mind when I addressed the Senate. . . . Our object now, as then, is to vindicate the principles of peace and justice in the life of the world as against selfish and autocratic power, and to set up amongst the really free and self-governed peoples of the world such a concert of purpose and of action as will henceforth insure the observance of those principles.[51]

Discarding the matrix of neutrality freed Wilson from many trammels. It made it possible for him to castigate the autocracies and insist upon democratic renovation of states as the means by which a "steadfast concert for peace" could alone be maintained. "Only free peoples can hold their purposes and their honor steady to a common end and prefer the interests of mankind to any narrow interest of their own." It was this which made Wilson say that "the world must be made safe for democracy," and that "its peace must be planted upon the tested foundations of political liberty." And in his final summation, the war President inter-knit the relationships of our objectives: "democracy, . . . the right of those who submit to authority to have a voice in their own governments, . . . the rights and liberties of small nations" and "a universal dominion of right by such a concert of free peoples as shall bring peace and safety to all nations and make the world itself

[51] *PPWW*, III, Pt. 1, 6-16, at 11.

at last free." [52] It is in this context that the great war aims of the United States actually took form and concreteness.

Up to this point Wilson had sedulously avoided—except for one brief reference to Poland—any mention of specific war aims, or concrete stipulations to be laid down in the peace at the close of the war. With the arrival of war missions in America, the business of concretization began. It is therefore necessary to turn to the territorial as contrasted with the institutional settlement and discover in how far the United States contributed to the solutions. Before doing so, it may be well to register, as of April 6, 1917, the degree of clarification which the United States, far more than any other nation, was successful in introducing into the world scene. It may be summed up by saying that Wilson was diligently at work in the creating of an international consensus as to the fundamentals of international organization. That organization was to be the result of the covenanting, by all the free peoples in the world, that they would establish a tribune and a tribunal, for the airing of grievances and the adjudication of causes. There must be major organized force behind both; there must be no contrarient alliances and there must be elaborate safeguards for human rights—credal, linguistic and cultural. This was the crystallized ideological nucleus at the time when neutrality went overboard and the United States at length drew the sword from its scabbard.

[52] *Ibid.*, 14-16.

APPENDIX IV

THE GENESIS OF THE PAN-AMERICAN TREATY

It is not my intention to give here, even in résumé, the narrative of the pourparlers concerning the instrument which President Seymour has called "A Pan-American Pact." [1] As elsewhere in these lectures, I am interested in genetic origins, for the document which finally emerges from a diplomatic conference almost invariably has a long line of distinguished—and some undistinguished—ancestors! Seymour attributes to Colonel House almost complete responsibility for the idea and for its implementation: "Colonel House was anxious" he writes, "to capitalize the advantage of the moment in order to develop a positive and permanent Pan-American policy, based on the principle of conference and cooperation." House assertedly early ascribed the European debacle of 1914 primarily to "the lack of an organized system of international cooperation. Such a system he was anxious that Wilson should develop for the Americas." [2] The idea was broadened indirectly on November 25, 1914, and followed by letter five days later, House being of opinion that "the opportunity to weld North and South America in closer union" was at hand and should not be neglected.[3] "What Colonel House had in mind,"

[1] Charles Seymour, *The Intimate Papers of Colonel House*, I, Chapter VIII, 207-234, hereinafter referred to as *IPCH*.

[2] *Ibid.*, 207.

[3] *Ibid.*, 208, November 30, 1914.

says Seymour, was nothing less than a rather loose league of American States which should guarantee security from aggression and furnish a mechanism for the pacific settlement of disputes." [4] "It was my idea," wrote House, "to formulate a plan, to be agreed upon by the republics of the two continents, which in itself would serve as a model for the European nations when peace is at last brought about. . . . My idea was that the republics of the two continents should agree to guarantee each other's territorial integrity, and that they should also agree to government ownership of munitions of war." As first drafted by Wilson and House—actually by Wilson—on December 16, 1914, the provisions were: "1st. Mutual guaranties of political independence under republican form of government and mutual guaranties of territorial integrity. 2nd. Mutual agreement that the Government of each of the Contracting parties acquire complete control within its jurisdiction of the manufacture and sale of munitions of war." [5]

Bryan appears to have taken little interest in the project save insofar as it would have automatically included the essential provisions of his "cooling off" treaties. By December 19, 1914, House had elicited from Wilson a statement that "the United States would not tolerate . . . aggression upon other republics." [6]

During Colonel House's absence in Europe in the winter and spring of 1915 there was no one at the

[4] *Ibid.*, 209, December 16, 1914.
[5] *Ibid.*, 209-210. [6] *Ibid.*, 213.

home base actively to push the idea, Lansing having been kept in ignorance of the matter, and Chile apparently being unwilling to undertake to abstain from aggressive policies.[7] With the return of House, Lansing was put *au courant* on July 24, 1915, and by the beginning of October the "pact" began to assume recognizable shape. The provision forbidding private manufacture of arms was dropped and "an automatic embargo on munitions in case of revolutionary attack upon an existing government" was added. The residues of Bryan's influence were ascertainable in articles which made provision for investigation and arbitration in the settlement of disputes. In this version Lansing, on November 18, 1915, submitted the pact to Colonel House who replied two days later that he thought the Secretary of State had got "the four propositions down to the best possible form."[8] "Indeed," remarks Seymour, "the matter seemed so close to completion that on January 6, 1916, Mr. Wilson in his address to the Pan-American Scientific Congress, stated publicly the gist of the proposals."[9]

During Colonel House's next sojourn in Europe, between December, 1915 and March, 1916, the project remained at a standstill in Washington, although the Colonel undertook to push for it from the sidelines. By the time of his return, Mexican-American relations were at such a pass that any prospect of success in the venture was extremely remote. Thus, on August 8, 1916, Frank L. Polk, then Under Secretary of State, wrote to Colonel House that the Pact

[7] *Ibid.*, 221-222. [8] *Ibid.*, 225-226. [9] *Ibid.*, 227.

"seems dead for the moment." [10] Due to the impending presidential election and the moves for peace at the end of 1916, "the Pan-American Pact was pushed to one side and," adds Seymour, "with the entrance of the United States into the European War in the spring of 1917, it slipped into a forgotten grave." [11]

Seymour's appraisal of the pact is pertinent here: "Even unfulfilled," he declares, "the plan occupies a position of historical significance. It was designed not merely to bring the American States more closely together but also to serve as a model to the European nations when they had ended the war. Both in its specific language and in its general intent the Pan-American Pact is the immediate prototype of the League of Nations." [12] Seymour claims for House a realization, even in 1916, that the United States would enter and vivify a larger concert than that of purely American States.

The Lansing Papers, published in 1940, serve to bring out, as was not fully done in the Secretary's *War Memoirs,* the share of Lansing, as Counselor and Secretary of State, in the genesis of the Pan-American Pact. They reveal the profound dissatisfaction of Lansing, while Counselor (1914-1915), with the existing status of the Monroe Doctrine, and his sincere belief, expressed in June, 1914, that the time was ripe for its restatement, since it was not "a Pan-American policy." Hence he wrote to Secretary Bryan:

[10] *Ibid.*, 231. [11] *Ibid.*, 232. [12] *Ibid.*, 233.

> The opposition to European control over American territory is not primarily *to preserve the integrity of any American State*—that may be a result but not a purpose of the Doctrine. . . . The primacy of one nation . . . is out of harmony with *the principle of the equality of nations* which *underlies Pan-Americanism*. . . . The equality of American republics and, in a measure, their independence, are legal rather than actual, but it is necessary to acknowledge their legal existence [i. e., their "existing political independence"] if the theory of Pan-Americanism is accepted. . . . Pan-Americanism is the joint policy of the American group of nations. . . . In its advocacy of the Monroe Doctrine the United States considers its own interests. The [territorial] integrity of other American nations is an incident, not an end. While this may seem based on selfishness alone, the author of the Doctrine has no higher or more generous motive in its declaration. To assert it for a nobler purpose is to proclaim a new doctrine.[13]

After discussing the extension of insidious financial controls as a problem requiring for its solution a restatement of doctrine, Lansing suggested as its object "not only the national safety and interests of this country, but also *the establishment and maintenance of republican constitutional government in all American states* . . ." [14]

Here the matter rested for a year and a half. Then, on November 24, 1915,—a week after Lansing had submitted to House the final boiled-down draft of the Pan-American Treaty—Lansing brought out the above memorandum, originally submitted to Bryan, and, refurbishing it with additional argu-

[13] *LP*, II, 461-462. (Italics mine.)
[14] *Ibid.*, 464. (Italics mine.)

ments, submitted it directly to President Wilson. In the interval the document had lost all its territorial guarantee character, and frankly looked to American intervention to create " stable and honest " governments in the Caribbean area.[15] Wilson replied on November 29, 1915, in a non-committal note agreeing with the analysis but not binding himself to the recommendations.[16]

The Lansing Papers further show that late in January, 1915, Wilson endeavored unsuccessfully to hybridize the territorial-guarantee idea imperfectly developed in Lansing's own mind, as shown in the June memorandum, with the conciliation or " cooling off " treaties which were Bryan's chief political passion. Wilson therefore asked [17] Bryan on January 28, 1915, to effect a working synthesis of the ideas. This was done overnight with Lansing's help, and the projected treaty thus took tangible form, with the territorial guarantees in Article I:

> That the contracting parties to this *solemn covenant* and agreement hereby join in a common and mutual guarantee to one another of *undisturbed and indisputed territorial integrity and of complete political independence under republican forms of government.*[18]

The solution of boundary disputes was provided for in Art. II, comprehensive munitions control was covered in Art. III, and general pacific settlement in Art. IV.[19]

[15] *Ibid.*, 466-70.
[16] *Ibid.*, 470.
[17] *Ibid.*, 472.
[18] *LP*, II, 472. (Italics mine.)
[19] *Ibid.*, 472-473. (Italics mine.)

The nature of guarantees of republican institutions and defined territories was comprehensively explained to the Chilean Ambassador on April 29, 1915, in a memorandum by Lansing which presented the situation as Wilson viewed it. Only two points deserve comment: First, the necessity of guaranteeing territory in order that there might be among the nations of the Western Hemisphere "*an understanding that force would not be recognized as a legitimate means of acquiring territory.*" It is obvious that both Wilson and Lansing, with the Chinese situation ever in the back of their minds, could not dissociate the non-recognition doctrine, then being announced, from their thinking about Latin America. Second, the guarantee to each State that it would not be deprived of its territory. "The United States is not only willing to give assurances of its purposes in this respect," declared the memorandum in typically Wilsonian language, "but is willing if desired to join with the Latin American republics in giving specific and definite assurances that no contracting State will be forced to part with any of its territory.[20] This obviously extended a guarantee found in the American constitutional system to this wider regional grouping.

In a memorandum delivered to Lansing on October 12, 1915,[21] Colonel House gave the Secretary of State his version of the genesis of the pact, ascribing to Wilson the definitive authorship of the territorial guarantee and munitions provisions, and thus

[20] *Ibid.*, 482-483. (Italics mine.)
[21] *Ibid.*, 486-488.

differing to a certain extent from Seymour's explanation. "Of course you understand," concluded House, "that the President's purpose is to broaden the Monroe Doctrine so that it may be upheld by all the American Republics instead of by the United States alone, as now."

In the period between January and October, there was time for examining Chilean objections which House, Lansing, and Wilson tried to overcome,[22] the Chilean Ambassador being virtually won over to the territorial guarantees at the very moment that negotiations were transferred to Santiago.[23] In the process of redrafting between November 3 and 11, 1915, national ownership of munitions plants disappeared and was supplanted by a new Article IV binding the parties not to assist insurgents or revolutionists.[24] By the end of 1915 Lansing had communicated the new draft to all the American States, but besought Wilson, at the very last moment, on January 6, 1916, to remove an explicit guaranty of a republican form of government from the programmatic address he delivered that evening.

I find a general idea prevails that the plan of a Pan-American treaty involved the guarantee of republican forms of government. It seems to me it would be well, therefore, if possible, for you to make clear tonight that *the plan does not contemplate a guaranty of republican forms of government, but removes from the benefit of the guaranty of territory and independence a nation which abandons the republican form.* The guaranty of a republican form would, of

[22] *Ibid.*, 488-491.
[23] Lansing to Wilson, November 3, 1915, *Ibid.*, 491.
[24] *Ibid.*, 492.

course, be a direct interference with the internal affairs of a country and entirely contrary to the views which we have expressed and the course which we have followed in regard to the sovereign rights of a people to decide their domestic affairs without outside interference.

I make this suggestion in view of the opposition which may be aroused not only in this country but in other American republics if it is thought that there is any plan to coerce the people of a sovereign state in the conduct of their internal affairs.[25]

Apparently Wilson acceded, for in his formal address there is reference only to "the States of America uniting in guaranteeing to each other absolutely *political independence and territorial integrity.*"[26] When it is recalled, however, that all existing regimes were republican in character, the statement actually did not recede from the position which President Wilson had deeply at heart.

Here the matter rested for some months. In April, 1916, Lansing let the Argentine Ambassador have a copy of the treaty[27] but no progress was made during a long absence of the Secretary from Washington owing to illness. Meanwhile the Mexican crisis and later the entry of the United States into the World War delayed and made increasingly difficult any affirmative action. After war came, Lansing began to have great misgivings as to different contingencies which might conceivably arise were the treaty in existence and in effect.[28] This did not

[25] *Ibid.*, 493. (Italics mine.)
[26] *PPWW*, II, Pt. 1, 444.
[27] *LP*, II, 495.
[28] Lansing to Wilson, April 17, 1917. *Ibid.*, 498-499.

greatly bother the President,[29] since he was convinced "that this is the very time when *such a league* would make the deepest impression and have the greatest moral effort on both sides of the water." It is evident from this that Wilson conceived of the treaty as creating at the very least an American League of Nations.[30]

There is an important epilogue. Although the treaty draft was officially buried, the idea did not die, particularly in the mind of Wilson. Hence when, in June, 1918, Wilson received a delegation of Mexican newspapermen, to explain to them the wartime and permanent objectives of this Government, he adverted to the Pan-American Treaty and stressed its ideological significance:

> Some time ago, as you probably all know, I proposed a sort of Pan-American agreement. . . . So I said, "Very well, let us make an arrangement by which we will give bond. Let us have a common guaranty, that all of us will sign, of political independence and territorial integrity. Let us agree that if any one of us, the United States included, violates the political independence or the territorial integrity of any of the others, all the others will jump on her." I pointed out to some of the gentlemen who were less inclined to enter into this arrangement than others that that was in effect giving bonds on the part of the United States that we would enter into an arrangement by which you would be protected from us.

[29] Wilson to Lansing, April 19, 1917, *Ibid.*, 499-500. (Italics mine.)

[30] Lansing's papers give a brief epilogue indicating that on May 24, 1917, he informed Ambassador Morgan in Rio de Janeiro that the draft treaty would not be forwarded by the Department "as it does not desire you to take up this question with the Government of Brazil at this time." *Ibid.*, 500.

"Now that is the kind of arrangement that will have to be the foundation of the future life of the nations of the world. . . . *The whole family of nations will have to guarantee to each nation that no nation shall violate its political independence or its territorial integrity.* That is the basis, the only conceivable basis, for the future peace of the world, and I must admit that I was ambitious to have the states of the two continents of America show the way to the rest of the world as to how to make a basis of peace.. . ." [31]

This elicited from the Government of Peru a formal "decision" to participate in the treaty—a step doubtless designed to revive the discussion.[32] The Government of El Salvador likewise expressed to President Wilson, through an autographed letter from President Melendez, its "firm adhesion" to the ideas propounded by Wilson: "Your great conception of an international convention that would guarantee the political independence and territorial integrity of the nations of this hemisphere carries the highest purpose that has struck the chords of American public law from the days of Washington to our time." It was the belief of the Salvadorean Executive that should Wilson follow up his "momentous initiative," it would undoubtedly "receive the support of the greatest sympathy and best will of all the statesmen and rulers of our continent who, like you . . . are convinced that conventions of that na-

[31] *FRUS*, 1918, 579; also *Official U. S. Bulletin*, No. 332; *PPWW*, III, Pt. 2, 223-228. (Italics mine.)

[32] Don Manuel de Freyre y Santander to Lansing from Washington, June 11, 1918. *FRUS*, *1918*, 580.

ture are the foundation upon which to build the future life of nations, after the present war." [33]

To this Wilson replied in a friendly message, asking the Salvadorean Executive to believe that the address expressed the real attitude of the United States and the policy which they would wish to see their Government adopt and pursue. The President concluded by reaffirming his highest hope and confidence in "such a union of minds and purpose in America as will lead to abiding peace and friendly cooperation." [34] At the moment the "First Wilson Draft" of the future League Covenant was intermittently occupying his attention. It is clear that the final transit from a regional to a world-wide Covenant was made in Wilson's mind some time between June 9, when he nostalgically referred to it in addressing the Mexican editors, and July 29,[35] on which date he penned his reply to President Melendez.

[33] *FRUS*, 1918, 597-598. President C. Melendez to President Wilson on July 4, 1918; The Salvadorean Chargé (Reyes Guerra) to Lansing, from Washington, July 18, 1918.

[34] President Wilson to President Melendez; Frank L. Polk, Acting Secretary of State to Minister Long at San Salvador, July 31, 1918. *Ibid.*, 600.

[35] The date of the note is given from Wilson's appointment books in Ray Stannard Baker, *Woodrow Wilson, Life and Letters,* VIII, 303, hereinafter cited as *WWLL.*

LECTURE V

The United States and the Territorial Settlement

While the thought of a general international system was uppermost in the minds of the policy makers of the United States from the outset of World War I, the idea of a territorial settlement was kept in the background, strictly subordinated to the status of that neutrality which the United States asked its citizens to practice " in deed and in thought." That pledge, so far as public pronouncements and policy are concerned, President Wilson kept until almost the bitter end of American neutrality. While our ambassadors abroad reported devastation, deportations, destitution; while civic groups in the United States urged this or that cause, the government was strictly impartial, except where humanitarian considerations were concerned. To these neutrality was no barrier, and, almost from the beginning of the war, the Government not only did not interfere with war relief activities in behalf of Europeans but in many indirect ways encouraged them, even going so far as to name days on which collections for specific groups of war refugees would be made.

Belgium, in particular, received special attention, and the work of organizing the Commission for Relief in Belgium elicited full diplomatic support. From the Levant, too, came reports through diplomatic channels concerning the treatment of Armenians by the Ottoman Porte. Protest after protest made during our neutrality against the inhumanities of the Turks apparently made no impression, and with the coming of war, it was obvious that we were no longer in a position to exercise influence of any kind upon the Government at Constantinople. With the breaking of diplomatic relations between Turkey and the United States,[2] however, we were estopped from any direct action, but we were likewise released from any particular regard for the territorial sanctity of the Ottoman Empire.

Only when the great endeavor was made at the end of 1916 to elicit a statement of peace terms, did the specific territorial alterations involved begin to assume importance. It will be recalled that the Central Powers refused to disclose their hand, and that the Allies, by contrast, were far more specific. In a trenchant note sent on behalf of all the Allied Governments by Premier Briand, the Allied war aims were summarized with the preliminary admonition that " Their objects in the war will not be made known in detail with all the equitable compensations and indemnities for damages suffered, until the hour of negotiations." " But the civilized world knows," continued the French premier, " that they imply in all necessity and in the first instance

> the restoration of Belgium, of Serbia and of Montenegro, and the indemnities which are due them; the evacuation of

[1] *FRUS, 1916, Supplement*, 846-848, *passim.*

[2] *FRUS, 1917, Supplement 1*, 598-603. The rupture, under heavy German pressure, came on April 20, 1917.

the invaded territories of France, or Russia and of Roumania with just reparation; the reorganization of Europe, guaranteed by a stable regime and founded as much upon respect of nationalities and full security and liberty of economic development, which all nations, great or small, possess, as upon territorial conventions and international agreements suitable to guarantee territorial and maritime frontiers against unjustified attacks; the restitution of provinces or territories wrested in the past from the Allies by force or against the will of their populations, the liberation of Italians, of Slavs, of Roumanians and of Czecho-Slovaks from foreign domination; the enfranchisement of populations subject to the bloody tyranny of the Turks; the expulsion from Europe of the Ottoman Empire decidedly foreign to western civilization. The intentions of His Majesty the Emperor of Russia regarding Poland have been clearly indicated in the proclamation which he has just addressed to his armies. It goes without saying that if the Allies wish to liberate Europe from the brutal covetousness of Prussian militarism, it has never been their design, as has been alleged, to encompass the extermination of the German peoples and their political disappearance. That which they desire above all is to insure a peace upon the principles of liberty and justice, upon the inviolable fidelity to international obligation with which the Government of the United States has never ceased to be inspired.[3]

A special plea was also entered on behalf of Belgium, emphasizing her particular desiderata, by her Minister for Foreign Affairs, Baron Beyens.[4]

Such was the war aim program of the Allied Powers at the moment that we became an associate. That it concealed much it is hardly necessary to note, for the Allies did not immediately and forth-

[3] *FRUS, 1917, Supplement* 1, 6-8.
[4] *Ibid.*, 8-9.

rightly disclose the details, even after we entered the war. It was impossible to figure from the Briand note how far "equitable compensations and indemnities for damages" would go. And the "territorial conventions and international agreements suitable to guarantee territorial and maritime frontiers against unjustified attack" left the door wide open for the resurgence of defensive alliances and strictly strategic frontiers. Owing to the existence of the autocracy in Russia, the program of the Allies had to tread softly as regards the nationalities in the great Russian fold. Finally, the denial of a design to exterminate the German peoples or to obliterate them from the map was not a positive index to the type of treatment to be meted out to the Germans.

All in all, the Allied answer was devoid of any idealism; it showed a myopic concern with the immediate business in hand, and it did not begin to envisage a solution in terms of an international order. By the time that the United States entered the lists, however, the fall of the autocracy in Russia removed a major obstacle to the application of the principle of nationality to the settlement. There is no question that much linen was quietly laundered between the different Allies in the weeks between January 10 and April 6, 1917, and that much was effected to sew up, beyond the point of reopening, settlements between Britain and France, between the Western Allies and Japan, etc. In proportion as the United States moved to enter the conflict, it was confronted with a number of minor *faits accomplis.*

What was the American reaction? Colonel House

supplies the answer in part, in telling of the genesis of Wilson's address to the Senate on January 22, 1917. In a conference at the White House on January 3, before Briand's detailed rejoinder was known, House and the President canvassed the whole ground and decided that,

> since Germany and Russia had agreed to free Poland, that should be put in. We naturally agreed upon Belgium and Serbia being restored. Alsace and Lorraine we were not quite certain of, but we agreed that Turkey (in Europe) should cease to exist.[5]

This created a core of agreement which covered points dealt with in Briand's note. In addition, Colonel House suggested "that something be put in regarding the right of Russia to have a warm seaport," adding with conviction that "If this were not done it would leave a sore which in time would bring about another war." According to Seymour,[6] however, Wilson finally decided not to include any statement of a desirable territorial settlement except to mention the necessity of a united independent Poland. Exactly a year later, adds Colonel House's biographer, Wilson "elaborated the chief items of this conversation with House into the Fourteen Points." The statement may be a tribute to Wilsonian tenacity, but it is difficult to believe that the House-Wilson conversation was kept integrally in intellectual cold storage for so hectic a period.

With the United States in the war and Allied missions arriving in this country, the normal course of

[5] *IPCH*, II, 415.

[6] *Ibid.*, 415 n.

diplomacy and intimate political conversations would have been to utilize to the full the opportunity to settle preliminarily the outstanding questions between the United States and each of its associates. This House was determined that Wilson should not do, at least insofar as it dealt with peace settlements.[7] In practice, however, it ultimately proved extremely difficult to avoid doing the obviously necessary. Wilson, on the other hand, wished to clarify and settle the situation, and agreed to have House go over the whole ground with Balfour privately, before Wilson indulged in detailed discussions with the British Secretary of State for Foreign Affairs. This was done in an hour and a half-long conversation on April 28, 1917.

Balfour apparently opened with a statement of assumed agreement—regarding the return of Alsace-Lorraine to France, and the restoration of France, Belgium and Serbia. Poland loomed first on the British agenda, and as the President had already announced an agreement in his speech to the Senate, it became not a matter of principle but of detail. House "warmly advocated a restored and rejuvenated Poland, a Poland big enough and powerful enough to serve as a buffer state between Germany and Russia"—an indication that he was himself

[7] "I hope you will agree with me," House wrote to Wilson, "that the best policy now is to avoid a discussion of peace settlements. Balfour concurs in this. . . . If you have a tacit understanding with him not to discuss peace terms with the other Allies, later this country and England will be able to dictate broad and generous terms—terms that will mean permanent peace." *IPCH*, III, 37-38 and 39-62, *passim.*

caught up in the balance of power diplomacy which Wilson wished to replace. The problem of Poland's access to the sea bothered both men, Balfour wanting to make Danzig merely a free port, House for the moment opposing such a solution.

They next dealt with Serbia and " it was agreed that Austria must return Bosnia and Herzegovina "— a strange arrangement, since Serbia had never possessed them, although the prospective expulsion of Turkey from Europe would leave no other beneficiary. Serbia in turn was to retrocede to Bulgaria " that part of Macedonia which the first Balkan agreement gave her "—an agreement so vague alike as to area and as to the specific treaty settlement to which it referred as to render precision most difficult. Rumania followed. " We thought," states House, that she " should have a small part of Russia which her people inhabited, and also a part of Hungary for the same reason." Seymour declares, in the absence of the map, that the references were " evidently to Bessarabia and Transylvania and the Banat," adding the critical comment that " They may have looked small upon Balfour's map, but the territories promised Rumania by the secret Treaty of Bucharest, signed August 17, 1916, would almost double the area of Rumania," and observing for unequivocal clarity that " Bessarabia, belonging to Russia, was not included in the territories then promised Rumania." [8]

Turning to the residues of the Dual Monarchy,

[8] *Ibid.*, III, 43 n-44 n.

House tersely remarks: "We thought Austria should be composed of three states, such as Bohemia, Hungary and Austria proper." It is clear in retrospect that this part of the settlement, to which House seems easily to have agreed, was not yet influenced by the force of Czechoslovak diplomacy, which eventually was able, through the personality of Thomas G. Masaryk, to bring Wilson from apathy to enthusiasm for the Czech cause. It is also clear that the United States, which less than two months before was endeavoring to entice Austria into a separate peace by guaranteeing her against disruption, had made little or no progress by way of a constructive solution with regard to the truncated Dual Monarchy.

Italy next absorbed the attention of the two conferees. Here Colonel House suddenly developed a profound interest in Trieste, but he and Balfour came to no conclusion on the subject. "I did not consider it best or advisable," declared House laconically, "to shut Austria from the Adriatic." Balfour countered with the Italian arguments, revealing at least tangentially his familiarity with the Treaty of London. "Italy," declared the Foreign Secretary, "claimed that she should have protection for her east coast by having Dalmatia. She has no seaport from Venice to Brindisi, and she claims she must have the coast opposite to protect herself." [9] Thereupon House elicited from Balfour a statement that the Allies "had treaties with one another, and that

[9] *Ibid.*, III, 43n-44n.

when Italy came in they made one with her in which they had promised pretty much what she demanded." In the ensuing conversation Balfour, according to House, explicitly promised to have copies of the treaties made for Wilson's confidential information.[10]

It is noteworthy that Colonel House sensed the extravagance of the Italian demands in the Adriatic. It is also not improbable that his conversations with Wilson were predestined to set Wilson in opposition to the integral fulfilment of Italian claims. Certainly by the time Wilson and Balfour really met, Wilson must have been fully aware of the extent of Italian claims and the Colonel's doubts as to Trieste. Thus what then appeared to Balfour as obtuseness turns out in 1946 to have been perspicacity.

From the Adriatic Balfour and the Colonel passed to the fate of the Ottoman Empire. "Constantinople was our next point. We agreed that it should be internationalized." This notwithstanding the earlier Allied pledge to give Constantinople to Russia. It is difficult to ascertain whether House made this suggestion and Balfour accepted it or vice

[10] The passage in question is most obliquely written in House's diary for April 28: "I asked him if he did not think it proper for the Allies to give copies of these treaties to the President for his confidential information. He thought such a request entirely reasonable and said he would have copies made for that purpose. He was not certain they had brought them over, but if not, he would send for them." It will be noted that the pledge by Balfour was implicit, rather than explicit, and that while he undoubtedly expressed himself broadly to House, the whole matter was left vague. Seymour comments that "House did not urge Balfour to give him complete details of the secret treaties, nor, being a private citizen, would he wish to ask for copies of the texts." *Ibid.*, III, 44, 46.

versa. Certainly it marked a disposition on the part of Great Britain, very early after the beginning of the Russian Revolution, to curtail her obligations in that quarter. Seymour endeavors to explain the discrepancy by suggesting that "House must have misunderstood Balfour, perhaps interpreting 'free port' as meaning 'free city.'" But the divergence between the outlook of both men was merely beginning.

Turning to the Anatolian settlement, House remarks initially: "It is here that the secret treaties between the Allies come in most prominently. They have agreed to give Russia a sphere of influence in Armenia and the northern part. The British take in Mesopotamia [and the region] which is contiguous to Egypt. France and Italy each have their spheres embracing the balance of Anatolia up to the Straits." This was the end of the area of agreement. "It is all bad," declares House drily, "and I told Balfour so." There was some questioning about the intent and content of spheres of influence, and Balfour proved evasive, "hazy," and "not altogether clear." In the circumstances to push the matter further would, perhaps, at this early a date in the common effort, have been hazardous. At all events the conferees did not touch upon the German colonies, Japan, China, "or the Eastern question generally."

Next there was a reprise of the Polish problem. Balfour's major objection was that an intervening Poland would rob the Franco-Russian alliance, which to Britain was second in importance only to the *entente cordiale*, of much of its force, since "it would prevent Russia from coming to France's aid in the event of an attack by Germany." Looking ahead a half century, House foresaw great changes: "While we might hope [she] would continue democratic and cease to be aggressive, yet if the contrary happened, Russia would be the menace to Europe and not Germany." Despite a further exchange of views, House records in his diary that "Balfour, however, was more impressed with the German menace than he was by the possible danger from Russia." [11] Here the conference ceased.

Two days later, on April 30, the ground was again covered in a tripartite conversation between Wilson, Balfour and House. The Colonel's diary is not at all helpful, nor is Baker able to throw any light on what went on at the time. Baker does, however, adduce from Balfour's own recollections the assertion that he thought the question of the secret treaties was raised by the President, but that there were no secrets between him and Wilson then or afterwards, on any of the many subjects that came up for discussion.[12] Here the situation stood at the close of the great Allied war missions to the United States. We were

[11] Fortunately the Lansing Papers contain, under date of May 18, 1917, an excerpt from the proceedings of the Imperial War Council (undated), which Balfour sent to the Secretary of State giving his own statement of foreign policy. It covers very largely the ground traversed with House and is distinctly revealing of Balfour's inherited balance of power ideas, which led him to be receptive to schemes of partition. Since the matter was officially communicated, Lansing at least cannot be said to have been unaware of the Allied commitments, nor is there any record of his protest or objection at the time. No effort is here made to evaluate the Balfour report, because it was not *inter partes*. *LP*, II, 19-32.

[12] Arthur J. Balfour, *Retrospect*, 243.

in possession of the essential information with regard to the European settlement, and House, but not Wilson, was generally favorable.

Before Balfour left the United States he did in fact send to Wilson, " as he had promised," [13] texts of the various agreements between Britain and her Allies. It had been necessary, he declared, to send to England for them because he had no copies with him. In a cover letter Balfour expressed doubt as to whether they added much to Wilson's existing knowledge. Since Balfour enclosed as a memorandum " the main points " of his statement to the Imperial War Council, it must be obvious that the subject matter was already known to President Wilson. In addition Balfour sent texts of the Treaty of London of April 26, 1915; the Sykes-Picot Agreement of May, 1916, togther with connected diplomatic correspondence between the Russian Minister for Foreign Affairs, Sergei Sazonov, and the French Ambassador in Russia, Maurice Paléologue; the exchanges of notes in March and April, 1915, " embodying consent of France and England to Russia's annexation of Constantinople, with England's demand for the neutral zone of Persia "; and finally the Treaty of Bucharest of August 17, 1916, with Rumania. Baker notes acridly that Balfour carefully omitted to mention the Grey-Cambon correspondence relating to the division of Togoland and the Cameroons [14] and concealed even from the Imperial

[13] *WWLL*, VII, 74-75.

[14] Ray Stannard Baker, *Woodrow Wilson and World Settlement*, I, 259, 268.

War Council two agreements with Japan regarding Shantung and the Pacific Islands. These did not come to light, so far as the United States was concerned, until the Paris Peace Conference in 1919.

The point of view taken by both House and Wilson, that it was preferable not to open up a debate on war aims as between cobelligerents, may have had values at the time, but the failure of the public to receive any information other than was given in the President's war message presently threatened to start a Congressional discussion of war aims, the range of which, if we recall the comparatively placid situations of 1826 and 1851, can hardly be imagined. Indeed President Wilson, while endeavoring as a diplomat to smooth certain matters with two of the principal belligerents—Britain and Russia [15] was

[15] While obviously Ireland was not an object of the peace settlement, nevertheless President Wilson recognized that Anglo-Irish relations were such that they could not but have an adverse influence on Anglo-American understanding. He therefore took the bold course of asking Page, on April 10, 1917, to convey to Prime Minister Lloyd George "in most confidential manner the information that the only circumstance which seems now to stand in the way of an absolutely cordial cooperation with Great Britain . . . is the failure so far to find a satisfactory method of self-government for Ireland." Citing the views expressed in the debates on the war resolution, Wilson declared that "If the people of the United States could feel that there was an early prospect of the establishment for Ireland of substantial self-government, a very great element of satisfaction and enthusiasm would be added to the cooperation now about to be organized between this country and Great Britain." Wilson's aim was to break up the combination of Irish and German malcontents. When Ambassador Page conveyed the message, Lloyd George declared "But the President's right. We've got to settle it and we've got to settle it now." Cf. *LP*, II, 4-5 Wilson to Lansing; Lansing to Page. Cf. also Page to Wilson, May 4, 1917, Burton J. Hendrick, *The Life and Letters of Walter H. Page*, II, 259-60.

Wilson's other overture was to send (at the suggestion of

compelled as a party leader to head off a unilateral definition, by debate in the Senate, of the war aims

---

Ambassador Francis conveyed to Lansing on May 17, 1917) a message to the Provisional Government of Russia on May 22. This came at a peculiarly significant moment, because by that time Wilson had become acquainted with the secret plans of the Allied Governments for the peace settlement. "The position of America in this war is so clearly avowed that no man can be excused for mistaking it. She seeks no material profit or aggrandizement of any kind. She is fighting for no advantage or selfish object of her own, but *for the liberation of people everywhere, from the aggressions of autocratic force*." This was the first pronouncement applicable to the conditions within both Russia and Austria Hungary, and presaged a degree of support to nationality movements. "We are fighting," the President continued, "for the liberty, the self-government and the undictated development of all peoples, and every feature of the settlement that concludes the war must be conceived and executed for that purpose. Wrongs must first be righted and then adequate safeguards must be created to prevent their being committed again." From caution, foresight or from fear of passing judgment on a situation in a flux, President Wilson abstained from making concrete any of the generalizations he was making. But the idea of creating a common consensus underlay his whole approach. His *credo* in this instance was concise and, on the whole, quite similar to the pronouncements he had earlier made to other groups and in other circumstances: "No nation must be forced under sovereignty under which it does not wish to live"—a pronouncement actively in harmony with the theses on self-determination which Stalin had already enunciated at the first general gathering of his party after the Revolution; "No territory must change hands except for the purpose of securing those who inhabit it a fair chance of life and liberty"—in embryonic form a stipulation underlying the later thinking in regard to the mandate system. "No indemnities must be insisted on except those that constitute payment for manifest wrongs done." Here the President undoubtedly moved on to new ground. By putting a limitation on a wholesale negative, he was enabled to subscribe to the general principle of no annexations and no indemnities—with a large King's X, as it were. Incidentally, this phraseology underwent very considerable expansion at Wilson's hands in later months. "No readjustments of power must be made except such as will tend to secure the future peace of the world and the future welfare and happiness of its peoples." This

problem.[16] It only served to defer the real debate to the end of the war, at the most inauspicious moment, with consequences which were ultimately dis-

---

was an ethical postulate invoked to fill the juridical vacuum which the Revolution had created in Russia. Finally, "the free peoples of the world must draw together in a common covenant some genuine and practical cooperation that will in effect combine their force to secure peace and justice in the dealings of nations with one another." Seen in the retrospect of thirty years, this amorphous conception can hardly have appealed to a people in the throes of revolution. Already Wilson, seeking to stave off discussion of the general mechanism, was unable to offer to those who were anxious to be convinced, anything more tangible that "some genuine and practical cooperation." In the light of this, the splendid affirmation that "The nations must realize their common life and effect a workable partnership against the aggressions of autocratic and self-pleasing power" was singularly devoid of real meaning. For the text of the message cf. *FRUS, 1917, Supplement 2*, 71-73; *PPWW*, III, Pt. 1, 49-51 (Italics mine).

[16] On June 2, 1917, Senator Owen of Oklahoma, spokesman for the Wilson Administration on financial matters in the United States Senate, conferred with Secretary Lansing, leaving with him a copy of a resolution which the Senator intended to introduce. It would undoubtedly have opened a rather extensive discussion in the Senate. Lansing's files, as gleaned by the Department of State, did not contain the exact text, or even a draft copy of the resolution, but it is to be inferred that the resolution ultimately introduced by Senator Owen on July 23, 1917, was substantially similar to the document presented to Lansing. On June 3, Lansing forwarded to President Wilson the draft resolution and the draft of an address which Owen intended to deliver. According to Lansing, Owen had "evidently given much thought to the subject" and was "strong in the belief that Congress should declare our war purposes." Feeling that only Wilson could restrain him from acting, Lansing suggested to the President that a personal conference between them would resolve the matter and that the President should give Owen his views orally, and not in writing. Lansing's view was that Owen's proposals were "based on the essential principles which will be the foundation of permanent peace." He questioned, however, the timeliness of inviting "controversy over the terms of peace in Congress and, as a consequence, throughout the world" not knowing how the various Allied Governments would view such a "formal declaration on our part of arrangements in which they

astrous both to the President and to the American public mind. There is no indication as to what Wilson replied, if indeed he replied at all.[17] It is noteworthy that at the moment of the peace note issued by His Holiness, Benedict XV, the whole discussion did in fact become injected into Congressional debate, although "squelched" and "steam rollered" by an administration majority. The wisdom of continually deferred discussion of war objectives, or peace aims, must, in the sad retrospect of history, seem open to the greatest question.

One of the major pronouncements of war aims

---

are so vitally interested, without our consulting them or giving them an opportunity to object to one or more of the provisions." This was a specific objection to a specific proposition, but Lansing made his own complaint general and sweeping: "In fact I believe that any resolution at the present time" he wrote the President, "would precipitate a debate in Congress which might give opportunity to those hostile to you to criticize your declarations as to the purposes which we seek to accomplish in the war. That would be very undesirable and might cause serious differences with our co-belligerents." Lansing to Wilson, June 3, 1917. *LP*, II, 34-35.

[17] Baker, reconstructing events with the aid of the Wilson date books, notes that on June 4, 1917, Senator Robert L. Owen called on the President in the evening with "copies of a resolution setting forth an American peace program laid before the President and Secretary Lansing." The interpretation given to this visit by Wilson's official biographer is that "The President dissuaded Owen, probably intimating his own intention of dealing with the subject in an address." *WWLL*, VII, 99. It is evident that Wilson was already contemplating a major address on Flag Day, June 14, (*Ibid.*, 97). Meanwhile Colonel House was elaborating with Sir Eric Drummond the bases for common pronouncements on Germany by British and American statesmen, noteworthily in the House-Drummond memorandum of May 20, 1917 (*IPCH*, III, 58). These eventuated in part in the Flag Day Address which is noted below, and found in *PPWW*, III, Pt. 1, 60-67, and in *FRUS, 1917, Supplement* 2, I, 96-100.

came in a powerful address of the President on June 14, 1917, when he reviewed the causes of the war in ways he had long been reluctant to essay. After surveying the immediate causes of American involvement, the Wilsonian mind reached into the deeper meaning of the war. His commitment to the principle of nationality, if it had come about waveringly and by stages, was complete:

> The war was begun by the military masters of Germany, who proved to be also the masters of Austria-Hungary. These men have never regarded nations as peoples, men, women, and children of like blood and frame as themselves, for whom governments existed and in whom governments had their life. They have regarded them merely as serviceable organizations which type could by force or intrigue bend or corrupt to their own purpose. They have regarded the smaller states, in particular, and the peoples who could be overwhelmed by force, as their natural tools and instruments of domination. Their purpose has long been avowed. . . .
>
> The great fact that stands out above all the rest is that this is a People's War, a war for freedom and justice and self-government amongst all the nations of the world, a war to make the world safe for the peoples who live upon it and have made it their own, the German people themselves included.

But Wilson was not specific. The generalities of this and other addresses had yet to become concrete and definite. Even the mid-summer appeal of Pope Benedict found Wilson in the valley of indecision with respect to either concrete peace terms or concrete proposals for the creation of a League of Nations. This came perilously close to lack of statesmanship.[18] The fact that Wilson would not participate in any inter-allied conferences of the period, not even allowing our generals and admirals and

[18] There can be no question that Balfour, after his experience in talking over with Wilson the various Allied commitments, foresaw great difficulties, were they to be discussed openly. Partly to avoid this embarrassment, and the still greater embarrassment of having to discuss with the Russians the same problem, Balfour counseled against any conference for the purpose, passing on his views to Wilson through Ambassador Page in London, who heartily concurred. (*FRUS, 1917, Supplement 2,* I, 119-120; *WWLL,* VII, 147.) This was on July 6. Balfour expressed the same views to the House of Commons on July 30 (*WWLL,* VII, 199). This may have operated as a deterrent to President Wilson in further clarification of war aims. There is further evidence, gathered chiefly by Baker, that Senator Owen continued to press his plans upon the President (*WWLL,* VII, 153, 171), using his important leverage on financial matters in that connection.

Meanwhile the French Government began to ask embarrassing questions: Premier Ribot, who was also Foreign Minister, asked Ambassador Jusserand to press for details as to the League of Nations. Just how, he asked the Ambassador on July 20, could such a society of nations be brought into existence? Ribot contemplated calling into being a governmental commission charged with the duty of examining the question. Wilson did not reply for a fortnight, and then most chillily: "The President" wrote Acting Secretary Polk on August 3, "expresses the fear that such a commission, if constituted at this time, would be premature and unnecessarily introduce new subjects of discussion and perhaps of difference of view among the nations associated against Germany," How fluid and uncrystallized Wilson's views really were can be indicated from the statement that "The President's own idea has been that such a society of nations would of necessity be an evolution rather than a creation by formal convention. It has been his hope and expectation that the war would result in certain definite covenants and guarantees entered into by the free nations of the world for the purpose of safeguarding their own security and the general peace of the world, and that *in the very process of carrying these covenants into execution from time to time a machinery and practice of cooperation would naturally spring up which would in the end produce something which would in effect be a regularly constituted and employed concert of nations.*" This we may regard as a colloid conception from which

ambassadors to be present,[19] indicates what a long way we had to go, including the whole American public, to reach the stage of constructive, positive, cooperation, at least with regard to the problem of the terms of peace.

A final test of this condition of political and diplomatic unpreparedness came in the Papal peace note, of August 1, 1917. In his appeal to the rulers of the belligerent peoples, the Pontiff declared:

> . . . we renew a pressing appeal to those who have in their hands the destinies of nations. But no longer confining ourselves to general terms, as we were led to do by circumstances in the past, we will now come to more concrete and practical proposals and invite the governments of the belligerent peoples to arrive at an agreement on the following points which seem to offer the bases of a just and lasting peace, leaving it with them to make them more precise and complete. . . . [20]

Actually the Papal suggestions were largely of a general nature, with specific references only to Armenia,

---

Wilson ultimately departed radically. " To begin with a discussion of how such a concert or society should be constituted, under the presidency of which nation, with what common force and under what common command, etc., etc., would be likely to produce jealousies and difficulties which need not be faced now. (*FRUS, 1917, Supplement 2*, I, 153; *WWLL*, VII, 203. (Italics mine.)

[19] Such was Wilson's stand in relation to the proposed conference on the military situation in the Balkans. Proposed by France to meet on July 16, the invitation was definitely rejected by telephone on July 13 (*FRUS, 1917, Supplement 2*, I, 118-119). An earlier invitation, issued by Balfour on July 2, four days ahead of the French, was likewise firmly declined on July 11, on the ground that " this government is not ready at this time to take part in the inter-Allied war conferences." *Ibid.*, 123-124.

[20] For the text of the Pope's appeal cf. *FRUS, 1917, Supplement 2*, I, 161-164.

the Balkan states and "the territories forming part of the old Kingdom of Poland." Before replying, Wilson endeavored through Lansing to collect the points of view of all the governments with which the United States was in diplomatic contact. He was further importuned by France,[21] Russia,[22] Belgium,[23] and possibly other countries, to join in concerted action, or at least bring about conference on the reply,

[21] On August 18, 1917, Jusserand besought Lansing to find out for him whether a reply was needed, and whether, if this was the case, an agreed reply should be sent. "My government consider that it would be appropriate to concert as to what should be said, so that a similar attitude be observed by those who fight on the same side of the trench" (*Ibid.*, 165). On August 21, Ambassador Sharp reported from Paris that "it was the opinion of both Mr. Ribot and Mr. Cambon that there should be a complete accord among the Allies in making their answer. They say that they would appreciate very much if I would express their desire that the President would first communicate his own views to them so that there might follow an exchange of opinion between them to the end that such accord might be arranged. . . . The question was presented as to whether it might be possibly thought best for the Allies to join together in making their answer." (*Ibid.*, 170-171.)

[22] On August 21, Ambassador Boris Bakhmetev importuned Lansing for an expression of opinion as to the American attitude on the Papal peace note. Lansing declined to give an answer, since the communication was still under consideration—a decision very disappointing to the Ambassador because Foreign Minister Tereschenko was desirous of acting, if possible, in a similar way to that chosen by the United States. How cooperative Lansing was at this stage may be noted from the fact that he informed the President that he told Bakhmetev "that similar but independent action seemed wise" (*Ibid.*, 166).

[23] On August 22, M. De Broqueville, Belgian Minister for Foreign Affairs, informed Brand Whitlock, the American Minister, of the general views of his Government, stating that he and the King "agreed that the Belgian Government should look especially to President Wilson for guidance," and that the Belgian Government "would therefore like to be advised of the President's views and to have his suggestions as to the nature and form of the reply eventually to be made" (*Ibid.*, 165-166, 172-175).

but did not do so. It is impossible to escape the feeling that Wilson still carried in the back of his mind a residue of the old non-interventionist mentality, such as he expressed on July 13, 1917, to Sir William Wiseman, pointing out "that while the U. S. was now ready to take her place as a world-power, the strong feeling throughout the country was to play a 'lone hand' and not to commit herself to any alliance with any foreign power." [24] Speaking in terms of universals, Wilson so phrased them as to subsume under his main premises the Central Powers and undercut the ground they stood on:

> Responsible statesmen must now everywhere see, if they never saw before, that no peace can rest securely upon political or economic restrictions meant to benefit some nations and cripple or embarrass others, upon vindictive action of any sort or any kind of revenge or deliberate injury. The American people . . . believe that peace should rest upon the rights of peoples, not the rights of governments—the rights of peoples great or small, weak or powerful—their equal right to freedom and security and self-government and to a participation upon fair terms in the economic opportunities of the world—the German people of course included, if they will accept equality and not seek domination. . . . Punitive damages, the dismemberment of empires, the establishment of selfish and exclusive economic leagues we deem inexpedient and in the end worse than futile, no proper basis for a peace of any kind, least of all for an enduring peace. That must be based upon justice and fairness and the common rights of mankind.[25]

The crushing character of this reply was every-

[24] *IPCH*, III, 71; *WWLL*, VII, 162.
[25] *FRUS, 1917, Supplement 2*, I, 177-179. (August 27, 1917.)

where lauded, but it is not impossible to see Wilson lashing out already against the exorbitant demands of the Allied Powers—" punitive damages " later to be rechristened reparations; " the dismemberment of empires," strangely reminiscent of the secret treaties; " exclusive economic leagues," echoing the resolutions of the Allied Economic Conference of Paris in June, 1916. Wilson had ceased to be a neutral, but he was certainly playing a " lone hand " in endeavoring to reshape the war aims of the Allied Powers.[26]

But the time for defining war aims in the " lone hand " way was sharply drawing to a close. After the reply to the Pope, it was obvious that the general discussion of war aims would continue in some fashion or other and that it could not, eventually, be avoided. Hence it is not altogether surprising that Wilson, in the same breath in which he chuckled at Allied discomfiture, turned to Colonel House with the idea of organizing the data for validating—or rejecting—the claims of the various belligerents to definite areas of the world:

---

[26] That this was Wilson's conscious desire is revealed by Baker, who gives the text of a letter from President Wilson to Colonel House under date of September 2, 1917, in which Wilson states unvarnishedly: " I did not dare to submit it to our Associates across the sea more than twenty-four hours before I made it public. I felt morally certain that they would wish changes which I could not make. I was confirmed in that view when Jusserand the next day went up in the air because it seemed to exclude economic punishment of Germany after the war. It will work out as well this way as any. The differences of opinion will be less embarrassing now than they would have been if I had invited them beforehand." *WWLL*, VII, 253-254.

I am beginning to think, [wrote the President,] that we ought to go systematically to work to ascertain as fully and precisely as possible just what the several parties to this war on our side of it will be included to insist upon as part of the final peace arrangements, *in order that we may formulate our own position either for or against them and begin to gather the influences we wish to employ,—or, at least, ascertain what influences we can use*: in brief, prepare our case with a full knowledge of the position of all the litigants. What would you think of quietly gathering about you a group of men to assist you to do this? [27]

In this way, and with the most utter informality, *The Inquiry* began. Thenceforth, in all matters of the basic settlement, it became a new factor in the American diplomatic tradition.[28]

A calm overview of the months of September, October, and November, 1917, quickly reveals the swift-changing situation. The steady decline of Russian power, the disaster of Caporetto, the nip-and-tuck tussle between shipbuilding and shipsinkings, all brought sharply home to the principal Allied nations the narrow margin by which they were escaping defeat. This dark period of the war generated its

[27] *WWLL*, VII, 253-254; *IPCH*, III, 168-173, at 169.

[28] *Ibid.*, 168-173; *FRUS, PPC 1919*, I, 9-118. The story of *The Inquiry* is in itself a fascinating one, and indicative, as a mere matter of method, of what can be accomplished by the conjoint effort of numerous scholars. The explanations by President Seymour and Sir William Wiseman give only the House side of the story; the Peace Conference volumes issued by the Department of State give the picture somewhat more clearly, with indications of the growing pains through which every rapidly expanding organization inevitably passes. It is impossible to detail here the growth of *The Inquiry's* program, hence, save in an evaluation of its positive contributions to the peace treaties, its work will come only occasionally under review.

own response to the problem, and while Wilson was firm in not allowing the United States to be represented in July [29] at the Allied Conference on Balkan affairs in Paris, by October the United States began actively to create that complex of international agencies which was—to borrow Wilson's own words—"of the very stuff of triumph." By November the Supreme War Council was already in being; by December, the United States was already hard at work on achieving a unified command of all Allied fighting forces.[30]

[29] On July 2, 1917, Balfour extended the invitation to President Wilson to have the United States represented at forthcoming Allied conferences; on July 11 President Wilson replied, declaring that "while Mr. Balfour's cordial invitation is greatly appreciated, this Government is not ready at the present time to take part in the inter-Allied war conferences" (*FRUS, 1917, Supplement 2*, I, 123-124). Similarly Balfour endeavored to act through Sir Cecil Spring-Rice in Washington by a despatch of June 21, 1917, which, for some unhappy reason or other, failed to be forwarded by the Ambassador to Lansing until July 24. The burden of the communication was that the President was to be impressed with the importance of American representation on Allied Conferences. In view of America's growing strength and importance, surely "President Wilson was deeply interested, not merely in the conduct of the war, but in the arrangements to be made at its conclusion, and he would certainly claim to be represented when important Allied interests were under discussion." Sir Cecil was instructed to lay before the President the problem of representation. Why the delay took place, and why Sir Cecil never followed it up, are mysteries which the published diplomatic documents to this day have not made clear (*Ibid.*, 142). Premier Ribot of France endeavored to get Wilson to be represented at the "so-called Balkan Conference" and failing, sought to obtain through Ambassador Sharp answers to important questions coming up for discussion (*Ibid.*, 144-148; 149-150). Even Ambassador Sharp was not present in an advisory capacity. Such was the situation in July, 1917.

[30] The story of the creation of the Supreme War Council and the Allied Conference of November, 1917, is told with a wealth of detail in the *Intimate Papers* by Colonel House, who along with

In this setting, the problem of defining war aims and objectives grew increasingly complex and important. The Bolshevik Revolution in Russia, the collapse of Italy, to mention but two aggravating factors, made a discussion of war aims imperative, but not easy. Far Eastern questions were kept out of the picture by the almost furtively secret negotiations between Lansing and Viscount Ishii. But the advances of the British forces in Palestine made the Zionist movement and the future of Palestine most important in the principal chancelleries of the world. On September 4, Lord Robert Cecil cabled to Colonel House that the British were being pressed in London for a declaration of sympathy with the Zionist movement. He therefore besought House to find out unofficially whether President Wilson favored such a declaration.[31] On September 7, House wrote the President, asking: "Have you made up your mind regarding what answer you will make to Cecil concerning the Zionist movement? It seems to me," added the Colonel, "that there are many dangers lurking in it, and if I were the British I would be chary about going too definitely into that question."

Apparently either them, or at an earlier date, House furnished Wilson with a memorandum on the Zionist

---

General Tasker H. Bliss represented the United States on the Supreme Council. Cf. *IPCH*, III, Chapter VII, "An American War Mission," 174-209, especially valuable for the genesis of the "Allied Council of War," "The Interallied (Food) Council," and the "Joint Embargo or Blockade Council"; Chapter VIII, "Conferences in London" 210-246; and Chapter IX, "The Supreme War Council," 247-290; as also Chapter X, "The Adjustment of Effort," 291-315.

[31] *WWLL*, VII, 256, 256 n.

movement, which Wilson "found" in his pocket on October 13,[32] whereupon he belatedly wrote to House: "I am afraid I did not say to you that I concurred in the formula suggested from the other side. I do, and would be obliged if you would let them know it." The Balfour Declaration of November 2, 1917,[33] was the result. Apparently the significance of the British move dawned on Secretary Lansing only some six weeks later, for on December 15 he instructed Ambassador Page in London to "investigate discreetly and report fully and promptly" to the Department the reasons for Balfour's statement.[34]

[32] *Ibid.*, 305.

[33] For the text of the Balfour Declaration see *FRUS, 1917, Supplement 2*, I, 317 and n.

[34] Lansing to Page, December 17, 1917. *Ibid.*, 473. The Lansing Papers are illuminating on this point. Before Lansing made inquiry of Page, he wrote President Wilson on December 13, 1917, indicating that the Department was under considerable pressure "for the issuance of a declaration in regard to this Government's attitude as to the disposition to be made of Palestine. This naturally emanates from the Zionist element of the Jews." Lansing's recommendation was that the United States should "go very slowly" in formulating a policy, and gave three reasons: (1) The fact that the United States was not at war with Turkey "and therefore should avoid any appearance of taking territory from that Empire by force"; (2) that "the Jews are by no means a unit in the desire to establish their race as an independent people" and that "to favor one or the other faction would seem to be unwise"; (3) that "many Christian sects and individuals would undoubtedly resent turning the Holy Land over to the absolute control of the race credited with the death of Christ." It seems almost incredible that a Secretary of State could have adduced a reason for policy on so subjective a motivation. However, being a realist, Lansing also stated that "For practical purposes I do not think that we need go further than the first reason given, since that is ample ground for declining to announce a policy in regard to the final disposition of Palestine."

Wilson's action was to return the letter to Lansing at the Cabinet meeting December 14, 1917, "saying that very unwillingly he was

This Page did, reporting on December 21 that "Lord Robert Cecil, in charge of the Foreign Office while Balfour is ill, informed us that the British Government has an understanding with the French Government that Palestine shall be internationalized. Mr. Balfour's letter, printed in the *Times* of November 9, merely [stated] that the British Government pledges itself to put [apparent omission] the Jews in Palestine on the same footing as other nationalities. No discrimination shall be made against them. This is as far as the British Government has yet gone." [35] So far this was indicative of official British policy and nothing more. But Mr. Page also reported:

Then followed an informal conversation. An internationalized Palestine must be under the protection of some great power. Lord Robert speaking only for himself feared that the continental powers would not agree that any one of them should hold the protectorate and some of them would object even to England's holding it. Still speaking informally and only for himself, he hoped that the United States would consent to be the protecting power when the time comes, and he felt sure that all the powers would gladly agree.[36]

The Palestine situation has been discussed with some detail principally because it brings out the inarticulate major premises of Allied diplomacy at the moment. The idea of internationalization—

---

forced to agree with me, but . . . that he had an impression that we had assented to the British declaration regarding returning Palestine to the Jews." This statement was an annotation on the letter itself with the initials RL. Cf. *LP*, II, 7 and note.

[35] Page to Lansing, December 21, 1917. *Ibid.*, 483.

[36] *Ibid.*, *loc. cit.*

whatever it might mean—was instantly coupled with a single-power protectorate, which could only have meaning if the protecting power were to be regarded as an agent for the Allies. And yet the great power function implied many other things—maintenance of the territorial integrity and administrative entity of the area, strategic security, enforcement of non-discrimination, etc. That the British hoped to share the responsibility with the United States or relinquish it to the United States is also apparent. . . . A war aim *was* being defined!

During this period Rumania also entered the diplomatic picture. The United States was not a party to the secret Treaty of Bucharest of August 4/17, 1916, and was presumably unaware of its existence, although it cannot have been unaware of the territorial aims of Rumania. In consequence, when, Rumania was left in a perilous position, after the Bolshevik regime seized power in Russia, the King of Rumania appealed behind the back of his ministers to the British and French ministers at Bucharest for assurances and advice. Simultaneously he sent his personal adjutant to convey to the American Minister the results of their deliberations, and ask further support:

> In order to increase the weight of this declaration the King would like the United States to join in it if not by adhering to the convention [i. e., the secret Treaty of Bucharest], at least by language implying the support of that power with a view to the realization of the national ideals of Rumania.[37]

[37] *FRUS, 1917, Supplement 2,* I, 309. Vopicka to Lansing from Bucharest, November 17, 1917.

While the results of this inquiry were pending, King Ferdinand besought the Anglo-French envoys to back their recommendations by representations at Washington—with what success, it is impossible even now to say.

In reply, President Wilson, on Nov. 28, 1917, sent to King Ferdinand a personal message which stressed the "warmest sympathy and admiration" of the American people for the courageous struggle of the people of Rumania "to preserve from the domination of German militarism their national integrity and freedom" and the determination of the United States to continue to assist Rumania in the struggle. Then came the pledge:

At the same time I wish to assure Your Majesty that the United States will support Rumania after the war to the best of its ability and that, in any final negotiations for peace, it will use its constant efforts to see to it that the integrity of Rumania as a free and independent nation is adequately safeguarded.[38]

Thus, without any explicit mention of definite territories, but by reference to "the best of its ability" and "constant efforts," the government of the United States in effect pledged itself to secure "adequate safeguards" for Rumania. The use of the passive verb with regard to safeguarding integrity lessened not one whit the fact that for all practical purposes the United States Government concurred in

[38] *Ibid.*, 325. Lansing to Vopicka, November 28, 2 p. m. It is interesting to note that Baker, who covers this period with exceeding care, and was always on the lookout for secret treaties, does not make any mention of this correspondence.

the guarantees of the Allies to Rumania. Another war aim crystallized in the process.

Similarly, during the summer and fall of 1917 the Polish question was on the *tapis*. Although it had been given considerable momentum by the declarations of President Wilson to the Senate, the United States lagged considerably behind other Powers in keeping in touch with the Polish national movement. When the integration of Polish political forces had gained sufficient strength, the various Allied governments began to deal with the Polish National Committee in Paris almost as though it were a provisional government. The United States was also repeatedly importuned to act, and finally decided, on November 10, 1917, to recognize "the Polish National Committee at Paris as an official Polish organization." [39] From this point on, financial and military commitments to the future Polish State were inevitable, and began to pile up incrementally. Thus, except for details, another war aim became in fact a reality.

Meanwhile the political situation in Russia, whose Provisional Government was drawing its last breath, began materially to affect the United States' plans and purposes. So deeply undermined was the authority of the Provisional Government that the Executive Committee of the Petrograd Soviet was issuing a program of peace terms, particularly with regard to territorial questions, for presentation at the Allied Conference in Paris [40] It is obvious in retro-

[39] *FRUS, 191 , Supplement 2,* I, 759-790, at 778.

[40] These proposed a "referendum for Alsace-Lorraine"; the restoration of Belgium with losses to be "compensated by an inter-

spect that the Russian situation was infinitely more serious for the whole Allied cause than any important leader outside Russia appreciated, and even the Provisional Government was gifted with no more perspicacity on its own part. That is why Russia really became the "acid test" of Allied diplomacy, and particularly that of the United States. With the information in hand that the Russian program was sharply veering in this direction even before the fall of the Provisional Government, Russia's aims warranted detailed, methodical, and perspicacious consideration. But no action was taken and the Bolshevik Revolution found the objectives of the United States in that quarter of the world confused and utterly unclear.

The failure of Colonel House to obtain from the Inter-Allied Conference at Paris an unequivocal expression of assent to the bases of peace [41] advocated

---

national fund; the restoration of the German colonies, etc."; "freedom of the seas which neutralizes Suez and Panama Canals and also straits leading into interior seas"; "contributions which prohibit belligerents demanding compensation for losses directly or indirectly"; "economic conditions which prohibit economic blockade after the war and accord rights of most favored nation to all states without distinction; guarantees of peace which abolish secret diplomacy and secret treaties; disarmament on land and sea; the way of peace, which requires that Allies enter upon peace negotiations as soon as adversary expresses willingness to begin under condition of renunciation by all parties of all violent conquests, and prohibit Allies undertaking secret peace negotiations except in congress where all neutral countries participate." Francis to Lansing from Petrograd, October 20, 1917. *Ibid.*, 276.

[41] "I find it will be useless," cabled House from London on November 16, 1917, "to try to get either the French or British to designate peace terms." (*IPCH*, III, 233.) Later, after the meeting of the Inter-Allied Conference at Versailles, House reported to Wilson his inability to get assent to common peace aims in a

by President Wilson, plus the reports which kept coming into the Department of State of plans for secret negotiation by Great Britain with Austria and Turkey, added to the appeal made by Signor Sonnino that the United States hearten the Italians after Caporetto by declaring war on the Dual Monarchy, led the Chief Executive, unrestrained by the presence of Colonel House, to act upon the Italian premier's suggestion with scarcely an advance notice to any one. On December 4, 1917, he addressed a joint session of the two Houses of Congress, and, after rejecting any peace by compromise, proceeded to a further definition of war objectives. Protesting against "vindictive action of any kind," against the punishment of nations or peoples because of the wrongs of irresponsible rulers, Wilson picked up the phrase: "No annexations, no contributions, no punitive indemnities" and gave it his own interpretation: "Peace on generosity and justice, to the exclusion of all selfish claims to advantage even on the part of the victors." But there must be responsible governments in enemy countries, and reparation of wrongs done. Thus,

They have done a wrong to Belgium which must be repaired. They have established a power over other lands and peoples than their own—over the great Empire of Austria-Hungary, over hitherto free Balkan states, over Turkey, and within Asia, which must be relinquished. The peace we make must remedy that wrong. It must deliver

declaration. "I wanted a clear declaration along the lines of my cable to you. . . . England passively was willing, France indifferently against it, Italy actively so." Hence—no resolution! *Ibid.*, 285. For this whole episode see 278-290.

the once fair lands and happy peoples of Belgium and northern France from the Prussian conquest and the Prussian menace, but it must also deliver the peoples of Austria-Hungary, the peoples of the Balkans and the peoples of Turkey, alike in Europe and in Asia, from the impudent and alien domination of the Prussian military and commercial autocracy.[42]

This on the negative, liberating side. As for the internal development of enemy countries, or those of the Quadruple Alliance, there was no wish " in any way to impair or to re-arrange the Austro-Hungarian Empire," the only desire of the United States being " to see that their affairs are left in their own hands, in all matters, great or small." In similar vein, the hope was expressed of securing " for the peoples of the Balkan peninsula and for the people of the Turkish Empire the right and opportunity to make their own lives safe, their own fortunes secure against oppression or injustice and from the dictation of foreign courts or parties." For Germany herself America's attitude and purpose were of like kind.

Clearly these were not global solutions in their content. Hence Wilson disclosed that these were " specific interpretations " of his address to the Senate on January 22. American entrance into the war had not altered objectives. One other amplification was more generic than territorial. Not only freedom of the seas, but freedom of access to the sea was essential—" assured and unmolested access to those pathways " for states not having a maritime

[42] *PPWW*, III, Pt. 1, 128-139, at 131.

frontier. "I was thinking, and I am thinking now, of Austria herself, among the rest, as well as of Serbia and of Poland." [43] It is obvious from this statement that Wilson was in fact familiar with the secret Treaty of London of April 26, 1915, because only on the supposition of the cession of Venezia Giulia to Italy could Austria have been cut off from the sea; [44] and only by the Italian annexation of the Dalmatian coast could Serbia be prevented from getting an access to the Adriatic. The reference may also have been to Serbian claims for an outlet on the Aegean, but the contexts are so far from indicating this, that only the Italian territorial settlement appears to have been involved. If one may accept this interpretation, it would appear that Wilson seized upon the overture from Sonnino and Salandra to declare war on Austria—at the price of procuring in advance a revision of the Allied understandings with Italy. This is the real *raison d'etre* of this move.

It will be noted that Wilson sought war only against Austria-Hungary and not against Bulgaria or

[43] *Ibid.*, 135.

[44] The *Life and Letters* throw an addiitonal light as to the genesis of Wilson's interest in access to the sea. When Dr. S. E. Mezes submitted an outline of the subjects to be treated by *The Inquiry*, Wilson replied on November 12, 1917, that there was an omission, although it might be only apparent: "It seems to me that it will be necessary to study the just claims of the larger states, like Russia and Austria, and Germany herself, to an assured access to the sea and the main routes of commerce not only, but to a reasonable access to the raw materials of the world which they themselves do not produce." In an additional paragraph the President declared: "Of course, what we ourselves are seeking is a basis which will be fair to all and which will nowhere plant the seeds of such jealously and discontent and restraint of development as would certainly breed fresh wars." *WWLL*, VII, 352.

Turkey. This caused a Congressional furore which could be held in check only by the interposition of Secretary Lansing, who supplied data and memoranda showing specifically why war against Bulgaria or against Turkey would be undesirable.[45] Simultaneously came reports as to the advisability of the Allies making peace with Turkey at this juncture, a course being urged on Lloyd George by some of his advisers, although naval and military circles definitely opposed it. Wilson thought the project chimerical and told Lansing so, asking him to convey that view to Ambassador Page. Then, applying his powers of analysis to the problem, the President declared:

> Arrangements must be made at the conference which closes the war with regard to Constantinople which could hardly be made if Turkey were first made peace with. Indeed, I suppose that *peace could only be made on terms which would preclude any radical changes of control over Constantinople and the Straits.* The only advantage to be gained would be to *prevent the bargains of the Allies with regard to Asia Minor from being carried out.*[46]

This indicates a strategic perspicacity not commonly attributed to the war President, and a political intuition of no lesser degree. After this there could be little doubt that the President knew of the secret

[45] *FRUS, 1917, Supplement 2,* I, 448-454. Lansing to Stone, December 6, 1917.

[46] *WWLL,* VII, 380. The text which Wilson wrote out on his own typewriter was intended for Lansing's guidance, hence it is not identic with Lansing's rephrasing, but there is no substantial difference, and Lansing also recognizes the existence of the secret agreements. *FRUS, 1917, Supplement 2,* I, 326. (Italics mine.)

treaties with regard to the Near East.[47] If any remained, it was dissipated by the recital, by our special agent at Cairo, William Yale, of the precise manner in which the British and French governments had handled the Levantine peoples in the Sykes-Picot agreements.[48] Yale's report was received in the Department of State on December 26, 1917, and was obviously available for Wilson in time to be considered with reference to the Fourteen Point address. Whether he actually used the Yale report may apparently remain a matter of conjecture forever, as there

[47] On November 20, 1917, Colonel House wrote in his diary: "The Prime Minister and Lord Chief Justice took dinner with us. We had a long and intimate talk afterward. . . . I pinned George down to British war aims. What Britain desires are the African colonies, both East and West; an independent Arabia, under the suzerainty of Great Britain; Palestine to be given to the Zionists under British, or, if desired by us, under American control; an independent Armenia and the internationalization of the Straits . . ." (*IPCH*, III, 235). This proves that once more the British disclosed their Hand to Colonel House, but there is no evidence in Seymour's account that House gave this information to Wilson before his return in December, 1917. On November 21, 1917, Colonel House recorded a conversation with Lloyd George and Balfour: "We then went into the question of war aims. Maps were brought and Mr. Balfour started in with his ideas of territorial division. . . . I thought that what we agreed upon to-day might be utterly impossible tomorrow, and it seemed worse than useless to discuss territorial aims at this time. What I thought was necessary, and pertinent at this time was the announcement of general war aims and the formation of an international association for the prevention of future wars" (*Ibid.*, 237). Apparently the truculent Colonel succeeded in fending off a British declaration of a character which would have made the Fourteen Points an utter impossibility. At least negatively, Point 5 was being solved!

[48] William Yale to Lansing from Cairo, November 12, 1917. *Ibid.*, 490-492. Here the decision was to ignore the secret agreements, and phrase Point XII as though they did not exist. Wilson's emphasis on free passage and international guarantee of the Dardanelles were practically pre-determined by November 28.

does not appear to be any direct evidence of the point, one way or the other.

Last scene of all, the "secret treaties," as published by the Soviet Government and relayed via both Petrograd and Stockholm, reached the State Department on December 27.[49] They were therefore literally "in the bag" and accessible to President Wilson in the period when the drafting of the Fourteen Points began.[50] The decision to set forth American war aims in a unilateral act, such as a message to Congress, was reached with unaffected reluctance but with little debate, at an historic moment when House, General Bliss, and Secretary of War Baker were all present, on December 18.[51] In the

[49] *Ibid.*, 493-507.

[50] On this the main authority is House (*IPCH*, III, Chapter XI, 316-349). See also *WWLL*, VII, 417-458, *passim.*

[51] House did not talk with the President for more than a quarter of an hour, and for the next five days Wilson was left to work on the problem without the aid of his confidant. Because the main genetic account of the origin of the Fourteen Points comes from the House Papers, as portrayed and interpreted by Seymour, with corrections—much needed ones—in perspective suggested by President Isaiah Bowman, and because there is no diary on the Wilson side, it is necessary to canvass a number of things and draw the possible correlations that indicate influence on the final product. Baker lists in each day that followed the official visitors and contacts, some of which are of undoubted influence.

Wilson spent his time in his study all morning on the 19th, the day immediately after the decision to make such an address. It is probable that all the preliminary sketching out was done at this time in Wilson's mind if not in his letter and papers (*WWLL*, VII, 417-419). Much of the correspondence with or concerning Edgar G. Sisson came under the President's eye that day. The only relevant influence noted for December 20th was the early afternoon conference with George Creel, who was primarily responsible for Sisson. (*Ibid.*, 422). Undoubtedly some discussion on Russian affairs took place at this time. A glance at the Sixth Point would seem to indicate that the general line which Wilson and Creel were

ensuing twenty days of milling, the program which had been building up as the result of isolated diplomatic transactions integrated, aided by *The Inquiry* and the omnipresent Colonel. It is significant that, once enunciated, on January 8, 1918, the Fourteen Points underwent no major change or amplification,

---

taking entered into this stage of the drafting. Friday, December, 21, was a cabinet meeting day, but there is no evidence that the idea of so comprehensive a statement was discussed with cabinet members, even with Lansing. However, it was a very Serbian day, the Serbian War Mission, headed by Dr. Milenko Vesnitch, being officially presented in the afternoon and feted by the President and Mrs. Wilson that evening. Since Vesnitch was a fine conversationalist in the English language, it is hardly likely that the transmitting of ideas was difficult. It is impressive, in the light of the information which Wilson had from our special envoy at Corfu, H. Percival Dodge, and the frequent correspondence with Cleveland H. Dodge on matters in the Near East, that the Eleventh Point was one of the most embroidered: first a generic statement: "Rumania, Serbia and Montenegro should be evacuated; occupied territories restored"—the latter probably a tangential dig at the Allies for their occupation of Albania—then "Serbia accorded free and secure access to the sea." Such must certainly have been the theme of Vesnitch's conversation on December 21. Certainly Serbia was the only one of the Balkan States singled out for special treatment. The rest of the point in question was generic, in order to be able to touch Bulgaria without creating animosity. Saturday, December 22, was a family day with the McAdoos, the Sayres, the Elliotts and a theater party.

Sunday, December 23, was likewise spent until the arrival of Colonel House at 6:30 with a sheaf of materials which the Inquiry had compiled. According to Baker, he "may have given the President at this time part of the material which the President wanted to see," though this is not certain. The Inquiry Report which was "basic" was not brought down until the Colonel's second visit, on January 4 (*Ibid.*, 424-426; *IPCH*, III, 320). What ground was covered by the President and Colonel House on the 23rd must, apparently, always remain conjectural, and there is no record of how long the conference lasted. Seymour's account fuses the impact of the two Inquiry reports, and adds very little to a comprehension of how the speech stood as the end of the first conference. Monday, December 24, yields no grist: The President

save as regards the future of the Czechoslovaks and Jugoslavs. The great presidential addresses of the period, involved in the debate at long range with Czernin and Von Hertling, brought forth no more crystallizations. The territorial program was methodical, complete. The "Force without Stint or

---

received, *inter alia,* the new Minister from Switzerland and Secretary Baker, but neither apparently had any direct influence on the slant of the President's thought. Christmas was a blank. Wednesday, December 26, was concerned with taking over the railroads and the President saw Baker and McAdoo at 5 p. m. on the matter and on permanent participation in the Supreme War Council, to which Bliss was named. However, the President managed to have almost the whole day free of appointments. It is fairly reasonable to assume that, having been at work on the address just before Christmas, he resumed work on it at this time. On Thursday, December 27, Jusserand presented Admiral Grasset of the French Navy in the afternoon; Colonel House and Mrs. House were guests at dinner. It is almost inconceivable that the address should not have been at least partly the subject of conversation. On Friday, December 28, which was the President's birthday, activities were wholly domestic or social, and nothing of international consequence transpired. Saturday, the 29th, there was an hour with Ambassador Jusserand, presumably on military matters; Sunday, the 30th, during great cold, the White House retreated into itself and there was no activity whatever. On December 31 there was a half day in the study and an interview with Sir Frederick Smith (Lord Birkenhead); and the Japanese Ambassador called (*WWLL,* VII, 428-441). Even New Years' Day was uneventful save for theater and family!

January 2 was a day of study. Whether on this day or on December 31 Wilson heard, through Lansing, of the policy assumed vis-a-vis Russia by the Allies is indeterminate, but it may be safely assumed that so important a dispatch was not allowed to escape the Presidential eye. It was a memorandum prepared by Milner and Cecil in Paris on December 22, approved by Clemenceau and Pichon and then transmitted to Wilson through diplomatic channels (*FRUS, 1918, Russia,* I, 330-331), reaching Washington on the morning of December 30. The Allies counseled that they should "continually repeat our readiness to accept the principles of self-determination, and this includes that of no annexation or indemnities." The Bolsheviks were to be urged unofficially to get

Limit" speech of April 6, 1918, commemorating our entry into the war, was a powerful philippic against the military masters of Germany, but not cast in the mold for war aims. The Mount Vernon address of July 4, 1918—possibly the finest among all Wilson's addresses—was only a powerful summation of the

---

definite terms from the Germans regarding Poland, Bohemia, the Rumanian parts of Transylvania, not to speak of Alsace-Lorraine and the Trentino. The Allies urged solicitous treatment of the Ukraine, if only to help save Rumania. Support was to be given to the Armenians and contingently the Georgians, so that they too might stem the German flood. Very little of this is reflected in Wilson's Sixth Point, hence it may be concluded that he depended on other sources for the formulation of that part of his address.

A very important sidelight on Wilson's thoughts in these days is given in the memoirs and letters of Sir Cecil Spring Rice, the British Ambassador, who, being recalled, paid Wilson a final visit on the afternoon of January 3. Cf. Stephen Gwynn, *The Letters and Friendships of Sir Cecil Spring Rice*, II, 422-425. Apparently Wilson unburdened himself to the veteran diplomat, discussing the difficult ways of American public opinion, and the growth of psychological unity in the country under war conditions. As reported by Spring Rice to Balfour on January 4, Wilson felt that agreement with the Allies on war aims "would be a very difficult thing to bring about and in the process very serious differences of opinion would develop themselves . . . it seemed to him that the American people were inclined to receive with favour a statement of a moderate and unaggressive character and would welcome such a statement. He had already in general terms indicated the general lines on which he thought American policy should be based. These statements had met with general approval. *Each one had been more detailed than the last, and it might be necessary, as the war continued, to define even more clearly those objects for which America was waging war* (Italics mine). In drawing up this statement, it would be necessary not only to follow the rules of logic and to draw reasoned conclusions from accepted principles, but also, so far as was possible, to give due consideration to the circumstances and the facts which actually existed." This is practically the only expression on record for this period in which the ways in which Wilson's mind was working are brought into relief, assertedly in his own words.

It is also evident that the President was under considerable

principles long before enunciated and previously traced here. It was only as the war entered the final six weeks that the President, in his Metropolitan Opera House address in New York, closed the circle by demonstrating the relationship of the Fourteenth Point to the full aims and formal terms of the settle-

---

pressure from those who knew the situation in Russia—men like Charles R. Crane—not to desert Russia in her extremity, and to elicit a formal statement of war aims from the Allies (*WWLL*, VII, 450 & n.). On January 4 there was a cabinet meeting but still no discussion of the war aims message. In the evening Colonel House arrived from New York about nine o'clock and the two worked on the message until 11:30, "discussing the general terms to be used, and looking over data and maps . . . some of which the Peace Inquiry Bureau had prepared (*IPCH*, III, 322). The conference was continued on the morning of January 5, interrupted for luncheon, and apparently continued in the afternoon despite an appointment with McAdoo on railway matters. During this time the papers carrying Lloyd George's speech of January 5 came out and the President first thought that it would be impossible for him to deliver the contemplated address. House, however, persuaded him otherwise. It is clear from the record that at this time Wilson was beginning the "final outline of his speech and the arrangement of his definite points" (*WWLL*, VII, 451-452; *IPCH*, III, 322-349), with many an addition at the suggestion of House and some subtractions, most of the latter, such as the omission of mention of Armenia, Syria, and Mesopotamia by name, being, in my opinion, unfortunate.

Over the week end House took up the Balkan point with Vesnitch, at the President's suggestion, and also saw Jusserand on a number of matters. In a rather polemic note, Vesnitch protested the maintenance of the Austro-Hungarian Empire but the Colonel vetoed change. This was, of course, in keeping with the Anglo-Austrian negotiations then furtively going on, and led Wilson into an impasse from which he had later, on the advice of Masaryk and others, to retreat. At this time, incidentally, the Inquiry Report recommended the maintenance of Austria-Hungary.

For the sake of precision it seems desirable to note that the President finished the exact terms of the Fourteen Points on Saturday morning, January 5, and completed the introductory and concluding parts the following afternoon. On Monday, January 7, he made an alteration in the statement regarding Alsace and Lor-

ment. It was the final philippic against the Hohenzollerns and the Habsburgs. In another week the Central Powers gave in ideologically and indicated their willingness to accept armistice and peace in terms of the Fourteen Points. That forthwith changed the nature of the discussions and made them conversations in camera with co-belligerents, rather than powerful open polemics with adversaries.

It was at this juncture that the President was called upon to define and specify to the Allies what the Fourteen Points really meant. This highly important work of political exegesis was intrusted by Colonel House to Walter Lippmann, then Secretary of The Inquiry, and to Frank I. Cobb, then editor of the New York *World*. Their elucidation was presented to the President by cable, with the request that he

---

raine "so as to give it a positive and definite character." He then called in the Secretary of State, and, upon his advice, made various verbal alterations in the final text.

A further crystallization of war aims around Wilsonian foci took place when the national conference of the Labour Party and the Trade Union Congress, on December 28, 1917, approved a memorandum on war aims. This document never passed through the channels of diplomacy but *may* have reached President Wilson's desk through the press. It proposed solutions of territorial problems almost identic with those eventuating in the Fourteen Points, but was more eloquent and explicit concerning colonial matters than was Wilson, who appears not to have been in any sense influenced by the phraseology. The Labour Party Memorandum was, however, strangely silent on Russia, very explicit on Albania and Palestine, and on the desirability of giving the Yugo-Slavs and Czechoslovaks a free hand. It further contained proposals which made their way into the International Labor clauses of the Treaty of Versailles.

Cf. K. Zilliacus, *Mirror of the Past; a History of Secret Diplomacy,* New York: Current Bookes, Inc. (A. A. Wyn, publisher), 1946, 180-184; H. W. V. Temperley, *A History of the Peace Conference of Paris*, I, 217-218.

indicate whether it met with his general approval.[52] This he did, though with some misgivings, declaring the analysis a "satisfactory interpretation of principles" though regarding the "details of application" "as merely illustrative suggestions," the real decisions being "reserved for [the] peace conference." In only one noteworthy respect did Wilson differ from the Lippmann-Cobb interpretations. To him the "admission of inchoate nationalities to [the] peace conference" seemed "most undesirable." [53] The Lippmann-Cobb document thus gained a degree of authenticity which no other interpretation of the Fourteen Points ever received.[54] And while the Allied Governments exhibited last minute reluctance to subscribe to them, they eventually gave in, adding their own reserved—and attenuating—interpretations of the Freedom of the Seas and Reparations.

* * * * *

[52] *FRUS, 1918, Supplement 1*, I, 405-413.

[53] *Ibid.*, 421.

[54] For a vigorous recent critique of Wilsonian principles, and particularly of the Fourteen Points, see Walter Lippman, *U. S. War Aims* (Boston, Little, Brown and Company, 1944), especially XII, "War Aims Then and Now," and XIII, "The Wilsonian Principles." It is only fair to note that the official commentary, to whose statements Lippmann takes strong exception, was written, as noted above, by Frank Cobb and Walter Lippmann. The identity of the authors is, however, carefully concealed in the more recent work.

That the Lippmann disavowal is not unchallenged may be noted in the no less vigorous defence of Wilson by Professor J. G. Randall of the University of Illinois in his *Lincoln, the Liberal Statesman* (New York, Dodd, Mead and Company, 1947, particularly VII, "Lincoln's Peace and Wilson's," originally written in 1943, approximately at the same time as the Lippmann recantation, and first published, unannotated, in the *South Atlantic Quarterly*, XLII, 225-242 (July, 1943).

From this point forward to and through the Peace Conference the Fourteen Points went their historic way. They have been written up by journalists and lawyers, historians and statesmen, each in his own way, and, with the gradual publication of the records of the Paris Peace Conference, their detailed application comes more and more clearly to light, although it is not yet complete. Yet it is not without some value to take note of the final metamorphosis from the American side. Between the bleak Christmas vacation days of 1917, with their news of apparently unmitigated disaster, and the paeans of triumph of the Allied cause a year later, only the political and military climate had changed, thus permitting the realization of the Fourteen Point Program by giving to the Allied and Associated Powers the margin of military victory by which alone they could enforce their will. It is therefore interesting to note the gradual mutation of the terms as the prospect of victory loomed large.

Taking the principal points serially, it is interesting to note that the First, dealing with the famous "open covenants of peace, openly conceived" was not intended to do more than prohibit secret treaties—a stipulation which passed into the preamble and Article 18 of the Covenant of the League of Nations and, without serious change, into Article 102 of the Charter of the United Nations. The "and openly arrived at" is a more difficult matter. It did not prevent the most recondite secrecy in the Paris of 1919, but bore exuberant fruit in the Paris of 1946, with a pitiless publicity which prevented accommodation and brought deadlock. Manifestly, even in attenuated form, it was then far too radical a change to be easily cushioned.

Point II, regarding the Freedom of the Seas, remains today probably the least controversial. In principle it promised free navigation in time of peace, as does Point 6 of the Atlantic Charter, but it meant closure in a League or United Nations war against an aggressor. The problem which bothered Lippmann and Cobb in 1918, viz., that the League might be neutral in a war, is today juridically meaningless, as the Charter in Article 2, Sections 5 and 6, definitely proscribes neutrality.

Point III, regarding the removal of economic barriers, was designed by Wilson to forestall an economic " war after the war " such as the Allies contemplated. In this it was only limitedly successful. Interpreted by Lippmann and Cobb to prevent economic discrimination among League members *inter se*, it operated only to a limited degree, as our own treaties with mandatories of the League reveal, to introduce the " open door " principle in backward areas.

Of Point IV, pledging the reduction of national armaments to the lowest level consistent with domestic safety, there remain only the phraseology of Articles VIII and IX of the Covenant and the mute and inglorious annals of the Geneva Disarmament Conference. Yet Lippmann and Cobb foresaw, long before the arrival of the atomic age, the absolute necessity of supra-national inspection. It is distinctly to their credit that they did so, and American policy, from Wilson, through Hoover, to Roosevelt and Truman has undeviatingly pursued this goal, even though the times have not been propitious enough to admit of attaining it.

The Fifth Point, dealing with colonial claims, was reduced by Lippmann and Cobb to apply only to colonial claims created by World War I—i. e., to the former German and Turkish possessions. This is probably the prime case of strict construction, which undoubtedly forestalled a reckoning at Paris on many colonial questions. Viewed in the retrospect of nearly thirty years, it is noteworthy that only at San Francisco in 1945 was a serious attempt made, on an international scale, adequately to survey the whole colonial problem.

With Point VI, dealing with Russia—the "acid test," according to President Wilson—the first of the major territorial settlements was reached. Here Lippmann and Cobb, while fearing that German evacuation of Russian territory might be followed by Bolshevist revolutions, recommended "nothing less than the [recognition] by the Peace Conference of a series of [*de facto*] Governments representing Finns, Esths, Lithuanians, Ukrainians." By distinguishing between "Russian territory" and "territory belonging to the former Russian Empire" they postulated, in correlation with Point XIII relative to Poland, that there could not be a "territorial reestablishment of the Empire." "What is recognized as valid for the Poles will certainly have to be recognized for the

Finns, the Lithuanians, the Letts, and perhaps also for the Ukrainians." Not only consistency to principle, but acceptance of realities counselled this view:

> Since the formulating of this condition, [they declared,] these subject nationalities have emerged, and there can be no doubt that they will have to be granted an opportunity of free development. . . . It is clearly to the interests of a good settlement that the real nation in each territory should be consulted rather than the ruling and possessing class.

There followed a complete code of procedure for giving effect to Point VI: National assemblies were to be called into being to create *de facto* governments, as soon as the Peace Conference drew their frontiers; those frontiers were to be, so far as possible, ethnic, but not to be closed to transit commerce; no dynastic connections with Russian, Austrian or German princes were to be permitted; federal reunion, particularly with Great Russia, was to be encouraged. Great Russia and Siberia were to be asked to create "a government sufficiently [representative] to speak for these territories," whereupon "any form of assistance," particularly for "economic rehabilitation" was to be offered. In the opinion of Cobb and Lippmann, "the Caucasus should be treated as part of the problem of the Turkish Empire," while some Power would have to be given a mandate to act as protector of "Mohammedan Russia, that is, briefly, Central Asia." The treaties of Brest-Litovsk and Bucharest must be "cancelled as palpably fraudulent," and all German troops in Russia must be withdrawn. With these preliminary conditions fulfilled, the Peace Conference would, in their opinion, " have a clean slate on which to write a policy for all the Russian peoples."

It is not material here to discuss the evacuation of Belgium (Point VII) or of France and Alsace-Lorraine (Point VIII), as they were already agreed upon and never became litigious.

By contrast, Point IX, dealing with the readjustment of the frontiers of Italy, along clearly recognizable lines of nationality, bristled with contentiousness. The Lippmann-Cobb interpretation conceded Italy a powerful strategic frontier on the Brenner, just in case " German Austria " should ever link her fortunes with those of the Reich, but also insisted, "for the protection of the hinterland, that Trieste and Fiume be free ports "—here reflecting a concern felt by Colonel House from the outset that the port arrangements were " essential to Bohemia, German Austria, Hungary, as well as the prosperity of the cities themselves."

With the demise of Austria-Hungary, Point X was no longer applicable, hence Lippmann and Cobb proposed to give Czechoslovakia her ethnic limits; to allocate Western Galicia to Poland but not Eastern Galicia, because it was " in a large measure Ukrainian " and did not " of right belong to Poland "; to join German-Austria " of right " with Germany despite France's strong objections; to allow Transylvania to go to Rumania, leaving a truncated " very democratic " Hungary, and a Jugoslavia with various historic territorial entities—Montenegro, Bosnia, Herzegovina, Croatia-Slavonia, Slovenia and Dalmatia—as her patrimony.

Point XI, covering the Balkans—perhaps the weakest and most unsatisfactory in the whole Wilson program—sought to accord maximum national unification to the Rumanian and Jugoslav States, their frontiers to be drawn along historically established lines of allegiance and nationality—when such lines were decidedly lacking! In the circumstances, the American commentators looked to the safeguarding of Albanian and Bulgarian rights against the excessive tailoring of the map by Jugoslav shearmen, though showing willingness to offer up Albania as a sacrifice to Italian nationalism. When it came to Macedonia, they were undecided as to its ultimate allocation.

The Twelfth Point, dealing with the Ottoman Empire, also required refashioning. By early November, 1918, the domains of the Caliph-Sultan were plainly in fission. Under the circumstances the official commentary recommended that Anatolia be reserved for the Turks, though suggesting that Greece be given control over the coastal lands and settlements; Armenia, under a British mandate, was to have a seaport on the Mediterranean; Syria was to be under France; Palestine, Iraq and Arabia under Britain. The most ingenious contribution of the journalistic team was the suggestion that

> A general code of guarantees binding on all mandatories in Asia Minor should be written into the treaty of peace. This should contain provisions for minorities and the "open door." The trunk railroad lines should be internationalized.

The resurrection of Poland as an independent state being pledged by the Thirteenth Point, and already accepted, the chief concern of the Lippmann-Cobb report was to avoid handing over non-Poles to Poland and to afford stringent minority guarantees for the inevitable minimum of non-Poles who would be caught up in the new state.

Above and over all, as the immanent, creative, and brooding spirit, was to be the League of Nations, formed under specific covenants for the purpose of affording mutual guarantees of political independence and territorial integrity to great and small states alike.

Here was the American program, simplified, clarified, rigidified. Of what worth was it to be at the peace table? As we look back at it today, almost exactly twenty-eight years after the fact, certain inescapable conclusions loom large: First, that the Fourteen Points did not succeed in effecting, at one jump, an integral revolution in the conduct of diplomacy, in the distribution of sea power, in the breaking down of the autarchical trend which the closed economies of wartime had set in motion, in the elimination of competitive armaments, or in the exorcizing of imperialism. These basic reforms in the functioning of a disordered community comprised a long-term program of which this and subsequent generations may well become the executors and beneficiaries.

It is to the shorter-range program that we must look in making a definitive appraisal: The United States having from its inception espoused the cause of nationality, the decision to apply that principle to Europe when the appointed time came was here given almost integral effect. From the restoration of Belgium and the restitution of Alsace-Lorraine on the West, through the completion of Italian unification and the liberation of the Habsburg nationalities on the South, to the liberation from Russian rule of the peoples long held in subjection by the Tsars, and the enfranchisement, partial or integral, of the peoples of the Arab world, we wrote large the program for which Washington, Lafayette, and Kossuth had alike contended. Yet we were careful, so far as we were concerned, to avoid giving it an anti-Russian slant. We were willing to disengage non-Russian nationalities from the great matrix of the defunct Russian Empire, but, from Petrograd to Vladivostok and Archangel to Batum, we were as much concerned in the maintenance of Russia's territorial integrity as any nation in the world, and for doing so, particularly in Siberia, we were destined to receive much, much later, belated, but unquestioned Soviet thanks.

For a quarter of a century it has been fashionable to malign the peace-makers of Paris, although the choice, then as now, was between the peace of imperial agglomeration and annexation, and the peace of liberated nationhood, between Brest-Litovsk and Versailles, and we chose Versailles. It was impossible for us to do otherwise, given our ideological inheritance and our own historical experience. At Paris we erected an edifice of national states on the foundations of legal equality and minority guarantees, and on top of that the first genuinely attempted superstructure of international government. If today we behold a Europe in which nationality has in large measure been annihilated, or thrown into a new flux, we can at least look back upon the promise which the America's program offered the world at the close of the first global war, of converting a Messianic hope into a vibrant reality, and say with pride of our statesmen, that, in the long annals of our diplomacy, this was their proudest hour.

LECTURE VI

THE UNITED STATES AND THE REORGANIZATION OF THE INTERNATIONAL COMMUNITY

In this final hour of our thinking together a rather forbidding task is set before me—to trace the broad course from the end of the Paris Conference to the convening of the General Assembly of the United Nations on our shores. What justice can we do to a subject of such scope, such magnitude? Much, I believe. Just as it is not necessary for the Alpinist to count the individual rocks in the way of his ascent, or to follow a strictly linear course to reach a panoramic height, it is possible to get a fair sense of the perspective, and, by determining objectively our starting point and the point at which we have arrived, to determine with some degree of accuracy the gains we have made and the goals we have attained. Let us, then, to the task.

In his first message to the Congress of the United States, on April 12, 1921, President Harding, reviewing the situation nearly two and a half years after the close of hostilities, declared:

> In the existing League of Nations, world-governing with its superpowers, this Republic will have no part. There can be no misinterpretation, and there will be no betrayal of the deliberate expression of the American people in the recent election; and, settled in our decision for ourselves, it is only fair to say to the world in general, and to our

associates in war in particular, that the League Covenant can have no sanction by us.[1]

With apparently crushing finality the new Chief Executive of the United States enunciated what was in effect a policy of non-intercourse with the newly formed international organization. Then, by contrast, he depicted the alternative conception of international organization:

The aim to associate nations to prevent war, preserve peace and promote civilization our people most cordially applauded. We yearned for this new instrument of justice, but we can have no part in a committal to an agency of force in unknown contingencies; we can recognize no super-authority. . . . The American aspiration, indeed the world aspiration, was an association of nations, based on the application of justice and right, binding us in conference and cooperation for the prevention of war and pointing the way to a higher civilization and international fraternity in which all the world might share. In rejecting the league covenant and uttering that rejection to our own people, and to the world, we make no surrender of our hope and aim for an association to promote peace in which we would most heartily join. We wish it to be conceived in peace and dedicated to peace, and will relinquish no effort to bring the nations of the world into such fellowship, not in the surrender of national sovereignty, but rejoicing in a nobler exercise of it in the advancement of human activities, amid the compensations of peaceful achievement.[2]

It is difficult in any attempt at juridical analysis to discover in the passage just quoted anything tangible on which to base policy; in fact, the whole passage

[1] *FRUS, 1921*, I, xvii-xviii. [2] *Ibid.*, xviii.

defies legal analysis and must be relegated to the limbo of discarded verbiage, for if there is one very definite thing that did not materialize between wars, it was the vaunted association of nations. But if the abjuration of the institutions of Geneva was formal and final, there was at the same time no disposition on the part of the United States to surrender rights or economic privileges:

With the supergoverning league definitely rejected and with the world so informed, and with the status of peace proclaimed at home,[3] *we may proceed to negotiate the covenanted relationships so essential to the recognition of all the rights everywhere of our own Nation* and play our full part in joining the peoples of the world in the pursuits of peace once more. Our obligations in effecting European tranquillity, because of war's involvements, are not less impelling than our part in the war itself. . . . We can be helpful because we are moved by no hatreds and harbor no fears. Helpfulness does not mean entanglement, and *participation in economic adjustments does not mean sponsorship for treaty commitments which do not concern us and in which we will have no part.*[4]

In these words may be found the touchstone to American policy in the ensuing twelve years. The formula might be stated even more tersely: *Negation of legal or moral concern; no political commitments; full economic participation.* Viewed thus, the *leitmotifs* of diplomatic policy from 1921 to 1933 are

[3] A reference to the proposed " peace " resolutions to declare the war at an end, and to enable the United States to negotiate a settlement with former enemy countries which would give to the United States all the rights accorded other signatories, but none of the responsibilities.

[4] *FRUS, 1921*, I, xx. (Italics mine.)

quite explainable. They might be characterized as the Compromise of 1920, stemming from the Presidential election of that year, and binding upon the administration, or the nation, until the next major political crisis, national or international.

Within the framework of this major premise, much that had meaning for the political and economic integration of the world was ultimately subsumed. While it was necessary to make a firm show of political abstention, by the withdrawal of the American representatives from the organic bodies set up under the peace treaties, and while there was ostentatious reduction of the role of fully empowered diplomats to that of inarticulate observers, it was not long before the United States was formally represented on international boards and commissions of a new character, and there was no lack of participation in the institutions of an economic character set up for the economic recovery of Europe and Asia.

To maintain this specious bifurcation of the economic from the political aspects of the modern world, it became imperative to suffer no discussion of the underlying premises of action lest the impossibility of the politico-economic dichotomy should become apparent. Therefore the President counselled:

It would be unwise to undertake to make a statement of future policy with respect to European affairs in such a declaration of a state of peace. . . . It would be idle to declare for separate treaties of peace with the Central Powers on the assumption that these alone would be adequate *because the situation is so involved that our peace engagements cannot ignore the Old World relationship and the settlements already affected, nor is it desirable to do so* in preserving our own rights and contracting our future relationships.[5]

Monopoly of policy-making by the Executive branch of the government, uncritical acceptance of the dogma of divisible responsibility, economic from political, were to be the landmarks of national policy. And yet with it all, instead of the vicious isolationism for which there were strident spokesmen in the party in power, there was formulated a doctrine of formal cooperation along humanitarian lines, which was to govern this country's attitude for more than a decade:

Prudence in making the program and confident cooperation in making it effective cannot lead us far astray. We can render no effective service to humanity until we prove anew our own capacity for cooperation . . . and no covenants which ignore our associations in the war can be made for the future . . . no helpful society of nations can be founded on justice and committed to peace until the covenants reestablishing peace are sealed with the nations which were at war. To such an accomplishment—to the complete reestablishment of peace and its contracted relationships, to the realization of our aspirations for nations associated for *world helpfulness without world government,* for world stability on which humanity's hopes are founded, we shall address ourselves, fully mindful of the high privilege and paramount duty of the United States in this critical period of the world.[6]

In this final, perorative paragraph, the President of the United States set forth the second pediment of

[5] *Ibid.*, xix. (Italics mine.) [6] *Ibid.*, xx. (Italics mine.)

official international policy: *World helpfulness without world government.* Like its twin pillar, it explains much of the minor actions of the United States within the framework of the existing international community. Yet it is clear that, while withdrawing from participation in political matters, the political postulates of the treaty settlement of 1919-1920 were at no point put in jeopardy, and in particular, *the United States Government accepted as an indisputable element of the international order the reconstruction of the map of the world along the principles of nationality.* This is worthy of reemphasis, a quarter of a century later, when there is a tendency to consider the United States' actions, in subscribing to the principle of nationality and all its corollaries, as somewhat *perimées* or out of fashion. For if there is any validity to the above analysis, it must be patent to all that run that the moment either the economic structure set up under the Paris peace treaties was threatened, or the territorial settlement was put in jeopardy, the United States would be bound, if only in its own self-interest, to bestir itself actively and renew, in one form or another, its active participation in world affairs, not merely at the " world helpfulness " level, but much more fundamentally.

It is therefore unnecessary to study the diplomatic minutiae of a decade, however rewarding that might be in other connections, to discover that, until the foundations of the policy thus enunciated by Harding were shaken, the United States would not, in fact did not, budge from the seat of complacency so pompously assumed. Three times within the decade the successive administrations in Washington were compelled to reckon with the addled economy of Europe, and brought forth the Dawes Plan, the Young Plan, and the Hoover Moratorium respectively—the first two to make workable the economic settlement, the third to scrap it altogether. For however distant and detached we might appear on the surface, there was no question that our fundamental interest was engaged if the economic foundations of the settlement crumbled. It was no less true in regard to the territorial settlement, whether as established at Paris, with our participation but not our ultimate support, or in the Far East, where the settlement had our entire countenance and approval.

It is interesting to recall that both pediments of our policy crumbled and went into dissolution almost coevally.[7] For the action of the militarists in Tokyo, in challenging frontally the territorial order in the Far East, was meticulously timed to coincide with the collapse of the gold standard in Europe, and the general economic upheaval and temporary political paralysis which it was bound in turn to produce. But while an inability to pay could be disposed of for the time being by a moratorium, an open military defiance of a treaty settlement could not. It was therefore at the beginning of the Man-

[7] "On September 18th, the very day—almost the very hour—of the outbreak in Manchuria, I was receiving word from the British chargé that Great Britain could no longer maintain the gold standard. It seemed as though from the Occident to the Orient, politically and economically, the world was rocking . . . If anyone had planned the Manchurian outbreak with a view to freedom from interference from the rest of the world, his time was well chosen." H. L. Stimson, *The Far Eastern Crisis*, 5-6.

churian crisis that the postulates of policy laid down by Harding were confronted by their severest test and the formula of *world helpfulness without world government* went down to ignominious defeat.

In the presence of the palpable collapse of the territorial order in the Far East, Henry L. Stimson, as Secretary of State, was faced with the same problem as had confronted Bryan and Lansing in 1915: How preserve legal rights when the legal situation is dissolving? In both instances the instinctive reply of the lawyer was to reaffirm the sacrosanct character of the antecedent legal order, to set it up as the sole criterion of international legality, and to declare anything at variance with it *hors de loi* and null and void. Nor was this new in human annals. Such has almost invariably been the response of king or pontiff, counselor or diplomat, to a course of action flagrantly at variance with historic tradition, current practice, or the spirit of a living order of affairs. The instances of refusal to face and accept as final the *faits accomplis* of crude violence are legion in human annals. Many of them, however morally exalted, have been the final affirmations of rectitude under circumstances of political and military impotence. It is necessary only to instance the final protest of Pope Innocent X against the Peace of Westphalia, pronouncing the treaty—" ipso iure nulla, irrita, invalida, iniqua, iniusta, damnata, reprobata, inania, viribusque et effectu vacua, omnino fuisse, esse et perpetuo fore " [8] under circumstances such as I

[8] From the bull *Zelo domus Dei*, issued November 20, 1648, by Pope Innocent X, quoted from Vol. XVII of the *Bullarium Romanum* by James Bryce, *The Holy Roman Empire*, 337.

have indicated, to make clear that neither Lansing nor Stimson was doing anything new in enunciating a doctrine of non-recognition. Yet it is no less true that this was not mere pique, or a *fin de non-recevoir*: what gives value to the announcement or intention not to recognize the legality of changes effected by violence is the implicit assumption of the persistence of law in spite of duress, whether that persistence derive from the all-pervasive character of an universal moral or natural law, or from the in-bred habit of respect for immemorial tradition, the *mos maiorum*. It must be assumed that when Lansing drafted the non-recognition memorandum by which we sought to limit Japanese aggressiveness in China in 1915, he was still supremely confident that, despite the assaults on the international order by Germany and her allies, right, juristically, would ultimately prevail over the disintegrative forces at large in the world. But Lansing faced a world of vanishing legality, a situation not entirely covered by recent and universally recognized treaties. It might have been brash in 1915 to uphold a toppling territorial order, but not so in 1931, when the Washington treaties were scarcely a decade old.[9] Hence the decision, under

[9] *Stimson*, op. cit., 94. "Since Mr. Bryan's day," wrote Stimson, "the relations of the powers with China had been crystallized in the Nine Power Treaty of 1922, which placed the commercial rights of the signatory nations upon the far-sighted principle of respect for [but, it should be noted, not guarantee of], China's territorial and administrative integrity. Furthermore, since Mr. Bryan's day this policy of self-denial of aggression by a stronger against a weaker power . . . had been powerfully reinforced by the execution of the Kellogg-Briand Pact . . . If our warning should be

analogous circumstances to those of 1915 insofar as an unwillingness to use force was concerned, "to find some way of formally expressing the moral disapproval of the world against the breach of the peace in Manchuria, and, if possible to put behind that expression a sanction which would bring pressure upon the party responsible to make amends." [10] The result was the note of January 7, 1932, which enunciated the non-recognition doctrine generally associated with the Secretary's name, declaring *inter alia* that the United States Government "cannot admit the legality of any situation *de facto* nor does it intend to recognize any treaty or agreement entered into between those governments [China and Japan] or agents thereof, which may impair the treaty rights of the United States or its citizens in China . . . and that it does not intend to recognize any situation, treaty or agreement which may be brought about by means contrary to the covenants and obligations of the Pact of Paris. . . ." [11]

It is interesting to note that this high act of "lone hand" diplomacy, while doctrinally of very high significance, was undertaken after only the most perfunctory last-minute consultation with Great Britain and France, and, as a move of diplomacy, proved a

extended as to include non-recognition of the fruits of a violation not only of treaties specifically relating to China, but also of the Kellogg-Briand Pact covering the whole world, it would not only rest upon a more elevated and broader principle, but it would appeal with greater force to a much larger number of nations in the world. . . . In this way it might possibly serve as the substitute for sanctions for which we all had been groping."

[10] *Ibid.*, 92.

[11] *Ibid.*, 96-97.

rank failure, being predestined to go down in ignominious defeat because of its spectacular unilateralism. The ground was not prepared for it, either by careful conversations between the principally interested Powers, or by the alerting of public opinion to the general situation. For all the high purpose which surrounded the note, it was the final fruitage of that system of diplomacy to which the United States had reverted after 1920, which avoided the consultative process, the collaborative venture or the cooperative action of the United States with other Powers.[12] The disembodied, organization-free character of the *modus vivendi* by which the United States lived, politically speaking, after 1922, here came to disaster at the first challenge. It is again important to put this of record, because the fundamental error of rejecting organization as a remedy against and a deterrent of, aggressive war persisted down to December 7, 1941, almost a decade later.

The petty expedients of the interim seem, to the

[12] "The purpose and character of such a note," said the Secretary of State, "obviously precluded a preliminary general conference in respect to it with other nations. Its primary purpose was to record the final decision of an influential government which had made earnest and patient efforts for a peaceful solution of this controversy; which had exercised great forbearance in the face of a long series of assurances, given and immediately disregarded and which had now been driven to a serious decision which was intended to be final. Any attempt to discuss such a note with a view to joint action . . . would inevitably have produced hesitation, delays and leaks to the press. These would have impaired, if they had not destroyed, the psychological effect of the note. From its nature and the circumstances surrounding its inception the note was thus necessarily the setting up of 'a standard to which the wise and honest may repair,' leaving 'the event in the hand of God.'" *Ibid.*, 97-98.

rather embittered world of our times, either strangely childish or senile. They are basically attributable to the fact that the government of the United States was itself a prisoner of its own provincialism, invoked in 1919 in the form of the non-intervention tradition to prevent the organization of the political life of the world under the aegis of the League, and perpetuated thereafter by a combination of forces shaping the domestic political climate. During this period no one had the intellectual audacity, the moral temerity, to attempt to alter that malignant climate of opinion, or to try to create a consensus as to the nature of the world and our place in it.

What, then, were the principal expedients of the period? The first and most obvious, as it was also the most difficult one to which to bring ourselves, was *passive cooperation with the League of Nations.* The classic statement of this position was made on October 9, 1931, by Secretary Stimson in a communication to Sir Eric Drummond, then Secretary General of the League:

> The American Government, acting independently through its diplomatic representatives, will endeavor to reinforce what the League does and will make clear that it has a keen interest in the matter and is not oblivious to the obligations which the disputants have assumed to their fellow signatories in the Pact of Paris as well as in the Nine Power Pact should a time arise when it would seem advisable to bring forward those obligations. By this course we avoid any danger of embarrassing the League in the course to which it is now committed.[13]

[13] Stimson to Prentiss Gilbert for Sir Eric Drummond, from Washington, October 9, 1931. *Peace and War: United States*

However classed as "independent cooperation," this course was one which left to the League all initiative and merely followed at a psychologically respectable distance. But it could not be indefinitely maintained. By late autumn of 1931 the United States was seated at the council table of the League, so-deliberating with it, and allowing one of its high-ranking military officers to serve as a member of a League investigating commission. The idea of exhausting League action first, and then,[14] and then only, falling back upon the Pact of Paris and ultimately on the Nine Power Pact seems to have actuated the United States throughout the period from 1931 to 1937. How far the United States would actually go was revealed in connection with the discussions at the Disarmament Conference.

The second expedient was disarmament. In the world situation of 1932 some indication of the course the United States would take toward the upholding of the existing international order and territorial settlement was imperative. At the opening of the Disarmament Conference, on February 9, 1932, Am-

---

Foreign Policy, 1931-1941 (Washington, USGPO, 1943) 157-8. Hereinafter referred to as *USFP.*

[14] In a communication to the British Secretary of State for Foreign Affairs, Sir John Simon, on February 12, 1932, Secretary Stimson made clear the endeavors of the United States to invoke the two jointly at a much earlier date than they were actually applied. "These two treaties represent successive steps taken for the purpose of aligning the conscience and public opinion of the world in favor of a system of orderly development by the law of nations, including the settlement of all controversies by the methods of justice and peace instead of by arbitrary force." *Ibid.*, 165-166. It is necessary to record that the move was not reciprocated by the British Government.

bassador Hugh Gibson indicated just how far the United States would go:

There is a feeling sometimes expressed that the convictions of the United States in this field . . . are a product of our geographical isolation and of our lack of experience of and exposure to the rivalries and strains of the European Continent. In answer the American people point to the fact that the system of competitive armament, of alliances and cross alliances . . . has failed to maintain peace and seems indeed to have been provocative of war. . . . The *altered conditions* of international relationships, the development of communication and transport *within the last generation* to a point where *the whole world is knit together* by strands of commerce, finance and *intimate contact*, have today produced *new international relationships which are utterly inconsistent with the older methods and formulas.* America is convinced that the world should not go on to new movements and new tasks *hampered by the garments of an older regime*, and that the problem is only how promptly and smoothly mankind will cast aside the weapons *and traditions* of the old.[15]

It is quite clear to all who read that the spokesman for the United States, himself a seasoned, veteran diplomat, fully realized that the two pediments of the Compromise of 1920 were both gone, and that there were active challenges alike to the economic structure and the territorial order set up under the Paris treaties. Yet for all the conviction that the conditions of international life were deeply altered, the United States Government was unwilling to enter into any commitments of a positive character with regard to the relationships between states. Willing-

[15] *Ibid.*, 162-163. (Italics mine.)

ness to accept restrictions on the exercise of military power, in terms of specific weapons, was certainly indicated; of willingness to concert for the coercion of aggressors there was none. Thus not until a basic change in this official stand came about, could any hope of affirmative action looking to repression of aggressors be envisioned.

How futile was this hope may be seen from the pronouncement, on May 22, 1933, by Mr. Norman H. Davis, Chairman of the American Delegation at the Disarmament Conference:

> We are ready not only to do our part toward the substantive reduction of armaments but, if this is effected by general international agreement, we are also prepared to contribute in other ways to the organization of peace. In particular, *we are willing to consult the other states in case of a threat to peace, with a view to averting conflict.* Further than that, *in the event that the states, in conference, determine that a state has been guilty of a breach* of the peace in violation of its international obligations *and take measures against the violator,* then, *if we concur in the judgment rendered* as to the responsible and guilty party, *we will refrain from any action tending to defeat such collective effort* which these states may thus make to restore peace.[16]

The highly contingent character of the declaration, giving a positive promise of inaction by the United States if four preliminary conditions—general disarmament, collective consultation, established guilt, and concerted retribution—were met, indicates how utterly frail and tenuous was the conception of collective security, and how extremely limited the

[16] *Ibid.*, 188-189. (Italics mine.)

American commitment. The chief constructive gain was the commitment to consultation for both preventive and punitive purposes. From this point forward, there was not, as in the antecedent period from 1928 to 1932, merely the "implication of consultation," but the express promise to enter into the cooperative enterprise, with a proviso so tenuous that its limitations were not, in fact, operative. How limited, in fact, was the intention of the United States to consult may be gathered from the fact that in discussing the idea of a consultative pact with the press on May 10, 1933, President Roosevelt hedged the idea of consultation about still further, perhaps to assuage reportorial fears:

Both platforms, I think certainly the Democratic platform, favored consultative pacts. Now what is a consultative pact? It means, and it meant in the platform, that if all the Nations agreed to set up some kind of machinery for consultation in the event of an act of aggression, we would be very glad to have somebody there to consult with. I consider that to be a step forward. *Do not get the idea that it means that we bind ourselves in the first instance to agree with the verdict.* Now that is a very different thing. We agree to consult. Therefore it does not tie the hands of the United States in any shape, manner or form and leaves our final action entirely up to us. Now, that is the simplest way of putting it. We in no way—*in no way*—are limiting our own right to determine our own action after the facts are brought out. . . . The position that I have taken . . . is that both parties here are entirely ready to sit at whatever kind of consultative meeting is provided for. The idea is to work out some sort of machinery and then, having sat there, there would be a report to Washington as to what the other Nations think and then we will be entirely free to do whatever we want to do. In other words, we would not be bound by the American who happened to be sitting in the consultative pact. He would report home.

Q. Mr. President, it seems to me that the consultative pact is almost identical to our relations with the League of Nations.

THE PRESIDENT: It is an entirely different thing. You cannot use comparisons in that connection.

Q. But we always took the stand that we would consult as things came up but do nothing obligatory—not be obliged to consult. With this new arrangement, would we be obliged to consult?

THE PRESIDENT: We would say quite frankly that we would sit in and consult. There is nothing particularly startling about that, when you come down to it.

Q. But we have that machinery now.

THE PRESIDENT: Sure. In other words, it sounds like a huge change in policy but it is very little change in policy. It is an announcement that we are going to do something that we would do anyhow.[17]

Along with the veiled offer of continuous consultation came the suggestion made by President Roosevelt

That all the nations of the world should enter into a solemn and definite pact of non-aggression: That they should solemnly reaffirm the obligations they have assumed to limit and reduce their armaments and, provided these obligations are faithfully executed by the signatory powers, individually agree that they will send no armed force of whatsoever nature across their frontiers.[18]

[17] *The Public Papers and Addresses of Franklin Delano Roosevelt,* hereinafter cited as *PPA-FDR,* II, 170-173, *passim.* (Italics mine.)

[18] This was the form in which President Roosevelt voiced his appeal to foreign nations on May 16, 1933 (*Ibid.*, II, 179-181).

It was clear to the Chief Executive that, with the status of peace so shaken in the world, the reaffirmation of existing boundaries would serve to create a firm basis of legality in relation to which further measures could operate. That was the principal reason back of his non-aggression proposal.

Meanwhile in Congressional circles attention focussed on the proposed joint resolution permitting the imposition of an arms embargo

> Whenever the President finds that in any part of the world conditions exist such that the shipment of arms or munitions of war from countries which produce these commodities may promote or encourage the employment of force in the course of a dispute or conflict between nations, and, after securing the cooperation of such governments as the President deems necessary he makes proclamation thereof.[19]

Urged upon the Congress by Secretary of State Hull for " the sole end of maintaining the peace of the world," " with a due and prudent regard for our national policies and national interests " it was believed

---

In transmitting the information to Congress the President used slightly different language, suggesting that " subject to existing treaty rights no nation during the disarmament period shall send any armed force of whatsoever nature across its own borders " (*Ibid.*, II, 182). Mr. Norman Davis paraphrased this offer by stating that " the President proposed an undertaking by the nations that subject to existing treaty rights, armed forces should not be sent across national frontiers," adding: " In the long run, we may come to the conclusion that the simplest and most accurate definition of an aggressor is one whose armed forces are found on alien soil in violation of treaties." (*Ibid.*, II, 189).

[19] *Ibid.*, 177n-178n. The recurrence of the problem in the spring of 1947, in almost the identical form, is noteworthy.

necessary, " in justice to the firm convictions of the American people " that the United States be empowered to support its diplomacy by embargoes of a very flexible character. In this form, the embargo legislation left it wholly to Presidential discretion to name the country or countries to which the embargo would apply. It was not long before the lines were drawn between the advocates of " impartial " embargoes and those favoring differential treatment as between aggressors and non-aggressors.

Something of the extreme cautiousness with which the Department of State approached the problem may be seen in the testimony that came before the Foreign Relations Committee regarding the proposed embargo legislation. Admitting that in many cases embargoes would be of little or no avail in preventing or putting an end to conflict, and that therefore the President would not act, there were other cases in which embargoes might be effective:

> It is conceivable that in certain cases the matured opinion of this Government might accord *with the opinion of the rest of the world* in fixing the responsibility for a conflict upon an aggressor nation. In such cases, an international embargo on the shipment of arms and munitions to one party to the conflict might be deemed an equitable and effective method of restoring peace. This method nevertheless would certainly not be adopted by this government *without such effective guarantees of international cooperation as would safeguard us against the danger of this country's being involved in the conflict as a result of such action.* In a case of this kind, this Government would naturally take into careful consideration the international law of neutrality, taking into account the definite, although perhaps

as yet undefined, effect of the Kellogg-Briand Pact and other treaties designed to prevent war upon the concept of neutrality.[20]

After brief references to the Bolivio-Paraguayan War and the Leticia controversy between Colombia and Peru, the spokesman for the State Department, Joseph C. Green, declared:

It has never been the intention and is not now the intention of this Government to use the authority which would be conferred upon the Executive by this Resolution as a means of restoring peace between China and Japan. . . . We do not, therefore, envisage the probability of proposals by the League or by its principal members to this government to cooperate with them in an embargo on the shipment of arms and munitions to Japan. Should such proposals be made, we would not be disposed to give them favorable consideration, and *we would not under any circumstances agree to participate in an international embargo of this kind unless we had secured substantial guarantees from the governments of all the great powers which would ensure us against the effects of any retaliatory measures which the Japanese might undertake. In brief, this government does not expect to take any action of this nature in connection with this case. . . .* [21]

The main reason, apparently, why the State Department wanted the resolution in hand was to protect itself against the possible charge that it was obstructing positive international action against aggressors. If action failed to be taken (this government having pledged itself to inaction under virtually all circumstances), this government, it was held, would not be

[20] *USFP, 1931-1941*, 183 (May 17, 1933). (Italics mine.)
[21] *Ibid.*, 184-185. (Italics mine.)

at fault for no action being taken. After the lapse of more than a decade, this position still fails to make elemental common sense. Read in the context of Ambassador Davis' pronouncement that we would refrain from defeating collective action, it gains a little, but not much more, respectability.

Along with the projects for a consultative pact and synchronous but independent embargoes came the idea of strengthening the existing organization of the American Community of States. Here, consciously or unconsciously, the United States was compelled to follow the course set by President Wilson. In addressing the Governing Board of the Pan-American Union on Pan-American Day, April 12, 1933, President Roosevelt began, in a historical sense, to lay down the principles on which the American Republics should find common ground. Moving from the familiar international helpfulness motif which prevailed throughout the 'twenties, the Chief Executive took actively in hand the removal of political difficulties, pointing out that "existing conflicts between four of our sister republics" constituted a backward step, and must be promptly removed if there were to be genuine solidarity and "continental self-defence."[22] To the removal of these difficulties and the closure of the breaches on which the Pan-American projects of the Wilson Administration had been wrecked, both President Roosevelt and Secretary Hull went to work with a will.

It is unnecessary to note in detail here what the fruitage of the "Good Neighbor" policy has been.

[22] *PPA-FDR*, II, 131.

Let it suffice to recall the broad stages through which it has evolved. It required a measure of internal fortitude to brave the frigid political climate and bring about a return to the spirit of confidence at the Montevideo Conference of December, 1933. Out of that came the special opportunity to convoke the American Republics at Buenos Aires, under the joint visible inspiration of President Justo and President Roosevelt, and push forward the Conference for the Maintenance of Peace in December of 1936. This, in turn, paved the way for the great Conference at Lima in December of 1938. All of these, through their deliberations, began to build up on the Western Hemisphere a separate, though narrower, system of security, along lines which were familiar, fully agreed, and part of a common fabric of thought.

It was thus that the foundation was laid for common action by the American Republics at the outbreak of World War II. An area of agreement, a great and living political consensus, was reached during the years of peace, which proved its viability and vitality during the years of war. Without Montevideo there would not have been Panama; without Buenos Aires, no conference at Habana; and without the Lima Conference there would have been no meeting at Rio de Janeiro after the Western hemisphere was itself involved in World War II. But here the analogy stops, for the Conference of Foreign Ministers of the American Republics at Chapultepec cannot be considered as activated solely, or even mainly, by strictly American reasons. Chapultepec implies Yalta; San Francisco implies Chapultepec. It is at

San Francisco that the American Republics join in the larger enterprise of erecting "a wider and permanent system of general security." So much for the overview. The particular means by which the Western Hemisphere security system advanced from the anomalous and amorphous condition in which World War I left it deserve some attention.

To Cordell Hull belong the responsibility and the honor of having piloted through a complex conference the idea of integrating into a common program the conventional relations, as expressed in signed treaties, to which the American Republics had formally subscribed during the preceding decade. To create a common platform of legally binding obligations, pledging the signatories to pacific settlement of their disputes was the *sine qua non* of progress in the creation of an inter-American regional system of security. This the Montevideo Conference accomplished in December, 1933, by knitting together four treaties: the Kellogg-Briand Peace Pact, the Argentine Anti-War Pact, the Gondra Treaty of 1923, aimed at avoiding or preventing conflicts between American States, and the General Treaties of Inter-American Arbitration and Conciliation signed in Washington in January, 1929. In addition, the Montevideo Conference adopted a very basic convention defining the rights and duties of States, building an over-all platform on the foundations of the foregoing treaties. By laying down the rule that no state has the right to intervene in the internal or external affairs of another, and by adopting, in the same convention "the precise obligation not to recognize territorial acquisitions or special advantages which have been obtained by force" the groundwork was laid as substantially as possible for the further erection of a Continental system.[23]

While the Montevideo Conference was winding up its work, President Roosevelt, in a pronouncement of singular clarity, defined before the Woodrow Wilson Foundation, on December 28, 1933, the position of the United States *vis-à-vis* the League of Nations. No explicit pronouncement had emanated from the United States Government since Harding's official utterances in 1921, and it was high time for a realistic attitude, more closely conforming to actualities than mere dissociation from the League of Nations, "world-governing in its super-powers."

Premising his pronouncement on the Montevideo Convention's provisions, by saying "that the definite policy of the United States from now on is one opposed to armed intervention," the Chief Executive stressed the fact that maintenance of constitutional government in the other American Republics, or in any other nations, was not a sacred obligation devolving upon the United States alone, but rather the "joint concern of a whole continent in which we are all neighbors." This doctrine of joint political concern was strictly Wilsonian, and Roosevelt built his position squarely upon it:

> Today the United States is cooperating openly in the fuller utilization of the League of Nations machinery than ever before. I believe that I express the views of my countrymen when I state that the old politics, the old alliances,

[23] *USFP, 1931-1941*, 199-204.

the old combinations and balances of power have proved themselves inadequate for the preservation of world peace. *The League of Nations*, encouraging as it does the extension of non-aggression pacts, of reduction of armament agreements, *is a prop in the world peace structure, and it must remain. We are not members and we do not contemplate membership. We are giving cooperation to the League in every matter which is not primarily political,* and in every matter which obviously represents the views and the good of the peoples of the world as distinguished from the views and the good of political leaders, of privileged classes and of imperialistic aims.[24]

In this manner the Chief Executive defined for another decade the general viewpoint of the United States toward the one organization with universal aims and objectives. It will be noted that, with singular finesse in timing, this pronouncement endeavored to link the progress of a new peace structure in the New World with the best remaining in the Old. And an exiguous loophole was left for future joint action: "in every matter which represents the views and the good of the peoples of the world"—surely not a narrow term of reference.

Before further progress could be made, it was essential that the United States implement the equalitarian system promised at Montevideo by abandoning its treaties of protectorate over Cuba, Panama, and other American Republics. This was done in the course of 1934 and 1935, so that promises became realities and confidence in the word of the United States was perceptibly restored. Meanwhile every diplomatic effort was bent to the solving of

[24] *PPA-FDR*, II, 544-549, at 547. (Italics mine.)

existing territorial conflicts in the Western Hemisphere.

Something of the measure of success attained along these lines may be gathered from the terms used by President Roosevelt in addressing Congress on January 3, 1936:

Among the nations of the great Western Hemisphere the policy of the good neighbor has happily prevailed. At no time in the four and half centuries of modern civilization in the Americas has there existed—in any year, in any decade, in any generation in all that time—a greater spirit of mutual understanding, of common helpfulness, and of devotion to the ideals of self-government than exists today in the twenty-one American Republics and their neighbor, the Dominion of Canada. This policy of the good neighbor among the Americas is no longer a hope, no longer an objective remaining to be accomplished. It is a fact, active, present, pertinent and effective.[25]

Once the peace protocols between Bolivia and Paraguay were signed in Buenos Aires, the way was opened for the American Republics collectively " to consider their joint responsibility and their common need of rendering less likely in the future the outbreak or continuation of hostilities between them, and by so doing, serve in an eminently practical manner the cause of permanent peace on this Western Continent." With this thought in mind President Roosevelt suggested to President Justo of Argentina " that an extraordinary inter-American conference be assembled at an early date in Buenos Aires . . . to determine how the maintenance of peace

[25] *PPA-FDR*, V, 8-9.

among the American Republics " might best be safeguarded. To Roosevelt the precise means to be employed were secondary, although for the first time in his Administration he envisaged something new—" the creation by common accord of new instruments of peace, additional to those already formulated." [26] With the impact of the Ethiopian war reaching Washington, it was already not too certain that the existing machinery for peace maintenance was strong enough to stand the test.

The Buenos Aires Conference was the result. It came at an auspicious moment, and not one hour too soon, for the purpose of realizing constructively the joint responsibility of the American Republics for the peace of the Western Hemisphere. Seizing the unprecedented opportunity given for " constructive steps . . . along lines heretofore untried " [27] President Roosevelt attended in person, stopping en route to consolidate the favorable ground existing in Brazil for the purposes of the conference.[28] Moving at a

[26] *Ibid.*, V, 72-73. Roosevelt to Justo, January 30, 1936.

[27] *Ibid.*, V, 583-584. Radio Message to the Twenty-one American Republics, November 7, 1936.

[28] *Ibid.*, V, 597-603. Addresses on November 27, 1936.

" The progress we have made must not be allowed to serve as a pretext for resting on our laurels; it should, on the contrary, stimulate us to new and increased effort. It is not enough that peace prevails from the Arctic to the Antartic, from the Atlantic to the Pacific; *it is essential that this condition be made permanent*, that we provide effectively against the recurrence of the horrors of war, and assure peace to ourselves and our posterity.

" All instrumentalities for the maintenance of peace must be consolidated and reinforced. *We cannot countenance aggression, from wheresoever it may come.* The people of each and every one of the American Republics—and, I am confident, the people of the Dominion of Canada as well—wish to lead their own lives

far faster pace than Wilson under analogous circumstances, and with the zeal of a consciously sought objective, he brought his own ideas as to the future of the Western Hemisphere to clear, sharp focus and relayed them to Brazil, Argentina, and Uruguay. The President's pronouncement before the Inter-American Conference amounted to a new *Credo*, an affirmative confession of faith in the viability of the democratic order in national states, in the principle of nationality itself, in the vitality of the processes of consultation and cooperation among the American Republics. Roosevelt's contribution came in stressing non-partisanly and non-contentiously the common ground, the consensus of the Americas, leaving it to Secretary Hull and others to embody in resolutions and conventions the actual arrangements for the evolution of an effective American system.

In a retrospective appraisal of the significance of Buenos Aires Conference President Roosevelt wrote, in a commentary on his own addresses:

Three main principles dominated the Conference: First, that no nation in the Western Hemisphere professed any right to threaten the peace of its neighbors; second, that

---

free from desire for conquest and free from fear of conquest; free at the same time to expand their cultural and intellectual relationships and to take counsel together to encourage the peaceful progress of modern civilization. . . .

"We are showing in international relations what we have long known in private relations—that good neighbors make a good community. In that knowledge we meet today as neighbors. We can disregard the dangerous language of rivalry; we can put aside the empty phrases of 'diplomatic triumphs' or 'shrewd bargains.' *We can forget all thought of domination, of selfish coalitions, or of balances of power. Those false gods have no place among American neighbors.*" (Italics mine.)

the integrity of every country, large or small, would be assured; third, that *renunciation of war required some method of obtaining instantaneously the cooperative effort of the entire Hemisphere.* The dominant idea was that *any threat to the maintenance of peace on this continent must lead to immediate consultation to seek common policies and take common measures to prevent conflict.* It was the basis of the major treaties and agreements negotiated at the Conference. *The agreements provide a complete consultative system intended to meet the menace of conflict by the quick and active cooperation of the twenty-one Governments.*[29]

Manifestly, the American Republics were creating, under the long-range threat of a small-scale war, the very system of preventive consultation under the League of Nations which the United States had officially rejected. It was all the more impossible for the United States to avoid it since every one of the other American Republics had at one time or another accepted the obligations of the League of Nations Covenant, with its Wilsonian Article 11, devoted to preventive action through quick consultation. On this rock the United States was privileged to build its own system,[30] and none of our enemies were historically able to prevail against it.

[29] *PPA-FDR,* V, 615-616.

[30] In the Declaration of Lima, the Eighth International Conference of American States, basing its action on the unity of the American Republics, deriving from their kindred republican institutions, affirmed the will of the Americas to "defend the peace of the continent and work together in the cause of universal concord." It reaffirmed the continental solidarity of the Americas and their purpose to collaborate in the maintenance of the principles upon which solidarity is based. It further reaffirmed their desire to defend the hemisphere against all foreign intervention or

From the close of the Disarmament Conference onwards, the United States found itself in an increasingly unsatisfactory position with regard to the general international situation. It had gone as far as possible toward the League of Nations without assuming active political commitments. Presently it found itself in an impasse from which there was obviously no exit without a sharp reversal of policy. During the Ethiopian war, during the Spanish civil war, while the country was blanketed by the successive neutrality acts largely originating with Congress, the first tendency, as was the case in 1914 and 1915, was to sink back not merely into an alert neutrality, but into an acute isolationism. The evidences of this are so numerous that it is hardly necessary to instance them.[31] What is more pertinent is to dis-

activity that might threaten them. Most important was the stipulation that " in case the peace, security or territorial integrity of any American Republic is threatened by acts of any nature that may impair them, *they proclaim their common concern and their determination to make effective their solidarity*, coordinating their respective sovereign wills *by the procedure of consultation . . .* using the measures which in each case the circumstances may make advisable." To safeguard " their juridical equality as sovereign states," it was understood that the American Republics would act " independently in their individual capacity." The actual means of consultation agreed on was that " the Ministers for Foreign Affairs of the American Republics, when deemed desirable and at the initiative of any one of them," would " meet in their several capitals by rotation, and without protocolary character." At most this meant the implementing of consultation. Actually the practice of four such gatherings has been to regularize and schematize and make uniform the procedures and habits of cooperation. Cf. *USFP, 1931-1941*, 439-441.

[31] Noteworthy instances can be found in the San Diego address of President Roosevelt, October 2, 1935, at the very outbreak of the Italo-Ethiopian war, when the President declared vigorously that " despite what happens in continents overseas, the United

cover the beginnings of the spread of the conviction that a new effort at basic reorganization of the international community was both necessary and inevitable. This is a much harder story.

Throughout the illucid interval of official neutrality policy it was scarcely possible for any representative of the United States, at home or abroad, to make any type of pronouncement of policy that did not wholly square with the strait-jacket neutrality enacted by the Congress and officially proclaimed by the President. It was this anomalous situation that, to cite but three examples, prevented protest, and forestalled cooperation in sanctions of a real degree of severity during the Ethiopian war; which kept the United States on the quiet side during the Spanish conflict; and which led to a passive acceptance of the annexation of Austria. Few indeed were the voices in authority that spoke in any alternative sense. In an apologia, Secretary Hull declared in September, 1936:

> At times there has been criticism because we would not depart from our traditional policy and join with other governments in collective arrangements carrying the obligation of employing force, if necessary, in case disputes between other countries brought them into war. That responsibility, carrying direct participation in the political relations of the whole of the world outside, we cannot accept, eager as we are to support means for the prevention of war. For current experience indicates how uncertain is the possibility that we, by our action, could vitally influence the policies

---

States of America shall and must remain, as long ago the Father of our Country prayed that it might remain—unentangled and free." *PPA-FDR*, IV, 410.

or activities of other countries from which war might come. It is for the statesmen to continue their effort to effect security by new agreements which will prove more durable than those that have been broken. This Government would welcome that achievement. It would be like full light overcoming dense darkness. *It is difficult to see how responsible governments can refrain from pushing compromise to its utmost limits to accomplish that result.*[32]

Clearly this was the road that led to Munich. Obviously another approach had to be made.

It was undertaken first by the Secretary of State within a fortnight of the renewed crisis in the Orient, in July, 1937, when Mr. Hull endeavored, by circularizing all governments, to bring about the maximum area of agreement on the kind of international relations which would be compatible with enduring and stable peace. The area of agreement which Mr. Hull was able to obtain was rather high. It began, even at the most difficult hour and without the moral authority that accrued to President Wilson, the difficult task of re-creating an international consensus, of establishing a platform, no longer for purely inter-American purposes, but for world-wide action. This received a powerful reinforcement by the thundering philippic of President Roosevelt in the now famous "Quarantine" speech at Chicago, October 5, 1937,—the first open act suggesting that "the peace-loving nations must make a concerted effort to uphold laws and principles on which alone peace can rest secure":

[32] *USFP, 1931-1941*, 335-336. Cf. also the Armistice Day address at Arlington National Cemetery, Nov. 11, 1935 (*PPA-FDR*, IV, 441-444 and the Chautauqua Address, August 14, 1936, *Ibid.*, V, 285-292.

The peace-loving nations must make a concerted effort in opposition to those violations of treaties and those ignorings of humane instincts which today are creating a state of international anarchy and instability from which there is no escape through mere isolation or neutrality. . . . There is a solidarity and interdependence about the modern world, both technically and morally, which makes it impossible for any nation completely to isolate itself from economic and political upheavals in the rest of the world, especially when such upheavals appear to be spreading and not declining. The situation is definitely of universal concern. . . . It is true that the moral consciousness of the world must recognize the importance of removing injustices and well-founded grievances, but at the same time it must be aroused to the cardinal necessity of honoring sanctity of treaties, of respecting the rights and liberties of others, and of putting an end to acts of international aggression. . . . . The will for peace on the part of peace-loving nations must express itself to the end that nations that may be tempted to violate their agreements and the rights of others will desist from such a cause. There must be positive endeavors to preserve peace.[33]

The task was continued with incessant purpose, and made long-run progress such as the Quarantine speech did not by itself achieve. In one of the most adroit and exacting addresses in his long career, the Secretary of State, in March, 1938, after the German annexation of Austria, made clear the golden mean which the United States Government was endeavoring to follow between excessive internationalism and perilous isolationism. It was clear that isolationism was no longer a means to security, but a fruitful source of insecurity; on the other hand, the United

[33] *PPA-FDR,* VI, 406-411; *USFP, 1931-1941*, 383-387.

States Government, at this point, steadfastly repudiated any intent to make pledges of a political character, and every imputation of alliance or military commitment. The time had not yet come when a substitute for the dissolving legal order could be envisaged. So the Munich crisis came and went, finding the United States on the side lines, with no commitments, no entanglements.

By the beginning of 1939 the President himself had matured a program to counter the collapsing military and territorial order in Europe and the Far East. Building, as Wilson before him, on the intangibles of faith, he appealed to the Congress for support. Defense of the Western Hemisphere "against storms from any quarter" was the sheet anchor of the program and revealed its initial territorial scope.[34] There was a broadened program of con-

[34] The President had given an inkling of what was in his mind along these lines in a radio address to the Herald-Tribune Forum, October 26, 1938—less than a month after Munich. In incredibly brief compass he outlined the conditions under which there could be no peace. Then, expanding the conception of neighborhood, he declared: "We covet nothing save good relations with our neighbors; and *we recognize that the world today has become our neighbor*. But in the principle of the good neighbor certain fundamental reciprocal obligations are involved." These the President proceeded to enumerate: Peaceful change, observance of treaties, lowering of armaments by agreements. Then, on the affirmative side: "We in the United States do not seek to impose on any other people either our way of life or our internal form of government. But we are determined to maintain and protect that way of life and that form of government for ourselves. And *we are determined to use every endeavor in order that the Western Hemisphere may work out its own interrelated salvation in the light of its own interrelated experience*." Here was a renewed form of the territorial commitments implicit in the Inter-American Conferences. Continental solidarity, hemispheric defence, are here

sultation "with all the other nations of the world to the end that aggression among them be terminated, that the race of armaments cease and that commerce be renewed." Still holding back from any pledge "to intervene with arms to prevent acts of aggression," the President pointed out that this did not mean that the nation must act as though there were no aggression at all:

Words may be futile, but war is not the only means of commanding a decent respect for the opinions of mankind. There are many methods short of war, but stronger and more effective than mere words, of bringing home to aggressor governments the aggregate sentiments of our people.[35]

With this pronouncement, the period of masterly inactivity which had characterized the actions of the United States Government in the face of increasing anarchy and disorder came to a close. The period of techniques and methods short-of-war had begun.

The first tactic along these lines was purely diplomatic—the subjection of the principal wrong doers in the family of nations to a needling process which would either bring clearly into relief their aggressive intentions, or else make them disavow by treaty or

---

found in nuclear form. But there is an important letting down of the limitations of our interest, a precursor to the aid-to-democracies program: "We affirm our faith that, whatever choice of way of life a people makes, that choice must not threaten the world with the disaster of war. . . . That statement applies not to the Western Hemisphere alone but to the whole of Europe and Asia and Africa and the islands of the seas." Palpably, the conception of direct interest was spreading! *PPA-FDR*, VII, 563-566. (Italics mine.)

[35] *PPA-FDR*, VIII, 2-3 (January 4, 1939).

open agreement any predatory tendencies. This was done in the aftermath of the conquest of Albania and the occupation of Czechoslovakia:

> Are you willing [asked the President,] to give assurance that your armed forces will not attack or invade the territory or possessions of the following independent nations: Finland, Estonia, Latvia, Lithuania, Sweden, Norway, Denmark, the Netherlands, Belgium, Great Britain and Ireland, France, Portugal, Spain, Switzerland, Liechtenstein, Luxemburg, Poland, Hungary, Rumania, Jugoslavia, Russia, Bulgaria, Greece, Turkey, Iraq, the Arabias, Palestine, Egypt and Iran? [36]

Unhappily, from the President's standpoint, the result was negative, as both Mussolini and Hitler disdained to reply.[37] But what was important in the inquiry was that President Roosevelt indicated enumeratively the system of national states, the recognized territorial order, disturbance of which must necessarily destroy the system on which peace, as it existed from 1919 to 1939, rested. This was digging down to fundamentals.

The second venture on new measures was the endeavor to repeal the arms embargo. It, too, was a failure as a deterrent, because the Congress, previous to the outbreak of war in Europe, was, despite all the admonitions from the President and the Secretary of State profoundly skeptical of the likelihood of war.[38] The recommendation for repeal "was one of the last formal efforts made by the administration to

[36] *Ibid.*, 201-205 (April 14, 1939).
[37] *Ibid.*, Introduction, xxx.
[38] Cf. *USFP, 1931-1941*, 458-460 (April 25, 1939).

prevent the war in Europe." On the clock of History it was, in fact, later than Congress thought!

With the coming of war, the United States was more concerned with "helping to maintain in the Western world a citadel wherein . . . civilization [might] be kept alive." The one thought of the President was for "the peace, the integrity, and the safety of the Americas—these must be kept firm and serene." [39] But repeal of the arms embargo was everywhere seen to be essential and inevitable and the Congress with retrospective perspicacity belatedly yielded.[40] For the initial period of the war it was sufficient, by the right of access given to the maritime belligerents, to keep the great land powers from our shores. Essentially the transition in American thought during the period of official neutrality but ideological rebellion at Nazi conquest can be indicated in the shift of emphasis from the conception of *citadel* to *arsenal.*

At the beginning of 1940, before the tremendous spread of the war, Roosevelt posed to the American people the potential courses of action open to them:

I hope that Americans everywhere will work out for themselves the several alternatives which lie before world civilization, which necessarily includes our own. We must look ahead and see the possibilities for our children if the rest of the world comes to be dominated by concentrated force alone. . . . We must look ahead and see the effect on our future if all the small nations of the world have their

[39] *Ibid.*, 461-465; 468-474.
[40] *PPA-FDR*, VIII, Introduction xxxi-xxxvii, and 381-393.

independence snatched from them or become mere appendages to relatively vast and powerful military systems. We must look ahead and see the kind of lives our children would have to lead if a large part of the rest of the world were compelled to worship a god imposed by a military ruler, or were forbidden to worship God at all; if the rest of the world were forbidden to read and hear the facts—the daily news of their own and other nations—if they were deprived of the truth that makes men free. We must look ahead and see the effect on our future generations if world trade is controlled by any nation or group of nations which sets up that control through military force.[41]

It is impossible to read these rhetorical queries thrust at the American public without noting therein the genesis of the Four Freedoms and parts of the Atlantic Charter. Indeed, before those could be enunciated, it was essential that the seminal ideas be deeply implanted. A further reiteration of these ideas came with the invasion of Norway and Denmark, on April 13, 1940, when, reiterating with undiminished emphasis his strongly expressed disapprobation of aggression, the President, with extreme understatement, declared that

If civilization is to survive, the rights of the smaller nations to independence, to their territorial integrity, and to the unimpeded opportunity for self-government must be respected by their more powerful neighbors.[42]

As protest, this was excessively moderate; as philippic, worthless; but as principle, it was essentially a cornerstone foundation for a post-war international

[41] *PPA-FDR*, IX, 3-4 (January 3, 1940).
[42] *Ibid.*, IX, 157.

order. And it was forewarning. On April 15, 1940, in addressing the Pan-American Union, the Chief Executive provided the first blueprint of that order:

Today the world and we, ourselves, are again face to face with the old problem. Universal and stable peace remains a dream. War, more horrible and destructive than ever, has laid its blighting hand on many parts of the earth. But peace among our American nations remains secure because of the instruments we have succeeded in creating. *They embody, in great measure at least, the principles upon which, I believe, enduring peace must be based throughout all the rest of the world.*

Peace reigns today in the Western Hemisphere because our nations have liberated themselves from fear . . . because we have agreed, as neighbors should, to mind our own businesses . . . because we have resolved to settle any dispute that should arise among us by friendly negotiation in accordance with justice and equity, rather than by force . . . because we have recognized the principle that only through vigorous and mutually beneficial international economic relations can each of us have adequate access to materials and opportunities. . . . We of this hemisphere have no need to seek a new international order; we have already found it. . . . The inter-American order was not built by hatred and terror. It has been paved by the endless and effective work of men of good will. We have built a foundation for the lives of hundreds of millions. We have unified these lives by a common devotion to a moral order.

This cooperative peace in the Western Hemisphere was not created by mere wishing; and it will require more than mere words to maintain. In this association of nations whoever touches any one of us touches us all. We have only asked that the world go with us in the path of peace. But we shall be able to keep that way open only if we are prepared to meet force with force if challenge is ever made against us.[43]

[43] *PPA-FDR*, IX, 160-161. (Italics mine.)

Here at last was an avowal, explicit and uncircumscribed, of the security value of rational organization, and, in the same breath, an admission that the same principles must underlie the peace of the future, in every part of the earth.

It is unnecessary here to repeat the chronology of failure which accompanied the efforts of the Allied countries throughout 1940. But there is one clear, unforgettable note uttered with intense calm, in a communication to the King of Greece on December 5, 1940. Without fanfare or warning, it became the *Leitmotif* of American policy for the remainder of the war: It was the announcement of "the settled policy of the United States to extend aid to those governments and peoples who defend themselves against aggression."[44] Though unimplemented as yet by legislation, it was the harbinger of the system of policy which was to transform defeat into victory and so reorder the map of Europe, and eventually, of the areas afflicted by the Nazi tyranny. Along with it, only a month later, came the Four Freedoms, hardily nailed at the masthead by the United States. These were predestined, if we may change the metaphor, to become not only touchstones to victory but buildingstones for future international order.[45]

In the future days, which we seek to make secure, we look forward to a world founded upon four essential human freedoms.

The first is freedom of speech and expression—everywhere in the world.

[44] *Ibid.*, IX, 599.
[45] *Ibid.*, IX, 672 (January 6, 1941).

The second is freedom of every person to worship God in his own way—everywhere in the world.

The third is freedom from want—which, translated into world terms, means economic understandings which will secure to every nation a healthy peacetime life for its inhabitants—everywhere in the world.

The fourth is freedom from fear—which, translated into world terms, means a world wide reduction of armaments to such a point and in such a thorough fashion that no nation will be in a position to commit an act of physical aggression against any neighbor—anywhere in the world.[46]

[46] A word may be in order concerning the genesis of the Four Freedoms. In a press conference on July 5, 1940, at Hyde Park, President Roosevelt, answering almost off-hand an inquiry by a newspaperman, Mr. Harkness, replied: " Now I come down to your questions. The first is—you might say there are certain freedoms. The first I would call freedom of information, which is terribly important. It is a much better phrase than freedom of the press, because there are all kinds of information so that the inhabitants of a country can get news of what is going on in every part of the country and in every part of the world without censorship and through many forms of communication. That, I think, is one of the objectives of peace, because you will never have a completely stable world without freedom of knowledge, freedom of information. The second, of course, is freedom of religion which, under democracies, has always— not always, but almost all the time—been fairly well maintained. It is not maintained in those nations which have adopted other systems of government. You have to take it as it comes, and that, in my mind, is an essential of permanent peace. Then, a third freedom is the freedom to express one's self as long as you don't advocate the overthrow of government. That is a different thing. In other words, the kind of expression that we certainly have in this country and that they have in most democracies. That, I think, is an essential of peace—I mean permanent peace. Fourth, freedom from fear, so that people won't be afraid of being bombed from the air or attacked, one way or the other, by some other nation. And, of course, we have maintained all along that freedom from fear must be based on a removal of the weapons that cause fear—in other words, disarmament. And that is an essential of peace. And so the question really comes down to whether we are going to continue to seek those freedoms or whether we are going to give up, at the behest of certain

All this has very long since become either so completely accepted, or a cliché, that it is important to note the ideological matrix in which this beatific mosaic was set:

This is no vision of a distant millennium. It is a definite basis for a kind of world attainable in our time and generation. That kind of world is the very antithesis of the so-called new order of tyranny which the dictators seek to create with the crash of a bomb. To that new order we oppose a greater conception—the moral order. A good society is able to face schemes of world domination and foreign revolutions alike without fear. . . . *The world order which we seek is the cooperation of free countries, working together in a friendly, civilized society.*[47]

This was corroborated shortly thereafter by Secretary Hull, when, addressing the American Society of International Law, he declared:

Although the task is huge, though time is pressing and though the struggle may continue for a long time, I am confident that at the end there will come a better day. We are at work not only at the task of insuring our own safety, but also at the task of creating ultimate conditions of peace with justice. We can help to lay a firm foundation for the independence, the security, and the returning prosperity of the members of the family of nations.[48]

---

elements, those freedoms in our system of government. . . . Does that cover it pretty well?

"Q. Well, I had a fifth in mind which you might describe as freedom from want—free trade, opening up trade?

"THE PRESIDENT. Yes, that is true, I had that in mind but forgot it. Freedom from want—in other words, the removal of certain barriers between nations, cultural in the first place and commercial in the second place. That is the fifth, very definitely." *Ibid.*, IX, 284-285.

[47] *Ibid.*, IX, 672.

[48] *Department of State Bulletin*, IV, No. 96 (April 26, 1941) 494 (hereinafter cited as *DSB*).

The next major pronouncement bearing on the future course of world affairs was the Atlantic Charter, a document of primordial importance for our purpose. Yet the Charter, no less than the Fourteen Points, was the irresistible culmination of attitudes long in the making and incrementally pronounced on other occasions. The Atlantic Charter has not, so far as I am aware, ever been given an intellectual pedigree, save for its most immediate forebears, and for its immediate timing. But it comes of a long lineage, of which the Fourteen Points are but a single ancestor. Tempting as it is to give the fuller setting and a sizable geneology, I must, in the circumstances, forbear from doing so.

Let it suffice to put on record the renunciation of territorial aggrandizement, the insistence on popular sanction of territorial changes, the vibrant reaffirmation of self-determination and the *voeu* for restoration of self-government and sovereignty to those forcibly deprived of them; the reassertion of equal access of all to trade and raw materials, the cooperative advancement of social security, the re-enunciation, for all the men in all the lands, of the fundamental freedoms; and the freedom of the seas. This in itself would entitle the Atlantic Charter to stand as a landmark in the minds and emotions of men everywhere. Only two points need detain us here: the hope of an established peace " which will afford to all nations the means of dwelling in safety within their own boundaries " and the promise of " the establishment of a wider and permament system of general security." This dual pledge was, during the war years, the principal hope held out to a world in travail and suffering.[49]

But to give body to this credal affirmation, to make concrete and real the dreams which it held out to those before whom lay the Valley of the Shadow of Death, was an infinitely more difficult procedure. It took almost a year to make even a beginning, so pressing were the other tasks before us. On July 23, 1942, Cordell Hull first attempted to put content into the promise of the Atlantic Charter:

> It is plain that some international agency must be created which can—by force, if necessary—keep the peace among nations in the future. There must be international cooperative action to set up the mechanisms which can thus insure peace. This must include eventual adjustment of national armaments in such a manner that the rule of law cannot be successfully challenged and that the burden of armaments may be reduced to a minimum.
>
> In the creation of such mechanisms there would be a practical and purposeful application of sovereign powers through measures of international cooperation for purposes of safeguarding the peace. Participation by all nations in such measures would be for each its contribution toward its own future security and safety from outside attack.
>
> Settlement of disputes by peaceful means, and indeed all processes of international cooperation, presuppose respect for law and obligations. It is plain that one of the institutions which must be established and given vitality is an international court of justice. It is equally clear that, in the process of reestablishing international order, the United Nations must exercise surveillance over aggressor nations until such time as the latter demonstrate their willingness and ability to live at peace with other nations. . . .

[49] *DSB*, V, 125.

> Building for the future in the economic sphere . . . means that each nation must play its full part in a system of world relations designed to facilitate the production and movement of goods in response to human needs. . . .
>
> To make full use of this opportunity we must be resolved not alone to proclaim the blessings and benefits which we all desire for humanity but to find the mechanisms by which they may be most fully and most speedily attained and be most effectively safeguarded. . . . The United Nations should, from time to time, as they did in adopting the Atlantic Charter, formulate and proclaim their common views, regarding fundamental policies which will chart for mankind a wise course based on enduring spiritual values.[50]

From this time forward for nearly two years there was a fundamental struggle, whose details are not yet fully revealed, between the believers in and opponents of a colloid Covenant, an amorphous and flexible arrangement between members of the United Nations, to be built up by incremental understandings and never at any time as a whole mechanism. There is no question that Sumner Welles was, if not the out-and-out leader of this school, certainly one of its most distinguished protagonists. And certainly, for the moment, time was on his side. It was, if we may infer from his contemporary utterances, vital for the United Nations to institutionalize their procedures, not globally but in a practical, matter-of-fact, established cooperation. Welles, would have salvaged for the future all the genetic impulses, the pain-born momentum which stinging defeat and long, costly struggle gave to the combatant members of the United Nations. And certainly there were many who leaned at the time to that view.

[50] *DSB*, VII, 639-647, at 645-646.

In sharp contrast to this evolutionary concept were those who must see the whole blueprint to appreciate it. It is difficult as yet, in default of memorabilia, to determine even approximately whence they came or who they were, but it cannot be gainsaid that they eventually constituted a majority and became the pervasive influence in the determination of policy. Rejecting absolutely all schemes for world governance that reposed on a balance of power,[51] such proponents of an entirely new international organization favored a unified plan, not " creating overnight a world government with sweeping and general power to invade the domestic affairs of sovereign states," but delegating to some international organization " certain carefully defined and restricted powers " and clothing the organization " with sufficient force to carry out effectively those restricted and limited powers." [52] Linked to such limited fed-

[51] " If we are to build for lasting peace, we must abandon the nineteenth century conception that the road to peace lies through a nicely poised Balance of Power. Again and again cold experience has taught us that no peace dependent upon a Balance of Power lasts. The Balance of Power theory rests upon the premise of utterly independent nations, owing no obligations of any kind to each other; and the peace of the world under twentieth century conditions cannot be made secure except through the activity of an organizd group, subject to common obligations and restraints. Whatever may be said in its favor under nineteenth century conditions, the Balance of Power theory is, under twentieth century conditions, the sure way to destruction." Francis B. Sayre, Special Assistant to the Secretary of State, speaking in his behalf, June 8, 1943. *DSB*, VIII, 510.

[52] " Presumably these would include among others the power to prevent by concerted action international territorial aggression and thievery, the power to regulate and control heavy armament-building in every country of the world, the power to administer and supervise the government of certain backward and colonial

eralism was the conception of guarantees of human rights, in the form of some fundamental enactment.[53] The governance of backward peoples was also caught up in this conception, in order to extend international controls over the colonial world and bring swiftly to an end the era of exploitation. With far greater bravery than the incrementalists, the advocates of full-panoplied international government came out into the open with their demands for an international governmental apparatus adequate to the complex social and economic problems of the day.

As we look back in retrospect upon a time even so recently past, it is clear that there was real perspicacity and foresight and a fundamental appreciation of historical realities in seeking to undertake the task on a global and integral scale. Long before the matter was discussed with foreign governments at all, the problem of future organization was made the object of the most intense study and programmatic planning. And by the time that the Moscow Conference on October 30, 1943, pledged the principal Allies

---

areas, and the power by concerted action to attack certain discriminatory and anti-social practices in the field of international trade and finance." Sayre, though sketching so comprehensive an organization, openly admitted that it too would have an evolutionary character: "The degree of power accorded to such an organization would naturally grow with time as experience proved its worth and competency" (*Ibid.*, 511).

[53] "The reasonable security of one's person and one's property, freedom of conscience, freedom of speech, the right to dispose of the fruits of one's own labor, equality of rights before the law, complete independence of thought, and reasonable independence of action—these are the basic human rights, on the safeguarding of which peace must be built if it is to be lasting (*Ibid.*, 511).

to establish at the earliest practicable date a general international organization, based on the principle of the sovereign equality of all peace-loving states, and open to membership by all such states, large and small, for the maintenance of international peace and security,

the plans were far advanced. Again and again during 1944 the Department of State reached out and sampled public opinion, took the American public into its confidence, until by the time of Dumbarton Oaks, the area of agreement was most substantial, and there was general agreement, both intra-nationally and inter-nationally, as to the nature and scope of the commitments about to be undertaken.

Here was the highroad to victory, the road which Woodrow Wilson so sadly neglected in 1917 and 1918. By preparing the public mind, by letting it sample the wares which international organization had to offer, by utterly abandoning the policy of the "lone hand" and taking the people into its confidence all along the line, the Department of State successfully surmounted the "critical period" that accompanied battle and death on the different military fronts, and exercised an almost clinical surveillance over the process of gestation and birth of a new international order. The result was the San Francisco Charter.

Into that document the United States wrote much that it had previously opposed, tacitly accepted, then openly espoused. All the institutions which President Harding declared we would not, could not, sanction, received our signature and obtained subsequent senatorial approbation. But we did more than that: We in part devised, and wholeheartedly accepted, principles of trusteeship, blueprints for the future of non-self-governing territories, and covenants for the incorporation of fundamental freedoms into the general framework of the international legal order. In the swift space of a few short months, we vaulted over the great abyss of a lost quarter of a century. Seldom is it vouchsafed to a generation of human beings so to retrieve the blunders of its immediate predecessor. Our generation, having found the high road the hard way, has thus far made good. We have come to agreement across party lines on the objectives, the procedures, and the conditions under which a viable future can be created for the Great Community of which we are now admittedly an organic part.

INDEX